Advances in Systems Safety

T0180663

Related titles:

Lessons in System Safety
Proceedings of the Eighth Safety-critical Systems Symposium, Southampton, UK, 2000
Redmill and Anderson (Eds)
1-85233-249-2

Aspects of Safety Management
Proceedings of the Ninth Safety-critical Systems Symposium, Bristol, UK, 2001
Redmill and Anderson (Eds)
1-85233-411-8

Components of System Safety
Proceedings of the Tenth Safety-critical Systems Symposium, Southampton, UK, 2002
Redmill and Anderson (Eds)
1-85233-561-0

Current Issues in Safety-critical Systems
Proceedings of the Eleventh Safety-critical Systems Symposium, Bristol, UK, 2003
Redmill and Anderson (Eds)
1-85233-696-X

Practical Elements of Safety
Proceedings of the Twelfth Safety-critical Systems Symposium, Birmingham, UK, 2004
Redmill and Anderson (Eds)
1-85233-800-8

Constituents of Modern System-safety Thinking
Proceedings of the Thirteenth Safety-critical Systems Symposium, Southampton, UK, 2005
Redmill and Anderson (Eds)
1-85233-952-7

Developments in Risk-based Approaches to Safety
Proceedings of the Fourteenth Safety-critical Systems Symposium, Bristol, UK, 2006
Redmill and Anderson (Eds)
1-84628-333-7

The Safety of Systems
Proceedings of the Fifteenth Safety-critical Systems Symposium, Bristol, UK, 2007
Redmill and Anderson (Eds)
978-1-84628-805-0

Improvements in System Safety
Proceedings of the Sixteenth Safety-critical Systems Symposium, Bristol, UK, 2008
Redmill and Anderson (Eds)
978-1-84800-099-5

Safety-Critical Systems: Problems, Process and Practice
Proceedings of the Seventeenth Safety-Critical Systems Symposium, Brighton, UK, 2009
Dale and Anderson (Eds)
978-1-84882-348-8

Making Systems Safer
Proceedings of the Eighteenth Safety-Critical Systems Symposium, Bristol, UK, 2010
Dale and Anderson (Eds)
978-1-84996-085-4

Chris Dale · Tom Anderson
Editors

Advances in Systems Safety

Proceedings of the Nineteenth Safety-Critical
Systems Symposium, Southampton, UK,
8–10th February 2011

Safety-Critical
Systems Club

The publication of these proceedings is
sponsored by BAE Systems plc

BAE SYSTEMS

 Springer

Editors
Chris Dale
Dale Research Ltd
33 North Street
Martock TA12 6DH
United Kingdom
chris.dale@scsc.org.uk

Prof. Tom Anderson
Centre for Software Reliability
Newcastle University
Newcastle upon Tyne NE1 7RU
United Kingdom

ISBN 978-0-85729-132-5   e-ISBN 978-0-85729-133-2
DOI 10.1007/978-0-85729-133-2
Springer London Dordrecht Heidelberg New York

British Library Cataloguing in Publication Data
A catalogue record for this book is available from the British Library

Printed on acid-free paper

Springer is part of Springer Science+Business Media (www.springer.com)

Preface

The Safety-critical Systems Symposium (SSS), held each February for nineteen consecutive years, offers a full-day tutorial followed by two days of presentations of papers. This book of Proceedings contains all the papers presented at SSS 2011.

The safety case has long been a cornerstone of the discipline, so the Symposium often debates advances in the creation, presentation and management of safety cases, and their associated arguments and evidence. This year is no exception, as will be clear from the three papers in the opening session of the event.

The management of projects developing safety-critical systems poses particular challenges, as do the delivery of systems safety in IT service organisations, and the preparation of safety cases for systems of systems. These important topics are brought together in the second session of the Symposium.

Three papers from healthcare form the third session: one on development processes for medical devices; a second on computer-based operational health systems; and the third on software testing for an artificial heart. The testing theme continues in the fourth session, with three papers on the testing of safety-critical systems.

Technological matters are dealt with in the fifth session: one paper discusses the challenges imposed by the use of multicore processor architectures in critical systems, and the second takes a pragmatic look at the use of formal methods.

The final session picks up on another recurring theme: safety standards. This year, we take a look at CE marking requirements, as well as reviewing significant updates to two important systems safety standards: IEC 61508 and DO-178C.

This year's authors have, as usual, delivered informative material touching on many topics that are of current concern to the safety-critical systems community, and we are grateful to them for their contributions. We also thank our sponsors for their valuable support, and the exhibitors at the Symposium's tools and services fair for their participation. And we thank Joan Atkinson and her team for laying the event's foundation through their exemplary planning and organisation.

CD & TA
October 2010

A message from the sponsors

BAE Systems is pleased to support the publication of these proceedings. We recognise the benefit of the Safety-Critical Systems Club in promoting safety engineering in the UK and value the opportunities provided for continued professional development and the recognition and sharing of good practice. The safety of our employees, those using our products and the general public is critical to our business and is recognised as an important social responsibility.

THE SAFETY-CRITICAL SYSTEMS CLUB

organiser of the

Safety-critical Systems Symposium

What is the Safety-Critical Systems Club?

This 'Community' Club exists to support developers and operators of systems that may have an impact on safety, across all industry sectors. It is an independent, non-profit organisation that co-operates with all bodies involved with safety-critical systems.

Objectives

The Club's two principal objectives are to raise awareness of safety issues in the field of safety-critical systems and to facilitate the transfer of safety technology from wherever it exists.

History

The Club was inaugurated in 1991 under the sponsorship of the UK's Department of Trade and Industry (DTI) and the Engineering and Physical Sciences Research Council (EPSRC). Its secretariat is in the Centre for Software Reliability (CSR) at Newcastle University, and its Meetings Coordinator is Chris Dale of Dale Research Ltd. Felix Redmill of Redmill Consultancy is the Newsletter Editor.

Since 1994 the Club has been self-sufficient, but it retains the active support of the Health and Safety Executive, the Institution of Engineering and Technology, and BCS, the Chartered Institute for IT. All of these bodies are represented on the Club's Steering Group.

The Club's activities

The Club achieves its goals of awareness-raising and technology transfer by focusing on current and emerging practices in safety engineering, software engineering, and standards that relate to safety in processes and products. Its activities include:

- Running the annual Safety-critical Systems Symposium each February (the first was in 1993), with Proceedings published by Springer-Verlag;

- Organising a number of full day seminars each year;
- Providing tutorials on relevant subjects;
- Publishing a newsletter, *Safety Systems*, three times annually (since 1991), in January, May and September; and
- A web-site http://www.scsc.org.uk providing member services, including a safety tools, products and services directory.

Education and communication

The Club brings together technical and managerial personnel within all sectors of the safety-critical-systems community. Its events provide education and training in principles and techniques, and it facilitates the dissemination of lessons within and between industry sectors. It promotes an inter-disciplinary approach to the engineering and management of safety, and it provides a forum for experienced practitioners to meet each other and for the exposure of newcomers to the safety-critical systems industry.

Influence on research

The Club facilitates communication among researchers, the transfer of technology from researchers to users, feedback from users, and the communication of experience between users. It provides a meeting point for industry and academia, a forum for the presentation of the results of relevant projects, and a means of learning and keeping up-to-date in the field.

The Club thus helps to achieve more effective research, a more rapid and effective transfer and use of technology, the identification of best practice, the definition of requirements for education and training, and the dissemination of information. Importantly, it does this within a 'club' atmosphere rather than a commercial environment.

Membership

Members pay a reduced fee (well below the commercial level) for events and receive the newsletter and other mailed information. Not being sponsored, the Club depends on members' subscriptions: these can be paid at the first meeting attended, and are almost always paid by the individual's employer.

To join, please contact Mrs Joan Atkinson at: The Centre for Software Reliability, Newcastle University, Newcastle upon Tyne, NE1 7RU, UK; Telephone: +44 191 221 2222; Fax: +44 191 222 7995; Email: csr@newcastle.ac.uk.

Contents

Testing Safety-Critical Systems

Technological Matters

Safety Standards

Safety Cases

A New Approach to creating Clear Safety Arguments

Richard Hawkins[1], Tim Kelly[1], John Knight[2] and Patrick Graydon[2]

[1]University of York, UK

[2] University of Virginia, Charlottesville, USA

Abstract We introduce *assured safety arguments*, a new structure for arguing safety in which the *safety argument* is accompanied by a *confidence argument* that documents the confidence in the structure and bases of the safety argument. This structure separates the major components that have traditionally been confused within a single safety argument structure. Separation gives both arguments greater clarity of purpose, and helps avoid the introduction of superfluous arguments and evidence. In this paper we describe a systematic approach to establishing both arguments, illustrated with a running example.

1 Introduction

In this paper, we introduce a new structure for arguing safety termed an *assured safety argument*. An assured safety argument has two components:

- a safety argument that documents the arguments and evidence used to establish direct claims of system safety
- a confidence argument that justifies the sufficiency of confidence in this safety argument.

These two components are both stated explicitly but separately. They are inter-linked so that the justification for having confidence in individual aspects of the safety argument is clear and readily available but not confused with the safety argument itself. This separation eliminates several difficulties with traditional approaches and provides several advantages.

The role of a safety case is to provide:

'a structured argument, supported by a body of evidence, that provides a compelling, comprehensible and valid case that a system is safe for a given application in a given environment' (MoD 2007).

C. Dale, T. Anderson (eds.), *Advances in Systems Safety*, DOI 10.1007/978-0-85729-133-2_1,
© Springer-Verlag London Limited 2011

A safety argument must explain how the available evidence supports the overall claim of acceptable safety. Best practice, risk-based, safety arguments decompose this claim into arguments that justify the acceptability of the risk posed by identified system hazards. For each hazard, the argument states what 'adequately' addressed means for that hazard and then identifies the evidence supporting the conclusion. This structure explains the purpose of each piece of evidence.

Unfortunately, both evidence and argument will typically be imperfect. For example, software testing may fail to support the claims for which it is cited for a variety of reasons including:

- inadequately defined test cases (e.g. that fail to fully capture the safety requirements)
- imperfect test coverage
- a faulty test oracle
- the failure of human testers to follow the test procedure faithfully
- testers inadvertently testing a different version of the system or component
- test results corrupted between collection and analysis.

There are numerous scenarios in which the reality of failures of the computer hardware and software together with the fallibilities of the test generation process could result in false conclusions (claims) being drawn from that evidence. Having sufficient confidence in safety claims is essential.

Any knowledge gap that prohibits perfect (total) confidence is referred to as an *assurance deficit*. In establishing an argument of safety it is first important to identify and acknowledge the assurance deficits that (inevitably) exist. Having recognised the assurance deficits, the goal is to explicitly manage them such that the overall confidence in the safety argument is considered acceptable.

Present practice is to develop a single, unified safety argument that does not distinguish the arguments of safety and confidence. This practice merges what are essentially two different but interrelated arguments. Both of these elements are essential to a *compelling* safety argument, but presenting both in an intermingled fashion typically results in a larger (often rambling) argument and makes grasping the crucial structures difficult for the reader. Clarity of presentation is important for all stakeholders even though their interests might differ. For developers, the distinction between the safety and confidence arguments would help provide clearer direction on the steps involved in constructing each argument and a better understanding of the necessary development and assurance steps. For reviewers, the distinction would help focus attention on those aspects of the argument that are weakly supported.

An assured safety argument separates the argument about assurance deficit into a separate confidence argument in order to address this problem. The *safety argument* documents the asserted arguments and evidence of risk reduction. The *confidence argument* documents the reasons for having confidence in the safety argument.

A truly risk-based safety argument must always be focused upon the identification and mitigation of hazards associated with the system. The safety argument demonstrates how the risks associated with each hazard are managed. Everything cited in the safety argument should therefore have a direct role as part of the causal chain to the hazard. That is, all of the goals in the safety argument must be claims about the system or parts, properties, or properties of parts thereof. Artefacts from system development (e.g. test reports and, by extension, their contents) may be referenced only in solution or context elements. Strict adherence to this tight definition of a safety argument ensures the focus of the safety argument is clearly on the (direct) management of risk. We will describe later how safety arguments may be structured.

A confidence argument demonstrates the justification for confidence in a safety argument. There will be uncertainties associated with aspects of the safety argument or supporting evidence. The role of the confidence argument is to explicitly address those uncertainties and explain why there is sufficient confidence in the safety argument. Figure 1 represents a complete assurance argument entailing the safety argument 'encapsulated' by a confidence argument. We will describe later how confidence arguments are used to create the overall assurance case for the system.

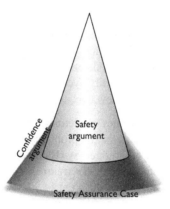

Fig. 1. A safety assurance case containing separate safety and confidence arguments

In the next section, we elaborate the difficulties that arise when both safety and confidence are argued in a single, integrated argument. In section 3, we discuss the construction of assured safety cases. In section 4, we illustrate our safety argument structure by presenting portions of a safety argument and confidence argument for a hypothetical drug infusion pump. Finally, we conclude in section 5.

2 The difficulties with a single argument

The present practice of including in a single argument elements that document both direct arguments of (product) mitigation and supporting arguments that are 'confidence-raising' leads to a number of difficulties including:

- Arguments tend to become large and unwieldy, because there is too much information in one argument. The entry criterion for the inclusion of an argument (or item of evidence) in the safety argument is often (too loosely), 'Does this have any possible bearing on the safety of the system?' Both direct arguments of risk reduction *and* (any) indirect arguments of confidence are admitted by this criterion. This can lead to voluminous, rambling, ad infinitum arguments.
- Both the safety argument and the confidence argument tend to be poorly prepared, because the lack of distinction between the two makes it more difficult to spot incompleteness or poor structure in either.
- Necessary elements of the argument are sometimes omitted, because the need for the specific elements is lost in the volume of the argument.
- Arguments become indirect and unfocused, and the link between elements of the argument and risk is often lost.
- Unnecessary material is sometimes included in arguments without proper consideration or explanation of its relevance – 'just in case'.
- Arguments become difficult to build, and weaknesses of the argument are sometimes not evident and so are easily overlooked.
- Arguments become difficult to review because of the size and lack of focus.

These difficulties are serious since they all detract from the basic purposes of using safety cases. We note that many of the problems with current practice in the application of safety cases were highlighted by (Haddon-Cave 2009).

Separation of the safety and confidence arguments offers the opportunity to mitigate these difficulties by providing different foci for safety and confidence. In addition, careful attention to linking the two arguments provides a mechanism for guiding analysis of the interrelationship between safety and confidence.

3 Constructing assured safety arguments

A safety argument must always be focused upon the identification and mitigation of hazards associated with the system. The safety argument demonstrates how the risks associated with each hazard are managed. Everything that is included as part of the safety argument should therefore have a direct role as part of the causal chain to the hazard. Anything that does not fulfil this role should not be included in the safety argument. Safety arguments are constructed by providing claims relating to the safety of the system. These claims are then broken into sub-claims that show how the top-level safety claim is demonstrated. The decomposition of claims and sub-claims continues until a point is reached where a claim can be supported by citing a development or assessment artefact (e.g. a design analysis report or test report) as evidence. The strategy adopted when supporting a claim should be made explicit in the argument. The argument should also clearly state the context in which the argument is made, along with any assumptions that have been made. When arguments are communicated solely through narrative text it can often be difficult for a reader to identify the individual elements (e.g. distinct claims) and structure (e.g. asserted inferences) of the argument. It is therefore often clearer to represent a safety argument graphically. Figure 2 shows a simplified example of how a safety argument structure may be captured using the Goal Structuring Notation (GSN). We refer readers unfamiliar with the GSN notation to (Kelly and Weaver 2004).

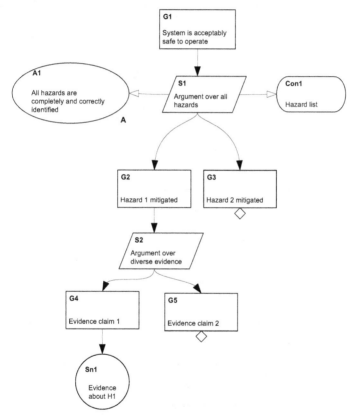

Fig. 2. An example safety argument represented using GSN

Although representing an argument graphically clearly disambiguates the structure and elements of the argument, it cannot ensure that the argument itself is 'good' or sufficient for its purpose. By exercising discipline over the permissible claims and evidence of the safety argument, and encouraging a systematic approach to the construction of a confidence argument, we can begin to address this issue.

A safety argument includes a number of *assertions*. These assertions relate to the sufficiency and appropriateness of the inferences declared in the argument, the context and assumptions used and the evidence cited. (A documented safety argument is merely a documented position that collects together these assertions.) To be compelling, the argument must justify the truth of the assertions made. If an argument assertion cannot be justified, then the argument will not be believed (it will not provide the required assurance). The confidence argument provides the justification for argument assertions. In order to indicate the assertion in the safety argument that the confidence argument is associated with, the confidence argument is tied to a number of *Assurance Claim Points* (ACP). An ACP is indicated in GSN with a named black rectangle on the relevant link. A confidence argument is developed for each ACP. Figure 3 shows ACPs named ACP1, ACP2 and ACP3.

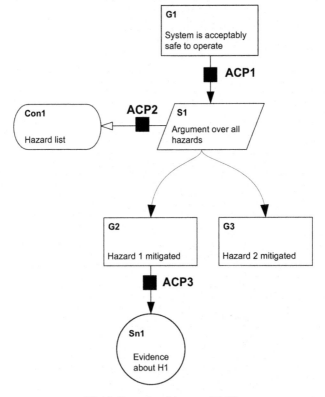

Fig. 3. Example of the use of ACPs

These ACPs correspond to three different types of assertion:

- asserted inference (ACP1)
- asserted context (ACP2)
- asserted solution (ACP3).

Below we discuss each of these three types of assertion in more detail.

3.1 Asserted inference

Each time a claim is said to be supported by other claims in an argument, an assertion is being made that the inference is appropriate and sufficient. Only in deductive arguments do premise claims *prove* a particular conclusion. Instead, for inductive arguments, the assertion is that the probable truth of the premises is sufficient to establish the probable truth of the conclusion. Although safety cases can contain a mix of both deductive and inductive arguments, inductive arguments typically dominate. For example, Figure 4 shows (in GSN) the assertion that, given the applicable context, the sub-claims put forward to implement the chosen argument strategy are, if true, a sufficient basis upon which to infer the conclusion stated in the parent claim. To gain assurance in the adopted argument strategy, it is necessary to provide a confidence argument that demonstrates why the asserted inference should be believed. The ACP for an asserted inference is the link between the parent claim and its strategy or sub-claims.

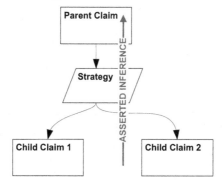

Fig. 4. Asserted inference

In the example shown below in Figure 5, the asserted inference is that if all hazards are mitigated then the system is acceptably safe to operate. The role of the confidence argument for ACP1 is to demonstrate why it should be believed that the two supporting claims of hazard mitigation are sufficient to draw the overall conclusion about system safety. We discuss how such a confidence argument may be constructed later.

3.2 Asserted context

Each time contextual information (represented by context or assumption elements) is introduced into the argument, it is being asserted that the context is appropriate for the argument elements to which it applies. For example, consider a context reference to a list of failure modes for a particular piece of equipment. The introduction of this context element when arguing about the safety of that piece of equipment implicitly asserts that the list of failure modes referred to is appropriate to the application and operating context in question.

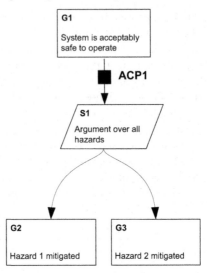

Fig. 5. ACP relating to an asserted inference

Figure 6 shows asserted context for an argument strategy. The assurance of the strategy depends upon the confidence that the context or assumption stated is appropriate for that strategy and its sub-goals. It is necessary to provide a confidence argument that demonstrates why it should be believed that the asserted context is appropriate. In addition to the appropriateness of the context, it is also necessary to provide an argument as to the trustworthiness of the context in question. The concept of trustworthiness relates to freedom from flaw. In the legal field the notion of integrity of evidence is often used to refer to the soundness or quality of the evidence put forward in a case. In considering the trustworthiness of an artefact, the processes used to generate that artefact are often considered (Habli and Kelly 2007). The ACP for asserted context is the link to the contextual element.

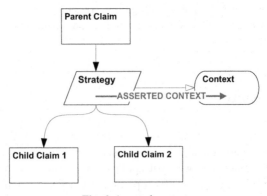

Fig. 6. Asserted context

In the example shown below in Figure 7 it is being asserted that the hazards given in the referenced hazard list are the relevant hazards. For this context to be appropriate there must be confidence that the hazard list is appropriate with respect to the system, application and context. The role of the confidence argument at ACP2 is therefore to demonstrate why it should be believed that citing this hazard list defines the appropriate context at this point in the safety argument. In addition, it is necessary to justify the trustworthiness of the hazard list. We discuss how such a confidence argument may be constructed later.

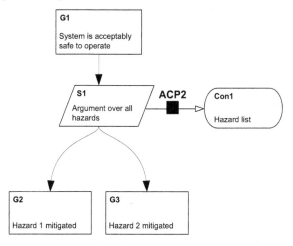

Fig. 7. ACP relating to an asserted context

For completeness, a confidence argument should be provided for both the inference *and* the context (ACP1 *and* ACP2), as shown in Figure 8. It is important to provide separate confidence arguments because each relates to a separate assertion.

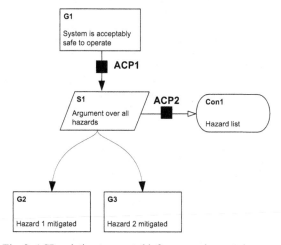

Fig. 8. ACPs relating to asserted inference and asserted context

3.3 Asserted solution

Each time evidence is referenced as a solution to the argument, it is being asserted that the evidence put forward is sufficient to support the claim. Figure 9 shows an asserted solution to a safety claim. The assurance of the solution depends upon the confidence that the evidence is appropriate to support the claim, and the evidence is trustworthy. The ACP for asserted solutions is the link to the solution element.

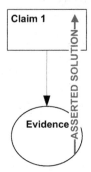

Fig. 9. Asserted solution

In the example shown below in Figure 10 it is being asserted that the stress testing results are sufficient to demonstrate that the defined operational forces can be tolerated. For this solution to be sufficient there must be confidence that the stress testing performed is good enough for this purpose. The role of the confidence argument at ACP3 is to provide this confidence. This will involve considering whether the stress testing of the type being referred to is adequate to support the claim and whether the stress testing procedure was followed faithfully. We discuss how such a confidence argument may be constructed later.

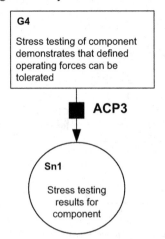

Fig. 10. ACP relating to an asserted solution

3.4 Confidence argument structure

In all but a very few situations, the truth of the assertions put forward within a safety argument cannot be demonstrated with certainty. It is necessary to demonstrate that there is sufficient confidence in each assertion. This is the role of the confidence argument.

The issue of sufficiency with regard to confidence in an assertion is complex. The notion of reducing risk to a level that is As Low As Reasonably Practicable (ALARP) has become widely accepted (HSE 2001). Risk is a quantifiable entity (i.e. the expected loss). Confidence is also quantifiable (i.e. the probable truth of a claim). However, except where purely statistical evidence is used, to reason about confidence quantitatively requires first qualitative reasoning about the sources of uncertainty in arguments. In our approach we focus on these qualitative arguments, and leave the subsequent 'encoding' and quantification of these to those who believe that quantification can reap further utility.

We require a qualitative argument to demonstrate sufficient confidence in an assertion. This argument demonstrates why a sceptical audience should believe three important things about the assertion:

- There are grounds to support the probable truth of the assertion.
- Residual uncertainties (assurance deficits) in the assertion have been identified.
- The residual uncertainties (assurance deficits) in the assertion are insufficient to cause concern.

The first aspect of this argument considers the reasons why the assertion should be believed. This aspect is realized as the decomposition of a goal of the form 'the assertion $<x>$ is true'. As in the safety argument, goal decomposition continues until the goal can be solved with evidence. Unlike the safety argument, however, the goals in this portion of the confidence argument are typically expected to be claims about properties of development artefacts (i.e. 'process' claims). For example, the decomposition of a solution assertion goal might contain arguments over the properties of test plans, development tools, and configuration management systems. Goal decomposition in this portion of the confidence argument should continue until no reasonable observer would deny that the artefact cited offers positive evidence in support of the goal claim.

The second aspect of the argument involves justifying that the uncertainties (assurance deficits) surrounding the assertion have been identified. The final (third) aspect of the argument, must argue the acceptability of the uncertainties (assurance deficits) that remain.

The identification of an assurance deficit identifies a gap in our knowledge relating to an assertion in the argument. One reason that assurance deficits are of interest is that they represent 'blind spots' in the argument – i.e. areas of the argument where no evidence has been presented. Should these 'blind spots' be eliminated (by providing the appropriate evidence) we may find that the evidence is positive (and supports the assertion made in the safety argument). However, we may also find that the evidence is negative and forms counter-evidence to the safety argument. Recognising assurance deficits, therefore, helps identify the possible areas in the argument where counter-evidence *may* exist. (This guiding of the otherwise boundless search for counter-evidence is a useful side-effect of the identification of assurance deficits.) For example, consider a case where there is no control flow analysis evidence of the absence of infinite loops in some source code. When arguing that a return value will always be provided, we should consider the probability of the existence of counter-evidence to our claim (i.e. if we were to provide the control flow analysis – how probable is it that an infinite loop will be detected?)

It is necessary to identify assurance deficits as completely as practicable and to justify that the residual assurance deficits can be accepted. Creating an assured safety argument in the manner we have described makes it easier to identify the important assurance deficits, since the structure demands a systematic consideration of the weaknesses in the argument. It is possible to mitigate any identified assurance deficits by taking one of four actions:

- making changes to the design of the system, e.g. adding a hardware backup when it is impractical to demonstrate with adequate confidence that software has the properties necessary to ensure system safety
- making changes to system operation, e.g. by limiting the conditions under which the system is used
- making changes to the safety argument, e.g. adding an independent source of evidence
- generating additional evidence for the confidence argument, e.g. increasing the coverage of software functional tests.

It is important to note at this point that completely mitigating all assurance deficits is not normally achievable. In many cases it would be possible to go on forever generating additional evidence to try to gain some additional confidence. It is therefore necessary to make a judgment on when assurance deficits can be tolerated. To do this it must be shown that the cost (effort) expended in addressing an assurance deficit reflects the risk associated with that assurance deficit. The risk associated with an assurance deficit can be assessed by expert judgment of the likelihood of any event chains that would lead to the assertion being false and of how damaging it would be to the main safety argument if the claim were false. Considering the likelihood and severity of counter-evidence may help in making such judgements.

We show the potential structure of confidence arguments using the GSN pattern notation (Kelly 1998). To create argument patterns, GSN is extended to support multiplicity, optionality and abstraction. The multiplicity extensions shown in Figure 11 are used to describe how many instances of one entity relate to another entity. They are annotations on existing GSN relational arrows. The optionality extension is used to denote possible alternative support. It can represent a 1-of-n or an m-of-n choice. In Figure 11, one source node has three possible alternative sink nodes.

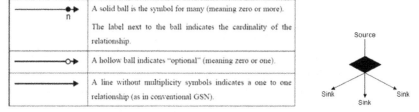

────────●▶ n	A solid ball is the symbol for many (meaning zero or more). The label next to the ball indicates the cardinality of the relationship.
────────○▶	A hollow ball indicates "optional" (meaning zero or one).
────────▶	A line without multiplicity symbols indicates a one to one relationship (as in conventional GSN).

Fig. 11. GSN multiplicity and optionality extensions

The abstraction extensions shown in Figure 12 allow GSN elements to be generalised for future instantiation. The uninstantiated entity placeholder denotes that the attached element remains to be instantiated, i.e. at some later stage the abstract entity needs to be replaced with a more concrete instance. The undeveloped entity placeholder denotes that the attached element requires further development, i.e. at some later stage the entity needs to be decomposed and supported by further argument and evidence.

Uninstantiated Entity   Undeveloped Entity

Fig. 12. GSN abstraction extensions

Figure 13 shows an example argument pattern for an asserted *inference* (e.g., ACP1 in Figure 5). This pattern demonstrates that there is sufficient confidence in the asserted inference by including a sub-argument:

- that the asserted inference is true
- that the assurance deficits relating to the asserted inference have been identified
- that any residual assurance deficits are acceptable.

The strategy used in the third sub-argument is to argue over the set of assurance deficits, and for each to show:

- the existence of significant counter evidence associated with the subject assurance deficit is considered unlikely
- the sensitivity of the remainder of the argument to the subject assurance deficit is acceptably low, i.e., the assurance deficit may be justified as acceptable when considered in the context of the other arguments and evidence in the safety case.

An example of how this pattern may be instantiated is included in section 4.

Figure 14 shows an example argument pattern for an asserted *solution* (e.g., ACP3 in Figure 10). The pattern demonstrates that there is sufficient confidence in the asserted solution by including a sub-argument that:

- the asserted solution is trustworthy
- use of the asserted solution is appropriate.

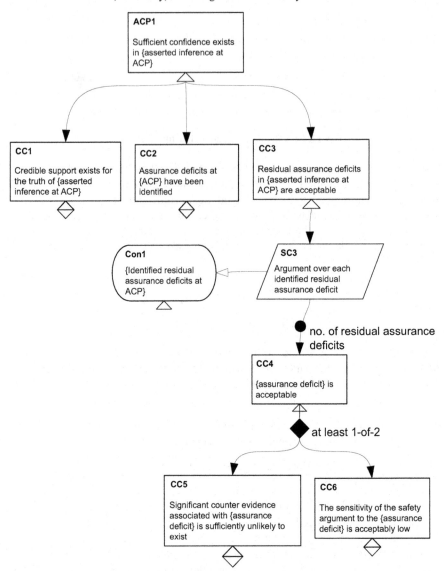

Fig. 13. Confidence argument structure for an asserted inference

Each of these sub-arguments has the same form as that used in Figure 13 and the same techniques for instantiation of the pattern could be used. The claims regarding the acceptability of the residual assurance deficits in each case (CC13 and CC23) would be supported using the same pattern as provided under CC3 in Figure 13. The distinction between these two sub-arguments is worthwhile since in general arguing the integrity of evidence is easier than arguing the appropriateness of the evidence. The explicit inclusion of both ensures attention is paid to both.

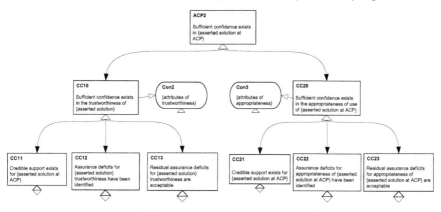

Fig. 14. Confidence argument structure for an asserted solution

3.5 The overall confidence argument

The individual fragments of confidence argument, each addressing a particular assurance claim point in the safety argument, should be assembled together to form
a single overall confidence argument (to accompany the single safety argument).
To be truly comprehensive in the construction of this overall confidence argument
would require that *all* of the assertions of the safety argument have an accompanying confidence (sub-)argument. This is illustrated in the three legs of the argument
shown in Figure 15 (arguing confidence for *all* inferences, *all* context and *all* evidence used in the safety argument).

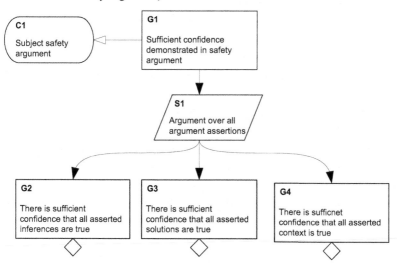

Fig. 15. Representing an overall confidence argument

In addition to this simple structure, there are a number of potentially important concerns at the level of the *overall* confidence argument. Firstly, arguing the sufficiency of the overall confidence in the safety argument can be more complex than the simple composition of arguments of sufficient confidence for each argument assertion (in the same way that arguing the acceptability of overall risk is more complex than simply arguing the acceptability of the risk posed by each individual hazard). For example, we have already highlighted in Section 3.4 that an assurance deficit for one argument assertion may be justified as acceptable when considered in the context of other arguments and evidence in the safety case. Such a justification of how shortfalls in one part of the safety argument are compensated by other arguments and evidence needs to be addressed at the level of the overall confidence argument. Secondly, it is useful to examine and justify whether the multiple lines of argument offered up in the safety argument (undesirably) share *common* underlying assurance deficits (i.e. there are common modes of failure in the argument). Thirdly, for large safety arguments it may simply not be practical to provide arguments of confidence for *every* assertion in the safety argument. Instead, some selection and prioritisation of the assertions of the safety arguments to be covered by the confidence argument may need to be performed. This prioritisation would be done most appropriately by addressing those assertions relating to the most significant arguments of risk reduction in the primary safety argument. Obviously, care must be taken when making any decisions regarding parts of the confidence argument to omit.

4 Example assured safety argument

To illustrate how an assured safety argument might be structured in practice, we show key aspects of an example argument created for a *hypothetical* insulin pump. Figure 16 shows the high-level structure of the safety argument. The claim that the insulin pump is adequately safe for routine use is supported by arguing over each of the identified credible hazards to which the patient might be subject.

To produce an assured safety argument, confidence argument fragments must be provided for each assurance claim point. In the example, the ACPs are:

ACP.S1. There is sufficient confidence that mitigating credible hazards will demonstrate that the insulin pump is adequately safe for routine use. Arguing over hazards is a widely accepted strategy in safety engineering, and this fragment of the confidence case is simple to construct.

ACP.A1. There is sufficient confidence that pump design is accurately documented. If the documented pump design does not faithfully represent the pump, then the argument presented may not be valid.

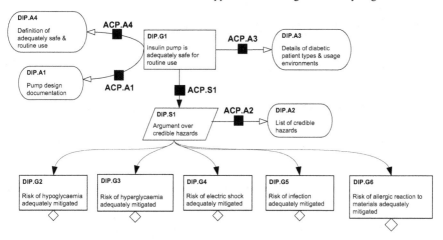

Fig. 16. High-level safety argument for an insulin pump

ACP.A2. There is sufficient confidence that the list of credible hazards is complete and correct. Inadequate definition of a hazard or omission of a hazard might invalidate the safety claim.

ACP.A3. There is sufficient confidence that the details of diabetic patient types and usage environments are accurately documented. Usage outside of the expected set of environments might invalidate the safety claim.

ACP.A4. There is sufficient confidence that the definitions of adequately safe and routine use are appropriate for the safety claim being made. If the scope defined by this context is not appropriate for the way in which the system is operated, for example if the device is used in an unplanned manner in a hospital, then the argument presented may not be valid.

We examine ACP.A1 in detail. A1 is a context, and to create a suitable confidence argument fragment we adapt the solution pattern shown in Figure 14. Figure 17 shows the sub-goals labelled CC1.3 and CC2.3 corresponding to sub-goals CC13 and CC23 from the pattern in Figure 14. The remainder of the pattern would be instantiated in a suitable way.

Subgoal CC1.3 states: 'Residual assurance deficits in the trustworthiness of the pump design document are acceptable.' The assurance deficits that we associate with the trustworthiness of the pump design document need to be enumerated and each included in the appropriate confidence argument fragment. In this example, we consider just two assurance deficits:

- the possible deficit introduced by the use of a commercial word processing tool (CC1.3.1), i.e., are we sufficiently confident that the document was not corrupted in some way by the word processor?

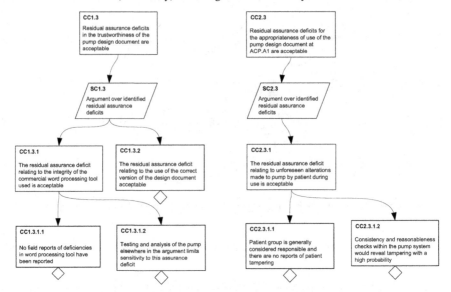

Fig. 17. Part of the confidence argument for ACP.A1

- the possible deficit introduced by the supply of the document for use (CC1.3.2), i.e., are we sufficiently confident that the correct document was actually referenced?

For both of these assurance deficits, we need to consider both counter evidence and sensitivity. In Figure 17, we show just a single claim for counter evidence and sensitivity and just for claim CC1.3.1. We argue a lack of counter evidence about the commercial word processor based on reported deficiencies, and we argue lack of sensitivity based on independent information about the design that will be generated by testing and analysis of the pump as built. Sensitivity is low because a defect in the document would be revealed from observations of the pump during testing and analysis.

A single assurance deficit for the appropriateness sub-argument is also shown in Figure 17 (claim CC2.3.1). The claim is: 'The residual assurance deficit relating to unforeseen alterations made to pump by patient during use is acceptable'. For this claim, the problem is that the documentation might be inappropriate because the pump has been locally modified. For lack of counter evidence in this claim, we cite the claim that there is no evidence that such tampering occurs. For sensitivity, we cite the claim that consistency and reasonableness checks by the pump during operation would reveal tampering with a high probability and would raise an alarm. Thus, the remainder of the safety argument is not especially sensitive to this possibility.

Part of the next level of the safety argument for the insulin pump, elaboration of goal DIP.G2, is shown in Figure 18. The strategy used in this elaboration is to argue over the hazard of excess insulin in different delivery modes. Five assurance claim points are defined by this (incomplete) version of the elaboration:

ACP.S2. There is sufficient confidence that considering the risk of excess insulin during each possible delivery mode will demonstrate that the risk of hypoglycaemia is adequately mitigated.

ACP.A5. There is sufficient confidence that the list of delivery modes is complete and correct.

ACP.S3. There is sufficient confidence that arguing over patient commanded and uncommanded infusions will demonstrate that the risk of excess insulin during meal/correction bolus infusion is adequately mitigated. We might argue that 'commanded' AND 'uncommanded' is a tautology.

ACP.A6. There is sufficient confidence that the definition of commanded infusions is appropriate. Some modern insulin infusion pumps use a Bluetooth network connection to communicate. This definition of commanded infusions might be inappropriate if it does not make clear whether infusions resulting from security attacks over Bluetooth are commanded or not.

ACP.A7. There is sufficient confidence that the definition of uncommanded infusions is appropriate.

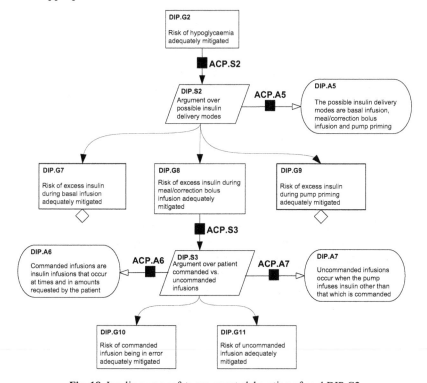

Fig. 18. Insulin pump safety argument elaboration of goal DIP.G2

5 Conclusions

It is currently commonplace for safety case authors to mix and confuse two types of argument within a single safety case argument structure – direct arguments of safety behaviour, and indirect 'confidence raising' arguments. There are a number of unfortunate consequences to this practice. Firstly, the confidence arguments are often weakly related to direct arguments of risk reduction. Secondly, the resultant arguments are often 'rambling', have poorly defined argument structure, and have unclearly defined stopping criteria. It is too easy to keep adding arguments and evidence ad infinitum, when the only entry criteria that seems to be being applied is, 'Does this have any possible bearing on the safety of the system?' Greater discipline is needed when deciding on how to structure the arguments of the safety case.

This paper introduces *assured safety arguments* as a mechanism to deal with this problem. This structure explicitly separates the safety case argument into two components – a *safety* argument and an accompanying *confidence* argument. The safety argument is allowed to talk only in terms of the causal chain of risk reduction, and is not allowed to contain general 'confidence raising' arguments. The confidence argument is constructed *relative* to this safety argument and clearly structured according to the assertions of the safety argument. Again, the confidence argument cannot be considered a 'free for all' and is not allowed to contain general 'confidence raising' arguments that cannot be clearly related to the structures of the core safety argument.

Of particular importance is the prospect of focusing the activities associated with certification on the two arguments in an assured safety case. Certification as defined by Defence Standard 00-56 (MoD 2007), for example, requires that a safety case provide:

> '... a compelling, comprehensible and valid case that a system is safe for a given application in a given environment'

The standard does not define 'compelling, comprehensible and valid', but intuition suggests that concern is with quality of the safety case. Using an assured safety case, officials charged with assessing a safety argument will have clear and distinct statements about the main properties of interest, the argument targeted at the primary safety claim and the argument targeted at the primary confidence claim.

We have limited our discussion in this paper to safety cases, but the concepts apply immediately to *any* property of interest. Thus, for example the notions of assured security cases or assured reliability cases are appropriate, and each would benefit from the explicit introduction of a confidence argument in the same way that a safety argument does. Naturally, the content of an assured security case would differ from the content of an assured safety case, but the overall structures and approaches would be identical.

Our preliminary experience of applying separation and developing explicit and separate confidence arguments has revealed that the approach yields the expected benefits – greater clarity in (and consequently comprehension of) the arguments, and a reduction in size of the core safety argument.

Acknowledgments The authors would like to acknowledge the financial support of the Royal Academy of Engineering (through the Distinguished Visiting Fellowship Scheme) for the work reported in this paper.

References

Habli I, Kelly T (2007) Achieving integrated process and product safety arguments. Proceedings of 15th Safety Critical Systems Symposium.

Haddon-Cave C (2009) The Nimrod review. The Stationary Office. London

HSE (2001) Reducing risks, protecting people. Health and Safety Executive. HSE Books

Kelly T (1998) Arguing safety - a systematic approach to managing safety cases. PhD Thesis. Department of Computer Science, The University of York.

Kelly T, Weaver R (2004) The goal structuring notation - a safety argument notation. Proceedings of the Dependable Systems and Networks Workshop on Assurance Cases

MoD (2007) Defence Standard 00-56 Issue 4: safety management requirements for defence systems. HMSO

Safety Cases – what can we learn from Science?

Steve Kinnersly

ESR Technology

Warrington, UK

Abstract Safety cases typically aim to show that a system is safe through constructive argument supported by evidence: 'the system is safe' is shown to be true as a logical (or at least compelling) consequence of appropriate evidence. This paper considers an alternative point of view based on scientific method. Specifically, 'the system is safe' is viewed as a hypothesis to be challenged. The hypothesis cannot be shown to be true but trust can be built up by it surviving extensive, rigorous challenge. This approach is shown to have implications that appear to go some way towards addressing certain criticisms of safety cases raised in the Haddon-Cave report into the loss of Nimrod XV230. Some safety standards and regulatory requirements are examined from the viewpoint of 'hypothesis and challenge'.

1 Introduction

Once in a while, it is useful to look at a familiar thing from a new point of view. It can challenge assumptions, generate new approaches to old problems and stimulate new ideas and developments.

This paper takes a look at 'the safety case' from what appears to be a new, but is at the same time an old, point of view: that of scientific method. The motivation for this is twofold. Firstly, it is a long-held belief of the author that the top-level claim in a safety case, namely that a system is safe, has much in common with a scientific hypothesis, yet this does not appear to have been explored. Secondly, the Haddon-Cave report into the loss of a Nimrod aircraft in Afghanistan (Haddon Cave 2009) made certain criticisms of safety cases and how they are used, noting that they are 'not new'. This suggests that new thinking about safety cases would be beneficial.

The scientific method, as currently understood, might not be familiar to engineers involved in system safety. A short introduction is therefore given here. Note that this addresses the process of science, not technical methods or scientific theories. This is followed by some comments on safety case fundamentals. The next section considers how a safety case can be seen from the viewpoint of scientific

C. Dale, T. Anderson (eds.), *Advances in Systems Safety*, DOI 10.1007/978-0-85729-133-2_2,
© Springer-Verlag London Limited 2011

method. Some comments on its compatibility with some influential standards and regulatory requirements are then made.

Some conclusions are drawn in the final section. However, it should be noted that the primary aim of this paper is to stimulate thought and discussion about the nature of safety cases. By doing so, it is hoped to make a small contribution towards removing the need to say, for any future criticisms of safety cases, that they are 'not new'.

2 How science works

2.1 Some history

Science is one of the most remarkable success stories of human endeavour. Remarkable, too, is that for most of the 350 or so years since the beginning of the scientific age, it was far from clear why science is so successful. It was generally agreed that looking at the real world (by observation or experiment) rather than trusting the writings of eminent people (simply because of their reputation) was the starting point and a defining characteristic of science. But how does that lead to seemingly universal truths?

For very many years, the standard wisdom was that science worked by induction. Observations and experiments were the starting point for extrapolation by an argument of the type:

- If it is true for N cases then it will be true for the (N+1)th case and thus for all cases.
- Observations or experiments show that it is true for N cases; therefore it must be true for all cases and thus be a universal law.

Taking this view, science was capable of finding absolute, universal truths, or 'laws of nature'. Once found, they were necessarily true for all time.

While there were always people who questioned this view of science, it did have a lot going for it. Induction is a rigorous and powerful method in mathematics and it was clear early on that mathematics was the language of at least a large part of science. And science did seem to have discovered universal truths. For example, Newton's laws of motion and gravity reigned supreme for over 200 years, while the theory of electromagnetism developed by Maxwell in the 19th century not only neatly explained all that was then known about electricity and magnetism but also successfully predicted other electromagnetic phenomena.

The current mainstream understanding of how science works was developed in the mid-20th century. It falls into two parts: 'knowledge through science' and 'the practice of science'. The biggest contributions to these were made by Karl Popper

(Popper 1959, 1963) and Thomas Kuhn (Kuhn 1962), respectively. (Note that there are, as always, people who disagree with the mainstream view, particularly regarding details. However, they will be ignored for the purposes of this paper.)

2.2 Knowledge through science

It is now recognised that science does not and cannot discover absolute truths. Rather than truth by induction, the essence of scientific knowledge is successive approximation. Knowledge and understanding can get better but never reach certainty or absolute truth. Specifically, science proceeds by:

1. formulating theories (also called hypotheses or conjectures)
2. challenging those theories by observations and/or experiments.

If the observations or experiments do not agree with the predictions of the theory, then the theory must be incorrect. However, if the observations or experiments do agree with the predictions of the theory, it cannot be concluded that the theory is correct. After all, making more observations may reveal some disagreement. The best that can be said of the theory is that it agrees with everything so far.

Of course, there are challenges and challenges. The most important challenges are those that push the limits of the theory, in particular where it makes an important prediction that lies beyond previous observational or experimental evidence. They extend 'everything so far'. Importantly, such challenges present the most severe challenge to a theory because they are where the theory might fall down and thus be shown to be incorrect – there are no similar or 'nearby' observations or experiments that already agree with the predictions of the theory. So theories that make predictions that can be subject to critical challenge are preferred to those that do not.

The importance of critical tests that can falsify a theory cannot be understated. Theories that do not permit such testing – the standard example is astrology – are usually deemed to be not part of science at all. (In fact, it was the search for a criterion to demarcate science from non-science that lead Popper to his discovery of 'hypothesis and challenge' as the basis of the scientific method.)

Even though a theory cannot be said to be absolutely true, can it nevertheless be given a probability of being true, for example 'likely' to be true? The answer is no (the reason is complicated and will not be explained here. See, for example, (Popper 1963)). On the other hand, one theory can be considered to be better than another. A theory that has been subject to wide-ranging critical challenges and is consistent with all the results is better than one that has not been so challenged or is not consistent with some results.

All this is neatly summed up by Karl Popper (Popper 1963, chapter 8):

'All we can ever hope to say of a theory is that it explains this or that: that it has been tested severely, and that it has stood up to all our tests. We may also compare theories in order to see which of them has stood up better to our severest tests – or in other words, which of them is better corroborated by the results of our tests. But ... degree of corroboration can never be equated with mathematical probability.'

(Note that Popper uses 'test' where this paper uses 'challenge'. 'Challenge' is used here to distinguish it from testing that is carried out during safety assurance.)

2.3 The practice of science

Science, however, is a human activity and subject to normal human practices. Furthermore, science would not get very far if every theory had to be tested against all historical observations and experiments. The remarkable progress of science has only been possible because of two important 'human' aspects as to how it is carried out. The first is the idea of a 'credible theory' (or hypothesis, conjecture, etc.). The other is the concept of 'normal science'.

The idea of a 'credible theory' is simple. It is a theory that deserves to be taken seriously (note, this does not imply that it is correct). Science requires time, resources and money. So unless a theory deserves to be taken seriously, it will not be challenged. 'Taken seriously' is to some extent a subjective matter. However, some factors add weight to a claim for credibility. For example:

- It addresses an important, outstanding issue or problem.
- It has a sound theoretical basis.
- It is consistent with the current best theories where they agree with observation or experiment.
- It has been subject to at least some significant challenges and has not been found wanting.

While these do not guarantee that a theory will be considered as deserving to be taken seriously, failing in one or more is likely to mean that it is considered as not deserving.

An effect of this 'credible theory' filter is that the need for, or even benefit from, challenges against historical observations and experiments is removed. A sound theoretical basis and consistency with current best theories (where they agree with observation or experiment) means that the proposed new theory will be no worse than the current best. Challenges can therefore focus on critical areas which can potentially show that the theory is wrong.

The idea of 'normal science' takes this idea further. This recognises that far from developing and challenging new theories all the time, for most of the time science and scientists are actually working out the implications of current theories or using them to solve problems. The theory itself is not being seriously questioned but is accepted as 'OK to use'. Thus, for instance, quantum mechanical calculations might be used to design a drug such that it should be effective against a certain disease. Or perhaps fluid flow and heat transfer equations, the laws of thermodynamics and chemical reaction theory are used to understand why a tricky nuclear reactor safety experiment gave some unexpected results. The point in both cases is that if there is a disagreement between the calculated results and observation or experiment, it would not be considered as invalidating the underlying theory (quantum mechanics, fluid flow, thermodynamics, etc.) but rather how it was being used or how the experimental results were being interpreted. The theory is, in effect, being regarded as accepted wisdom which is not to be challenged.

However, sometimes there is a need to challenge accepted wisdom. This will typically only be when there is no alternative. If such a challenge is successful, the accepted wisdom must change and a new accepted wisdom be found. This has become known as paradigm change. In essence, work is carried out within the existing paradigm until pressure to change is irresistible. A new paradigm is then developed and work continues within the new paradigm until pressure builds up for more change.

3 Some comments on safety case fundamentals

The purpose and nature of a safety case is well known and will not be considered in detail here. However, a few points are made in order to provide context for the rest of this paper.

Safety cases entered the UK safety world as a result of the Control of Industrial Major Accidents Hazards regulations (CIMAH regulations) in 1984. Safety case principles were further examined and developed by Lord Cullen in his report into the Piper Alpha disaster (Cullen 1990) in which a major accident in an offshore oil facility in the North Sea resulted in 167 deaths. As a result of this report, the approach to offshore safety shifted from compliance to achievement of safety objectives. A safety case would demonstrate through argument and evidence that the required safety objectives would be met. Regulations laid down what must be addressed in a safety case.

Safety cases were subsequently extended to other sectors, particularly those in which there is the potential for major loss of life such as rail, nuclear and defence. While the scope, content, structure, regulation and organisational aspects of safety cases and safety case regimes necessarily varies among the different sectors, the overall purpose and nature of a safety case remains the same: to demonstrate by argument and evidence that a system is safe.

The widening use of safety cases stimulated consideration of what should constitute a safety case. This was particularly important in areas where there were no regulations that prescribed what should be addressed in a safety case. Definitions vary in detail, but an influential definition which is consistent with general usage comes from the military domain (MoD 2007). A safety case is:

'a structured argument, supported by a body of evidence that provides a compelling, comprehensible and valid case that a system is safe for a given application in a given operating environment.'

This view of a safety case as comprising structured argument with evidence that provides a compelling case for the safety of a system is now deeply rooted in most sectors.

Of course, complex systems require large, complex safety cases. Producing and documenting a structured argument with evidence that is both compelling and comprehensible for the intended reader is a major challenge. Thus, various approaches to structuring an argument, identifying appropriate evidence and presenting them in a comprehensible manner were investigated. A current de facto standard in the UK is Goal Structuring Notation (GSN). In this approach, the safety argument is based on the idea that the top-level claim of the safety case (usually 'the system is safe') is a goal to be achieved. An argument (consisting of subgoals, strategies, etc.) is developed as a branching (and sometimes cross-linked) tree, with evidence requirements identified at the end of each branch. The argument thus provides the logic by which the top-level goal can be shown to be achieved if suitable evidence is provided. When suitable evidence is provided, the top-level goal is necessarily achieved.

By and large, safety cases are quietly providing a valuable contribution to safety, primarily by helping to ensure that safety is seen and addressed in the round rather than as a matter of minimum compliance with technical safety regulations. However, once in a while, 'safety case' becomes a high profile topic, typically as a result of an inquiry into a major accident. In spite of there being a structured argument and evidence for safety that was (presumably) considered to be compelling, an accident happened. The inquiry looks at the safety case and finds problems. Most recently, the Haddon-Cave report on the broader issues surrounding the loss of Nimrod XV230 (Haddon-Cave 2009) made a number of criticisms of safety cases. Many of them are matters of attitude rather than technical issues. Referring back to previous inquiries into major accidents, he makes the disturbing comment that many of his criticisms are 'not new'. This suggests that there may be something deficient at a fundamental level in how safety cases are currently viewed and understood.

4 Safety cases from a scientific viewpoint

At first sight, it may seem that safety cases and science have little in common. A safety case is about proving that a system is safe; science is about formulating and challenging hypotheses. However, for hundreds of years it was generally believed that science was about proving that particular 'laws of nature' were true. Only relatively recently did it become clear that this was not, in fact, possible and that hypothesis and testing is the basis of science. This section therefore considers how a safety case can be looked at from the scientific perspective. It addresses three topics:

- how a safety case can be seen in terms of hypothesis and challenge

- 'normal science' and paradigm shift in the context of safety cases
- implications of seeing safety cases in terms of hypothesis and challenge.

4.1 Safety cases, hypotheses and challenges

4.1.1 The safety case hypothesis

Where is the hypothesis in a safety case? Not the safety case itself; that is a mixture of argument and evidence. Rather, the hypothesis is the thing that the safety case attempts to prove, namely 'the system is safe'. This should not be unexpected. When work starts on a safety case, 'the system is safe' is merely a hypothesis. The next step in the traditional approach to safety cases is to assert that 'the system is safe' is a goal to be proven. Here, however, we keep it as a hypothesis, not a goal.

According to the point of view we are taking here, a hypothesis is not proven, only challenged. So what, then, of the argument and evidence that makes up a traditional safety case? It must have some value. Indeed it does, but not as proof of the hypothesis. Rather, it corresponds to the argument and evidence that a scientist puts forward to provide justification for their hypothesis being worthy of serious consideration. Typically, before a scientific hypothesis hits the streets, it will have been subjected to checks and challenges by its originator(s) to ensure that it cannot easily be dismissed. The argument and evidence put forward by the originator(s) of a safety case can be seen in the same light. It says that the hypothesis 'the system is safe' must be taken seriously and cannot easily be dismissed. This is, of course, not the same as a proof. It is more akin to a reasonableness argument. But for systems where a complete, rigorous proof of safety is not possible (which is the case for all but the simplest systems), the 'proof' provided by a safety case is simply a 'compelling argument': in other words a reasonableness argument for a hypothesis.

4.1.2 Challenging the safety case hypothesis

We now turn to challenging the hypothesis. Challenging, in the sense used in science, means a challenge that is independent of previous argument and evidence. For a scientific hypothesis, this would typically be done by other members of the scientific community after the hypothesis is made public (usually by publication or public presentation). However, the situation is not quite as simple for a safety case. Reasons include:

- Safety cases are not usually made available for wide scrutiny.

- The time available for accepting (or rejecting) a safety case is usually quite limited.
- The scope for independent challenge is usually limited because the system itself needs to be involved.

It is useful to consider the independent challenge to the hypothesis in a safety case as falling into any or all of three parts:

1. during independent assessment activities carried out while the safety case is being developed
2. during independent assessment of the safety case itself
3. after the safety case has been accepted and the system has entered service.

These are now considered in turn.

4.1.2.1 While the safety case is being developed

Independent safety assessment may be carried out (by an Independent Safety Assessor (ISA), functional safety assessor or whoever). Some of that may challenge the hypothesis 'the system is safe'. For example, an independent identification of hazards may identify hazards that are not adequately addressed by the system and thus refute the hypothesis 'the system is safe'. Note that not all independent safety assessment activity involves challenging the hypothesis. For instance, assessing conformance with a process standard is not a challenge because the system may well be safe even without adherence to the standard. In some cases, a challenge may conclude that the design as it is at the time is not adequately safe and the designers respond by making changes to the design. This can be regarded as the hypothesis failing a critical challenge and a new hypothesis being produced (note that the hypothesis 'the system is safe' implies a specific design; changing the design changes the hypothesis). Such a refinement of hypotheses before publication is not unknown in science: the overall thrust of the hypothesis remains intact but details are modified in response to observation or experiment.

4.1.2.2 Independent assessment of the completed safety case

This may (and should) include challenging the hypothesis 'the system is safe'. Indeed, it is arguable that this should be the main purpose of such an assessment. Again, not all assessment activity may challenge the hypothesis. In particular assessing conformance to process requirements is not such a challenge since non-conformance does not in itself mean that the system is not safe. Activities that may challenge the hypothesis include assessment of existing test results (which may lead to conclusions different from those in the safety case), independent testing of the system, analysis of system attributes and behaviour, and assessment against operational experience of similar systems. These challenge the hypothesis because any of them may result in the system being considered not safe (or at least not as safe as is claimed by the safety case). The most important challenges are those which are independent of the evidence given in the safety case and for which failure would result in at least severe questioning of the validity of the hypothesis 'the system is safe'. If the challenge is met successfully, then the validity of the hypothesis 'the system is safe' is strengthened in the sense that it has been severely challenged and not found wanting.

4.1.2.3 After the system has entered service

The hypothesis 'the system is safe' can be challenged by something akin to a scientific experiment: operational experience. It is important to recognise here that challenging the hypothesis means examining the operational experience for evidence that 'the system is safe' is *not* true rather than for confirmation that it is true. 'The system is safe' gains and retains credibility on the grounds that it has been subjected to stringent challenges and has not failed. As with much scientific endeavour, a direct challenge to the hypothesis may not be possible (although an accident might show that the system is not safe). It is therefore necessary to establish indirect criteria for refuting the hypothesis. Examples include component or subsystem failure rates (which may show that the system does not meet quantitative safety requirements) and system inspections (which may show that the system has changed with respect to that described in the safety case – or perhaps that it never was like that). The key point is that the collection and analysis of operational experience should be based on *challenging* 'the system is safe' rather than confirming it.

4.2 'Normal science' and paradigm shift

The great insight provided by the concepts of 'normal science' and paradigm shift is that for the most part, science actually works within a set of accepted rules, data, concepts etc. that are *not* challenged until and unless there is good reason to do so. In other words, there is accepted wisdom which lasts for as long as it seems to work. It is, in fact, hard to see how science could progress at all if everything had to be challenged all the time. Challenge is reserved for hypotheses that are important and, for some reason or other, no longer seem as sound or trustworthy as before. Then, if the hypothesis is challenged and found wanting, it must be replaced by something better – a paradigm shift.

A similar approach needs taken in respect to safety cases when seen from a scientific viewpoint. Development of a safety case – and, indeed, the interpretation of 'safe' – relies on a lot of rules, data, concepts, etc. that are regarded as accepted wisdom. They may vary from domain to domain, but each domain has its own. While it would be possible in principle to challenge any or all that could affect the validity of the hypothesis 'the system is safe', it would be impractical, wasteful and counter-productive to do so for most systems and safety cases. Accepted wisdom is accepted wisdom for good reason: it has been tried many times and not found wanting.

However, 'tried and not found wanting' does not mean right. It is a characteristic of accepted wisdom that the reasons why it is appropriate wisdom are rarely questioned. Thus it is both legitimate and necessary to consider whether accepted wisdom might not apply to a specific case and to question it if appropriate. Reasons for challenging the accepted wisdom for safety cases include new technology used by the system; improved understanding of the strengths, weaknesses and limitations of standard tools and techniques; and new insights into safety and risk. If necessary, the accepted wisdom should be changed – a paradigm shift. Two examples:

- Use of software in systems meant that the accepted tools and techniques for assessing the safety of hardware systems were no longer sufficient. New approaches had to be developed, in particular to address systematic faults and failures. New technology had required the safety assessment paradigm to change.
- Until about 20 years ago, the safety risk from civil nuclear power stations was considered to be dominated by operation at power. Then a study of one plant showed that the risk from low power and shutdown states was comparable to that from operation at power. All comprehensive safety assessments from then on had to consider low power and shutdown states. New insight into risk had required a change of paradigm.

4.3 Implications

As might already be clear from the above, the implications of adopting a scientific viewpoint for safety cases are not primarily in respect of the technical aspects of safety cases. Rather, they relate more to principles and interpretation. That does not mean they are unimportant. Many of the criticisms of safety cases raised in the Haddon-Cave report (Haddon-Cave 2009) concern attitudes, and attitudes can be conditioned or significantly affected by such things.

Implications of adopting a scientific viewpoint for safety cases include:

- 'The system is safe' is always to be regarded as a provisional statement that may yet be shown to be invalid, rather than something that has been proven or shown to be true by a safety case. 'It's safe, there's no point in looking any further' has no place here.
- The validity of 'the system is safe' lies in the extent to which it has been subjected to critical challenge and found not to be wanting. Thus challenge should

be welcomed, even encouraged, as the means by which trust in the safety of the system can be built up.

- The stronger the challenge, the more it should be welcomed. The most valuable challenges are those which have the potential to falsify the hypothesis, i.e. to show that the system is not (or is not necessarily) safe.
- The search for counter-evidence is king. A single, strong item of counter-evidence can show that a system is not safe, irrespective of the amount of evidence and argument that it is safe.
- The convincing argument and evidence in a safety case should not be regarded as proof of safety, but rather as the grounds for regarding the safety case hypothesis (i.e. 'the system is safe') as a credible proposition. The argument and evidence gives a basis for determining how the hypothesis may be challenged.
- The value of a challenge in respect to its potential for adding credibility to a hypothesis is strengthened by the degree of independence of the challenge. Critical, independent challenge should be encouraged.
- Accepted wisdom may need to be challenged. However, there should be good reasons for doing so and any challenge should focus on where there is significant potential for invalidating the hypothesis 'the system is safe' if the challenge is successful.

It is interesting that the above addresses a number of criticisms of safety cases raised in the Haddon-Cave report on the broader issues surrounding the loss of Nimrod XV230 (Haddon-Cave 2009). These criticisms include:

Compliance only. Safety cases are drawn up for compliance reasons only, and tend to follow the same, repetitive, mechanical format … Such safety cases tend also to give the answer which the customer or designer wants, i.e. that the platform is safe.

Audits. Safety case audits tend to look at the process rather than the substance of safety cases.

Self-fulfilling prophesies. Safety cases argue that a platform is 'safe' rather than examining why hazards might render a platform unsafe, and tend to be no more than self-fulfilling prophesises.

Not living documents. Safety cases languish on shelves once drawn up and are in no real sense 'living' documents or a tool for keeping abreast of hazards.

Wood-for-the-trees. Safety cases do not see the wood for the trees, giving equal attention and treatment to minor irrelevant hazards as to major catastrophic hazards, and failing to highlight, and concentrate on the principal hazards.

Haddon-Cave notes that these criticisms are 'not new'. Perhaps a change of viewpoint towards the 'hypothesis and challenge' approach found in science is due.

5 Compatibility with standards and regulatory requirements

Having considered how safety cases could be viewed in terms of the 'hypothesis and challenge' approach used by science, this section looks briefly at its compatibility with three well-known system safety standards or regulatory requirements. Note that this is intended to illustrate how the 'hypothesis and challenge' approach can fit (or not) existing standards and regulatory requirements; it is not a complete analysis.

5.1 Def Stan 00-56 Issue 4

Def Stan 00-56 Issue 4 (MoD 2007) defines a safety case as:

'A structured argument, supported by a body of evidence that provides a compelling, comprehensible and valid case that a system is safe for a given application in a given operating environment.'

It then defines a safety argument (which is presumably the argument in the safety case) as:

'a logically stated and convincingly demonstrated reason why safety requirements are met.'

A Def Stan 00-56 safety case is therefore constructive, starting from safety requirements, proceeding via argument and evidence and culminating in the conclusion that the system is safe (for the application, etc.).

The guidance to Def Stan 00-56 Issue 4 (MoD 2007) expands on what a safety case argument should comprise. Key points are explicit argument, structure, hierarchical argument and deduction starting from explicit, objective evidence (this is preferred to induction – which is stated to involve extrapolation beyond available evidence – and judgement). The overall view of a safety case is therefore a logical proof of safety, something to which 'QED' can be appended.

The 'logical proof' view is somewhat modified by the need to adjust the rigour of the argument to the potential risk, complexity and unfamiliarity of the system. However, there is still the over-riding need for it to be 'compelling'. This begs the question 'Compelling to whom?' (It is tempting to regard all of this as a consequence of the influence on the safety case of accident inquiries conducted by senior lawyers. A case made by the prosecution (or defence) has to be compelling (beyond reasonable doubt) to a judge or jury with a degree of rigour that is appropriate for the severity of the charge and the complexity and novelty of the argument and evidence.)

This view of a safety case does not reflect the scientific approach of 'hypothesis and challenge' with 'the system is safe' always being open to challenge. It tends to support a view in which safety is proven once and for all. Nevertheless, there is a hint of the scientific approach in the guidance to Def Stan 00-56 (MoD

2007). Specifically, the need to consider counter-evidence (i.e. evidence with the potential to undermine a previously accepted argument) is noted. However, this is an isolated instance and is not developed far. Indeed, the exhortation to seek out and consider counter-evidence in a safety case might be seen as sitting uncomfortably in the otherwise dominant view of a logically argued proof derived from evidence.

5.2 IEC 61508

IEC 61508 (IEC 2002) is a safety process standard which does not require or even mention 'safety case'. Nevertheless, it is interesting here because it requires one thing that is a fundamental part of the scientific approach, namely independent assessment (called functional safety assessment in IEC 61508). The stated purpose of this assessment is to 'arrive at a judgement on the functional safety achieved …' It therefore focuses directly on the safety case hypothesis 'the system is safe'.

IEC 61508 does not say how the assessor should arrive at their judgement about the functional safety achieved. However, it does say that a functional safety assessor is required to 'consider the activities carried out and the outputs obtained during each phase of the overall, E/E/PES and software safety lifecycles and judge the extent to which the objectives and requirements in this standard have been met'. The strong implication (and its usual interpretation) is that the judgement about safety is to be based on conformance to the IEC 61508 process and requirements.

While the IEC 61508 approach to safety assessment is not the 'challenge the hypothesis' approach, the requirements on a functional safety assessor do not appear to preclude it. For example, IEC 61508 requires that the likelihood and potential consequences associated with hazardous events are determined. If this has been done, then the requirements of the standard have been met. Depending on the system and the analysis already carried out, though, it may be appropriate for the assessor to 'challenge the hypothesis' by challenging some of the likelihoods and potential consequences. Rather than asking 'do the numbers seem reasonable', a challenge might be 'here is a bigger likelihood or worse potential consequence, why is it not reasonable?' It is a challenge in the scientific sense because it has the potential to show that 'the system is safe' is not necessarily true (because a likelihood or consequence has been underestimated). If there is a good reason why it is not reasonable, all well and good. If good reason cannot be found, all well and good too – something important to safety has been discovered and it can be dealt with.

5.3 CAP 670/SW01

CAP 670/SW01 (CAA 2003) sets regulatory objectives for software assurance in ATS (air traffic service) equipment. As well as giving the objectives themselves, SW01 provides non-mandatory guidance on how compliance with the (mandatory) safety objectives may be demonstrated. While limited in scope to software, SW01 notes that demonstration of satisfaction of its requirements (i.e. safety objectives) may be used in support of a system safety case.

The five SW01 safety objectives take a constructive approach to assurance of safety, starting with requirements then requiring argument and evidence for how and where they are achieved. While not prescribing the type of argument and evidence, the language used leans towards proof ('… show that it satisfies …') rather than challenge. However, there is one objective for which challenge might be the natural response: 'to ensure that functions implemented as a result of software safety requirements are not interfered with by other functions implemented in the software'. Whatever else might be done to satisfy this objective, it would be reasonable to expect part of the demonstration to be something like, 'we have looked hard for possible interference (i.e. critically challenged the hypothesis) and can find nothing that might interfere with the ability of the software to carry out its safety functions (i.e. hypothesis not refuted)'.

The concepts involved in arguing requirements satisfaction are given in terms of primary arguments and secondary arguments. Primary arguments are the main arguments for showing that the requirements are satisfied. Secondary arguments 'compensate for the possible lack of completeness and uncertainty in the primary argument' and 'need not demonstrate the claim completely, but the result should not contradict the result of the primary argument'. These do not preclude arguments based on critical challenges. However, their emphasis on demonstrating that requirements are satisfied does not appear to recognise the importance of challenge by searching for counter-evidence. A single item of counter evidence can outweigh any amount of argument and evidence for requirements satisfaction. Rigorous search and failure to find counter-evidence may not directly demonstrate requirements satisfaction but it is evidence that there is no credible reason to disbelieve it.

The guidance to SW01 provides a methodology for how compliance might be demonstrated. It introduces the concept of Assurance Evidence Levels (AELs). An AEL (in the range 1-5) expresses the safety criticality of the software safety requirement (5 being the most critical). The AEL determines the minimum set of assurance evidence that is required to be available to the regulator. Evidence is considered as coming from three sources: field service, testing and analysis, and is classed as either direct or backing evidence.

The role of field service evidence is interesting. SW01 generally limits it to providing evidence for lower AELs, higher AELs relying on evidence from testing and analysis (particularly analysis). The reason appears to be that for practical and logical reasons it is usually difficult to make a rigorous argument for satisfaction of requirements from field service experience. However, the converse is not necessarily true. Field service can readily provide a compelling argument that a requirement is not met: a single instance when a system fails to meet the requirement during field operation can be sufficient, irrespective of any amount or rigour of testing and analysis. In effect, field service experience provides a critical challenge for 'the software is safe' in that it can invalidate it, although it cannot rigorously prove it. On that basis, it is surprising that field service experience is not called on as evidence for higher AELs – not as evidence that a requirement is satisfied but as evidence that there is no reason to doubt that it is satisfied.

6 Conclusions

The main purpose of this paper is to stimulate thought and discussion about the nature of safety cases. That does not depend on specific conclusions. However, all papers need conclusions, so:

- The scientific approach of 'hypothesis and challenge' has been described and shown to be significantly different from the viewpoints usually adopted for safety cases.
- Regarding 'the system is safe' as a hypothesis (i.e. provisional claim) that is never fully proven has been examined and shown to be a reasonable viewpoint.
- There appear to be a number of benefits from adopting this viewpoint. The chief one is that it makes very clear that a questioning, challenging attitude towards the safety of a system is expected even when there is a safety case that claims to show that the system is safe.
- Brief consideration of some influential standards and regulatory objectives (Def Stan 00-56 Issue 4, IEC 61508 (2002), CAP 670/SW01) shows that while they do not, in general, exclude a more scientific approach, they tend to regard a safety case as proving or demonstrating that a system is safe rather than that there is no good reason to believe that it is not safe. This may discourage inquiry and challenge with respect to safety.
- While 'challenge' is important, so is accepted wisdom, i.e. what is usually accepted without question. Challenging accepted wisdom should be rare but may, however, be needed (for safety cases as well as science) and might result in a paradigm shift.
- Adopting a more scientific viewpoint for safety cases appears to go some way towards addressing a number of criticisms of safety cases raised in the Haddon-Cave report on the broader issues surrounding the loss of Nimrod XV230 and which he notes are 'not new'. It is noted that many of them are criticisms of attitude rather than safety engineering technique.

References

CAA (2003) CAP670 Air traffic services safety requirements. Civil Aviation Authority

Cullen (1990) The public inquiry into the Piper Alpha disaster. HM Stationery Office, London

Haddon-Cave C (2009) The Nimrod review. The Stationery Office, London

IEC (2002) IEC 61508 Functional safety of electrical/electronic/programmable electronic safety-related systems, Part 1. International Electrotechnical Commission

Kuhn TS (1962) The structure of scientific revolutions. University of Chicago Press

MoD (2007) Defence standard 00-56 Issue 4. Safety management requirements for defence systems: part 1 requirements; part 2 guidance on establishing a means of complying with part 1. Ministry of Defence

Popper KR (1959) The logic of scientific discovery. Routledge, London

Popper KR (1963) Conjectures and refutations. Routledge, London

Accounting for Evidence: Managing Evidence for Goal Based Software Safety Standards

Vivien Hamilton

Viv Hamilton Associates Ltd

Wethersfield, Essex, UK

Abstract   Goal-based safety standards require an evidence-based approach from suppliers and the large volume of evidence for safety assurance that is generated by a software project needs to be effectively assessed and managed. A structured safety argument needs to be created and agreed with regulators and other stake-holders early in the project lifecycle so that project processes can be designed to produce the required evidence. This safety argument needs to be abstracted in that it should define the requirements for evidence without attempting to explicitly identify the concrete evidence generated. A means of traceability between abstract requirements for evidence and concrete realization needs to be provided: an SQL database which can be hyperlinked to the argument is an efficient means of managing both the status of evidence and the traceability to the argument. The safety case is completed once the evidence has been successfully generated and assessed by an evidence report in which the assessment of limitations in evidence and counter-evidence can be effectively managed.

1 Introduction

This paper is concerned with the practical issues of managing the evidence that is created during the development of large software products and is required as part of a safety case before the software can be put into service. A number of research papers have discussed safety arguments but very few discuss the evidence specifically. This paper is principally applicable to projects working to goal-based standards such as Defence Standard 00-56 (Ministry of Defence 2007) and EC 482/2008 (European Commission 2008) for air traffic control that is implemented in SW01 in the UK (Civil Aviation Authority 2010). These standards are not prescriptive about how safety of software is achieved, but require instead a structured safety argument, supported by evidence for why the software product is safe and generated within the context of an overall safety management system. Of course large volumes of evidence are also generated when complying with other stan-

C. Dale, T. Anderson (eds.), *Advances in Systems Safety*, DOI 10.1007/978-0-85729-133-2_3,
© Springer-Verlag London Limited 2011

dards so some of the issues discussed in this paper may be relevant to projects using more prescriptive process based standards such as DO-178B (RTCA 1992) or IEC 61508 (IEC 2000).

Goal based standards require an evidence based approach from the supplier (Hamilton 2006) for, although the argument structures and makes sense of the evidence, it is the evidence that delivers the assurance. Ultimately the safety case must argue that there is adequate evidence to demonstrate that the product is acceptably safe.

On a small project, the volume of evidence produced is more tractable, but when the effort for development and verification of the software can be in the hundreds of man-years, the evidence generated by these processes will be correspondingly large, and the effort needed to ensure that evidence is properly assessed could be excessive.

In the context of a regulatory system that requires that the risk must be ALARP (As Low As Reasonably Practicable), there is an implied corollary, that the effort to achieve assurance needs to be applied as efficiently as practicable, since if it is inefficient, or includes nugatory effort, that wasted effort could potentially have been applied elsewhere to achieve further reduction in risk. Effective management of the evidence is crucial to achieving this, as well as potentially delivering savings to the project and ensuring that regulatory approval can be achieved in a timely manner.

2 Managing the argument

A safety argument is a complex piece of analysis which has to be scrutinized and checked for validity through manual scrutiny. Although the introduction of structuring notations, such as *Goal Structuring Notation* (GSN) (Kelly 1999) and *Claims Argument Evidence* (CAE) (Adelard 1998), enables a more rigorous analysis of the argument, verification of the correctness of the argument still requires human review. The argument therefore needs to be presented in a way that promotes readability. An argument that is cluttered with detail is difficult to comprehend and incurs the risk that it is considered in a piecemeal way such that interactions across different parts of the argument are not noted. In managing arguments and evidence, safety engineering needs to learn lessons from software engineering and adopt the principles of abstraction and of separating the requirements from the implementation: the argument needs to define the requirements for different types of evidence abstracting away from the details of the realization of the evidence. This approach enables the safety argument to be produced and agreed at an early point in the lifecycle, but in order to complete the safety case, an evidence report that traces back to the argument will need to be produced at the end of the assurance process.

An additional problem for gaining agreement on the safety argument is that typically consensus is required amongst a large number of stakeholders, including regulatory authority, operating authority, system integrator, software producer and independent safety assessor. Moreover the safety argument is a critical document for both safety and project risk, so it is likely, and desirable, especially given the focus in this paper on large software projects, that it is approved at a senior level in each of the organizations involved. It is highly desirable for the argument to be agreed at an early point in the lifecycle and preferably as part of the planning stage alongside the production of the safety management plan and technical plans, such as software development and verification plans: any later and it will be more difficult for the needs of safety assurance to influence the development and verification activities. By making a concise argument that is restricted to the requirements of the evidence to be produced and avoids implementation detail it should be easier to achieve this consensus at an early stage. Moreover, the requirements from the evidence can then be stated as objectives in the software development and verification processes and the concrete detail of how the evidence will be generated and presented can then emerge from the design of the software processes. This is far more efficient than having a safety team dictate the detailed form of the evidence to the software engineers which may result in unnecessary changes being made to the established and mature processes of the software supplier.

The large number of stakeholders who are generally required to agree the safety argument means that it is likely to be costly and time-consuming to update it. Changes to the safety argument may be unavoidable, for example if new safety requirements or safety constraints emerge in the course of system development, if significant counter-evidence is uncovered or if the intended design and implementation processes undergo significant change. A good safety argument however needs to be written in a way which means that minor changes can be absorbed within the detail of the delivery of evidence, so that only such significant changes require corresponding changes to the argument. The safety argument will need to make reference to the safety case evidence report and since, as described later in this paper, the safety case evidence report addresses limitations in the evidence and counter-evidence, this reference to the evidence report provides a further example of abstraction of unnecessary detail, making the safety argument robust to minor inconsistencies in the processes followed and evidence generated.

Given that the argument should only address the abstract requirements for evidence, a means of tracing from those requirements to the concrete realization of evidence will be needed. A simple method is for the argument to identify placeholders in the configuration management system: these placeholders can later be filled either with a single document or a hierarchy of folders and evidence. However, a more satisfactory approach is to use a relational database to link nodes of the argument to items of evidence. The advantage of a database is that it can hold additional metadata: e.g. the person responsible for producing the evidence, date created, its status in terms of completeness and also in terms of assessment against the argument. The Object Management Group (OMG) has recently generated a standardized schema for safety arguments as the Software Assurance Evidence Metamodel (SAEM) (Object Management Group 2010). A database that is accessible through hyperlinks, e.g. implemented in SQL, can also enable hyperlinks to the database entries for the evidence to be embedded in the argument.

3 Managing the processes that create evidence

As already discussed, the safety argument needs to be agreed at the earliest practicable stage of the project. In order to understand what needs to be argued, significant systems engineering and safety assessment will need to be undertaken before the safety argument can be created, but it is desirable for the argument to be in place at the planning stage before software development. This ensures that the processes that generate the largest volumes of evidence (detailed software specification; software development; software verification; system verification and system validation) can be designed to produce evidence that is suitable to provide assurance.

The abstract requirements for evidence as stated in the safety argument should be explicitly identified in the documents that define the processes that will generate that evidence: e.g. references in the safety argument to the identification and assessment of hazards will presumably be addressed by safety engineering processes; reference to demonstration of software behavior will presumably be addressed by software testing or analysis processes. By stating the requirements for evidence as objectives of the process, the process can be designed to generate evidence of the required form and verification of the acceptability of the evidence can be made a normal part of the verification of the process. This also has the added benefit that every member of the project can see how their work contributes to producing a safe (and assured) product.

A previous paper (Hamilton 2006) discussed how there are two types of properties of evidence: those that can be objectively assessed and those that are subject to (expert) judgment. Processes can often be defined such that many of the objective properties of the evidence are automatically achieved. For example, in software engineering, the development environment can be configured to ensure that correctly named objects are stored in the configuration management system with the appropriate meta-data fields completed. An example from safety engineering could be a tool to support HAZOP that ensures that entries are recorded for all of a defined set of guidewords. The properties that are subject to judgment cannot be automated in this way, for example the software engineering object will need to be reviewed to ensure that it is appropriately designed and the HAZOP will need to be reviewed to ensure that all the entries are correct and meaningful; however it may still be possible to provide tool support to provide an audit trail, for example to enforce that a person of a defined role completes a review field. From the perspective of good safety engineering, evidence, and the assessment of evidence, should be as objective as possible. It is not possible for expert judgment to be removed entirely but it should be relied on only for those properties of evidence that are necessarily subject to judgment. An argument that uses subjective judgment for objective properties that could have been objectively assessed may appear 'handwaving' and unconvincing. To ensure that these objective properties can be objectively assessed, processes need to be designed to systematically produce the evidence and verify its properties.

In the CAE notation for safety cases, evidence is linked to claims through arguments that explicitly justify why the evidence is adequate to discharge the claim. GSN does not have such an explicit argument: it does have an optional justification notation but in general the goals should be decomposed sufficiently that the relationship between the evidence and goal is obvious. In either case thought needs to be given as to why the evidence is adequate to fulfil the safety claims, why this approach has been selected and how possible weaknesses have been addressed. These are also the questions that need to be considered when planning the processes to be adopted in the project, so the document that provides the process definition is also the obvious place to record the justification for the approach, bearing in mind from the previous discussion that the process document should explicitly state, as objectives of the process, the requirements for evidence as defined in the safety argument. So in the planning stages of the project, the safety engineer should be actively in discussion with each of the other technical experts in the project, covering software design, coding, testing etc. to ensure that each process definition meets the needs of safety assurance in addition to the other technical goals of the project.

There is one further area in which the project processes can be optimized to deliver evidence in a form suitable for the safety case and that is in the final form of documentation. Each project process on completion should produce some form of summary document that confirms successful completion of the process, achievement of the objectives of the process (including the objectives to generate the safety assurance evidence) and also makes explicit reference to the body of evidence generated by that process. Of course most projects already do this for testing, but it is not necessarily the case that such a summary report exists for specification, design and coding processes. On a small project this may not be such an issue: if, for example, the entire specification can be encompassed in a single document, then the final issue of the document implicitly provides such a document. On a large project however the specification is likely to be spread over multiple documents and whichever is the latest such document to be issued or updated is relevant only to one area of the software and says nothing about the specification process as a whole. Imposing an additional requirement for such a summary document provides a convenient means of simplifying traceability from the argument to the body of evidence. It also has the benefit that formal documents normally have a defined process of document review and approval with signatories so a formal document provides a means of generating evidence that the appropriate persons, who were both competent and accountable for the delivery of a part of the evidence, have confirmed that the evidence is correct.

Figure 1 illustrates how the reference to evidence, using summary documents and process definitions that justify the process, might appear in a safety argument constructed using GSN.

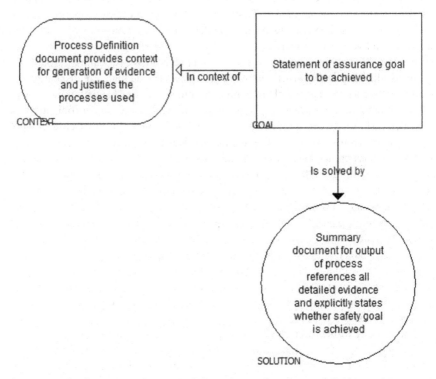

Fig. 1. Example of argument using GSN relating safety goals to process definitions and summary evidence documents

4 Assessing the evidence

4.1 Overall process of assessment

The process for assessment should ensure that the assessment is as objective as possible and that any anomalies, limitations, assurance deficits and counter-evidence are dealt with transparently and at an appropriate stage of the assessment. Software engineering uses a V model to explore the relationship between requirements and implementation and between test evidence produced at progressive stages of integration, and a similar model can illustrate how evidence should be progressively assessed.

Figure 2 illustrates, on the left hand side, how the requirements for evidence are refined from the safety argument through the definitions of the processes that generate the evidence. The right hand side illustrates the progressive assessment from individual items of evidence in their raw state, to an overall judgment of the acceptability (or otherwise) of the safety case. Each individual item of evidence is first verified against the exit criteria of the process to produce pass/fail results, e.g. was a test result within the defined tolerances, did a code file pass static analysis checks, did a design document successfully pass its review process? For most of these the assessments are being made against objective criteria defined in the process definition; the verification is a normal part of the process and the involvement of safety experts should not be necessary.

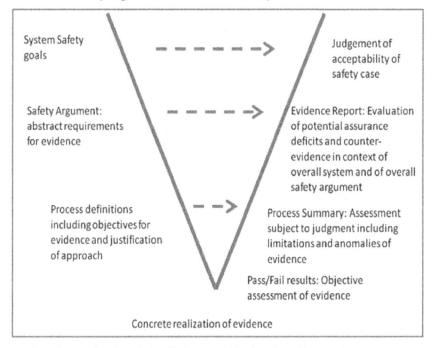

Fig. 2. V diagram showing relationship between objectives for evidence and assessment stages

The process summary document then identifies the extent to which the outputs of that process have met the safety objectives. Did all of the tests pass? If not, what was the pass rate and where are the failures recorded and analyzed? Were all of the tests carried out exactly as specified? If not what were the deviations and what are the consequences for the safety objectives? Were all of the tests completed? If not where is it stated which parts of the software are not tested? Since this part of the assessment of evidence is concerned with process compliance, additional backing evidence for the safety case can be provided through quality auditing to check that processes are being properly carried out.

Both Defence Standard 00-56 and EC 482/2008 require the safety argument to be produced within the context of a safety management system. Objective evidence of the correct operation of the safety management system and also project quality management system should also be recorded and summarized and audits carried out to confirm the effectiveness of these management systems. Assuming that the quality management system contains methods of managing deviations to processes and that the safety management system contains systems for managing potential safety issues in the product or the evidence, then these too are processes that need to be summarized, with any observed limitations recorded.

The title of this paper is *accounting for evidence* since this reflects that what should occur is systematic recording and objective assessment. Moreover all of the limitations with evidence should be recorded so that the overall presentation of the evidence shows transparently exactly what has been achieved, and what still remains unproven. As the processes continue up the right hand side of the V model, more safety judgment is required in assessing the impact on the safety case of the individual faults and limitations uncovered in the detailed evidence.

4.2 Limitations, counter-evidence and assurance deficits

Life is not perfect and neither is evidence. Software will contain faults; tests will fail; documentation will contain errors and audits will find deviations in processes. The problem for assessment of the safety case is how much of this actually matters to safety.

In this paper the word *limitation* has been used as a general term to describe any difference from the ideal state of the evidence. *Counter-evidence* is defined in Defence Standard 00-56 as evidence with the *potential* to undermine safety claims. As Defence Standard 00-56 requires a pro-active search for counter-evidence, a limitation needs to be considered as possible counter-evidence unless or until it can be shown that the safety claims are not undermined by that limitation. Suppose for example that a test has failed, and as a result a fault has been found in the software, this limitation (in the correctness of the software) might be counter-evidence. On the other hand if the fault is in some functionality that is not safety related, then it is likely that, from a safety perspective, the existence of the fault is acceptable, and so this limitation is not counter-evidence. Any member of the project who is competent in a particular process area could record limitations and assess their impact in relation to the scope of that process. However, counter-evidence is wholly related to the safety of the product and must be assessed by a competent safety professional. Hence it is important that limitations are accurately and transparently recorded in the evidence generated by all of the project processes and identified in the summary process documents, so that they can be assessed by a safety engineer.

What if a problem with a test meant that instead of identifying a fault in the software, the test simply could not be executed? Here the problem is not that the software is known to be incorrect: the problem is that because the test could not be executed there is no evidence that the software is correct. The term *assurance deficit* (Menon et al. 2010) is used where such uncertainty exists. However, as with counter-evidence, a limitation in evidence is not automatically an assurance deficit when considered in the overall context of the safety case. Suppose the software verification was being done in an automated test environment in which some test could not be executed, so that there is a limitation in the extent of the software verification, but it is possible to execute a test that achieves the same test objectives in the overall system environment: in this case a limitation in software testing is addressed through system testing so there is no assurance deficit. Assurance deficits are concerned with the overall uncertainty in the safety case, so as with counter-evidence, assessment of whether or not limitations constitute assurance deficits should be determined by a competent safety professional.

By freeing the safety engineers from having to scrutinize a large amount of low level raw evidence, they should be able to better concentrate on the issue of safety on the overall context. In particular, as required by Defence Standard 00-56, the search for counter-evidence should be pro-active and look beyond the immediate project. Additionally, by seeing the whole picture presented by the evidence, the safety engineers may be in a better position to identify the 'counter-intuitive' possibilities identified by Littlewood and Wright (Littlewood and Wright 2007) in which being more successful in generating evidence can occasionally reduce confidence overall, an example of which is that if the entire test programme fails to find any faults, it may be suspected that the test system is ineffective.

The safety management system should have specific objectives to manage the identification, assessment and mitigation of assurance deficits and counter-evidence. The output of that activity will be recorded in the safety case evidence report.

4.3 Safety case evidence report

The safety case evidence report is the final deliverable of the assurance process. Since the safety argument should be designed to be abstract, it is possible for a single version of a safety argument to cover multiple software installations, or multiple deliveries of a phased-delivery project. However, the safety case evidence report will need to address a specific software version and a specific installation. The safety case evidence report will identify the unique set of relevant evidence for the safety case. It will need to refer to the baseline of the software (which may be addressed by standard documentation such as a release note) and it will need to relate this to the appropriate set of safety evidence, including system level evidence. Each installation may have unique evidence: specific site constraints; a unique history of field experience perhaps using previous versions of the software, and different experiences of commissioning.

The safety case evidence report is the output of the process of assessment of limitations, assurance deficits and counter-evidence. It provides the summary of the assessment process and the resultant identification of assurance deficits and counter-evidence in the context of the overall safety case. It will also confirm the successful operation of the safety management system.

Since it assesses the complete set of evidence it is able to evaluate which parts of the argument are supported by evidence that is compelling and which parts are less convincing and therefore where the residual risk lies. Although an extension to the GSN notation exists to identify the relative contribution of different parts of the argument, it does not appear to be used in practice. This is possibly because it adds notational complexity to what are already complex pieces of analysis. The safety case evidence report would appear to be a more suitable place in which to note the relative weights of different parts of the argument, since this can be stated in the context of the actual evidence delivered. As the final output of the safety assurance process, the safety case evidence report is issued to those who need to make the decision to accept or reject the safety case.

5 Conclusion

This paper is not a theoretical study but instead attempts to give pragmatic guidance on the issues of managing a large body of safety assurance evidence, since for large software projects any inefficiencies in this area will be at best costly and at worst lead to a weak or incorrect safety case or severe delays to delivery into service of the product.

It is the responsibility of the project manager to deliver a product that is both safe and seen to be safe through the body of safety assurance evidence. One of the goals embedded in the approach in this paper is to establish a culture such that all members of the project team are accountable for delivery of safety assurance evidence in their area of responsibility. In such a culture, the safety engineer works not in isolation retrospectively reviewing and judging project artifacts, but as a partner working in dialogue with other technical experts to establish processes that enable the project as a whole to deliver the safety assurance in an efficient manner.

The approach has drawn on three principles learned from software engineering: information hiding; separating requirements from concrete realization, and progressive integration. The safety argument should address the abstract requirements for evidence, deferring unnecessary detail on the realization of evidence to a safety case evidence report. A means of traceability is needed between the nodes of the argument and the eventual evidence, perhaps using a relational database which can also record the status of evidence. Finally the evidence needs to be assessed as it is generated, working progressively from detailed anomalies specific to the type of evidence, to understand how this might contribute potential assurance deficits or counter-evidence, and then sentencing this information in the overall system context to evaluate whether or not the evidence delivers a satisfactory safety case.

The process of accounting for evidence includes the systematic recording and objective assessment of evidence that generates, through the exercise of appropriate judgment, an accurate overall picture in which any problems with evidence are transparently stated in order that the safety case shows exactly what has been achieved, and what still remains unproven.

Acknowledgments   The author gratefully acknowledges the discussions on safety arguments and insight into the SAEM provided by Dr Tim Kelly, University of York.

References

Adelard (1998) ASCAD – Adelard safety case development manual
Civil Aviation Authority (2010) CAP 670 ATS safety requirements
European Commission (2008) Commission Regulation (EC) No 482/2008 Establishing a software safety assurance system to be implemented by air navigation service providers and amending annex II to regulation (EC) No 2096/2005 http://www.caa.co.uk/docs/952/SESESARR%28482-2008%29.pdf. Accessed 12 September 2010
Hamilton V (2006) Criteria for safety evidence – goal-based standards require evidence based approaches. Safety Systems 16:1 September 2006. http://www.vivhamilton.co.uk/Papers/SCEvCriteria.pdf. Accessed 12 September 2010
IEC (2000) ISO/IEC 61508 Functional safety of electrical/electronic/programmable electronic safety related systems, Parts 1 to 7. International Electrotechnical Commission
Kelly T (1999) Arguing safety – a systematic approach to safety case management. PhD thesis, University of York YCST99/05
Littlewood B, Wright D (2007) The use of multi-legged arguments to increase confidence in safety claims for software-based systems: a study based on a BBN of an idealized example. IEEE Trans Softw Eng 33:347-365
Menon C, Hawkins R, McDermid J, Kelly T (2010) An overview of the SOBP for software in the context of DS 00-56 issue 4. In: Dale C, Anderson T (eds) Making systems safer. Springer-Verlag, London
Ministry of Defence (2007) Defence Standard 00-56 Issue 4: Safety management requirements for defence systems
Object Management Group (2010) Software assurance evidence metamodel (SAEM) Sysa/10-02-01 http://www.omg.org/cgi-bin/doc?sysa/10-02-01. Accessed 23 March 2010
RTCA (1992) RTCA/DO-178B: Software considerations in airborne systems an equipment certification. RTCA

Projects, Services and Systems of Systems

Distinguishing Fact from Fiction in a System of Systems Safety Case

Zoë Stephenson[1], Christian Fairburn[2], George Despotou[1], Tim Kelly[1], Nicola Herbert[2] and Bruce Daughtrey[2]

[1]University of York, UK

[2]BAE Systems, Preston, UK

Abstract Based on our recent experience, 'distinguishing fact from fiction' in relation to System of Systems (SoS) safety has emerged as a pertinent topic in a number of senses. From an analytical perspective, we recognise that it would be a mistake to treat a SoS as 'just another complex system'. The defining properties of a SoS mean that traditional analysis methods may fall short if applied without additional support. On the other hand, we also argue that the structured and comprehensive analysis of a SoS need not be so complex as to be impractical.

We draw on an internal BAE Systems development project, Integrated Aircrew Training (IAT), as an exemplar. IAT interconnects multiple systems and participants – air and ground assets – into a training SoS. As would be expected we have identified a number of sources of complexity in the analysis of this SoS, chiefly the exponential impact of interactions among increasing numbers of system elements on analysis complexity. However, the training domain provides constraints which may be captured as feature models to structure the analysis.

We outline a SoS hazard assessment process and associated safety case approach that are the subject of ongoing research and development and as such, are not yet formally recognised. They acknowledge that the presence of human decision-makers in a SoS means that human factors analysis contributes significantly to SoS safety assessment. We discuss the human element in SoS safety analysis and show how its treatment in the case of IAT has caused us to recognise that augmented-reality training brings with it both novel sources and consequences of human 'error'. In this particular SoS, the 'fact versus fiction' differential also applies to SoS users and the notion of participant 'immersion' is a key area of interest.

1 Introduction

The System of Systems (SoS) term is increasingly used to describe classes of systems, such as the Air Traffic Management (ATM) and Network Centric Warfare (NCW) paradigms, which exhibit a combination of the following characteristics:

C. Dale, T. Anderson (eds.), *Advances in Systems Safety*, DOI 10.1007/978-0-85729-133-2_4,

- common overall objectives
- multiple elements which are systems in their own right and which demonstrate varying degrees of autonomy
- geographically dispersed elements
- dynamic collaboration of elements to achieve common objectives
- heavy dependency on network communications
- ad-hoc communications networks (Alexander et al. 2004)
- independently developed constituent elements (Despotou et al. 2009)
- emergent behaviours (Maier 1998)
- system complexity.

This definition helps us to differentiate 'fact' from 'fiction' in an analytical sense as it illustrates that the SoS term is about more than just complexity and scale. Consider for example an aircraft. Under the SoS definition presented above, an aircraft would be considered as a complex system but it would be wrong to view an aircraft as a SoS. An aircraft is a complex system whose components perform distinct roles, but these components are not independent systems in their own right in a SoS sense; an aircraft engine provides propulsion and is something of a 'hub' with regard to onboard power generation, however it is co-located with other system elements on the aircraft platform and the way it interacts with these other elements is well defined, predictable and relatively invariable.

Comparing the aircraft complex system with, for example, an ATM or NCW SoS, it is clear that the degree of 'openness' and flexibility with regard to membership and role within the system is quite different. The aircraft engine does not have a 'life of its own' outside the complex system. Aircraft systems are designed to work together in one or a relatively small number of fixed and well defined configurations. The way in which they are integrated takes account of this. Nodes in an NCW network, on the other hand, may or may not always be present and the functions that are performed within an NCW SoS may be allocated in quite different ways across the nodes which are members of the SoS at a particular point in time.

From a safety point of view distinguishing a SoS from complex systems is necessary. Recognition of the fact that a SoS is not just a large complex system and that a complex system such as an aircraft is not a SoS leads us to realise that the safety analyses applied to 'traditional' systems may fall short of exhaustively revealing hazards in a SoS context. Whereas our understanding and the methods used to demonstrate the safety of an aircraft are considered sufficient, it is difficult to identify the hazards in a SoS following the NCW paradigm. The inherent characteristics of SoS affect the ability to understand hazards and apportion safety related requirements (Despotou et al. 2009).

In exploring SoS safety assessment, this paper makes reference to an internal BAE Systems development project, Integrated Aircrew Training (IAT), as an exemplar. IAT is a SoS training system for training and developing combat aircrew. It allows pilots and navigators to be trained by combining Live, Virtual and simulated Constructive (LVC) elements into realistic multiplayer training scenarios that closely resemble those encountered in operational experience. For the purposes of this paper, 'Live' elements of the IAT SoS are real people operating real equipment (e.g. aircrew flying in fast jet aircraft). 'Virtual' elements of the IAT SoS are real people operating simulated equipment (e.g. aircrew 'flying' a ground based simulator) and 'Constructive' elements of the IAT SoS are simulated people or simulated equipment under computer control (e.g. a computer generated synthetic hostile aircraft or surface to air threat).

IAT provides a common training environment, with the ability to coordinate multiple assets. IAT interconnects multiple systems and participants: aircrew in real aircraft, Virtual participants in ground-based simulators and training devices. Geographically dispersed participants can train side-by-side. IAT can thus be described as a SoS that consists of various interconnected standalone systems. The obvious advantage of adopting such an architecture is that it provides a flexible training system that is able to adapt according to training needs and the required numbers of participants in a training scenario. However, the systems in the IAT SoS are of diverse types and build standards, and will include aircraft, simulators, communications and ground equipment that were not originally designed to be interconnected. Furthermore, the complexity and variability of such a SoS has the potential to make safety analysis problematic.

Having established that SoSs are not the same as complex systems, and that complex systems such as aircraft are not SoSs, we need to establish which existing techniques/approaches can be utilised in support of SoSs, which cannot and what else is required in addition (i.e. distinguishing fact from fiction when moving from complex systems to SoSs). Based on this, the paper will therefore outline a SoS hazard assessment approach, detailing some of the steps we are taking to handle the difficulties of safety analysis for our exemplar, IAT. Despite the fact that a SoS like IAT raises a number of challenges, analysts can still use existing principles to structure the SoS safety lifecycle; however, there can be a certain amount of hazard attributed to the distinct combination of SoS characteristics that will require problem specific approaches (Despotou and Kelly 2010). One of the most challenging parts of this project is the variation in human behaviour; and so we also describe aspects of our approach that are specific to the modelling of how human behaviour contributes to safety. Finally, we conclude with our plans for future development, particularly in the use of automated techniques and in the validation of our proposed method as an adequate and practical response to the 'facts' of SoS analysis.

2 Hazard assessment approach

Rigorous, traceable and comprehensive hazard assessment is required in the production of safety involved systems, regardless of the specific type of system in question. Assessment techniques and processes are well established for this purpose, however knowing what is known about SoSs, it could be a mistake to apply these existing methods in exactly the same way as they applied in the case of complex systems.

For this paper we treat hazard assessment as a combination of two interrelated concepts: hazard identification, in which the possible hazardous events at the system boundary are discovered, and hazard analysis, in which the likelihood, consequences and severity of the events are determined. The hazard identification process is based on a model of the way in which parts of a system may deviate from their intended behaviour. Examples of such analysis include Hazard and Operability Studies (HAZOP, Kletz 1992), Fault Propagation and Transformation Calculus (Wallace 2005), Function Failure Analysis (SAE 1996) and Failure Modes and Effects Analysis (Villemeur 1992). Some analysis approaches start with possible deviations and determine likely undesired outcomes (so-called inductive approaches) while others start with a particular unwanted event and try to determine possible causes (so-called deductive approaches). The overall goal may be safety analysis, to assess the safety of a proposed system (a design, a model or an actual product) or accident analysis, to determine the likely causes of an incident that has occurred.

The challenge for hazard assessment in a SoS is the inability of current techniques to convincingly account for uncoordinated interactions between the various systems. Such interactions typically involve a coincidence of events that are otherwise not hazardous, and which may (as noted by Alexander 2007) be of rather different types, involving information from multiple domains studied by a diverse range of experts. Without specific techniques to address the complexity, the likelihood is that many hazardous interactions will remain unaddressed.

Approaches that try to address the phenomenon of unknown variation include:

Modelling the variation. A description such as a feature model (Kang et al. 1990) can be created to explicitly detail the configurations that will be encountered. The resulting safety assessment is contingent on every configuration that is subsequently encountered being represented in the feature model, something known as the *oracle hypothesis* (Weiss and Lai 1999). The approach is generally applied in product lines in which the risk of not modelling the variation is greater than the risk of an incorrect model. This use of modelling goes some way towards meeting the suggestion of (Raheja and Moriarty 2006):

> 'System safety needs to pay more attention to hazard analysis on the structure and architecture of the system-of-systems.'

Product-line safety assessment typically generalises from individual safety analyses to produce a configurable analysis result that is then customised to the particular product in question. The process may involve annotation of an existing model, such as fault trees (Dehlinger and Lutz 2005), or it may involve the creation of a new model (Stephenson et al. 2004). In contrast to these relatively simple approaches, (Habli 2009) describes a complex meta-model that relates design variation, context variation, events, consequences and severities. It is important to note that each of these bodies of work assumes the existence of hazard assessment information relating to particular products that can be used to populate and validate the model.

Focusing the analysis with decision support tools. Tools can cut down a complex search space by highlighting important aspects of the space for further analysis. (Alexander 2007) proposes such a tool for SoS hazard assessment. The tool uses agent-based simulation to suggest likely unwanted events and explain their causes. In cases where the complexity is so high that analysis is impossible without some filtering of the events, such an approach provides useful support; while it does not claim to discover all of the unwanted events, it does provide a tractable starting-point for manual training scenario analysis.

Creating a richer model of causation. (Leveson and Dulac 2005) propose the STAMP accident model and the STPA hazard assessment approach. STAMP is based on systems-theoretic concepts of hierarchical control, internal models of the environment and a classification of control errors. STPA takes that classification as the basis for iterative integrated control system safety assessment. At each design iteration the design is assessed and constraints are derived (equivalent to derived safety requirements) and imposed on further design iterations.

We base our choice of hazard assessment approach on the recognition that the scope of variation in IAT is limited and well-defined due to its reuse of existing training infrastructure and equipment. The key additions with IAT – the augmented reality/synthetic elements – are small modifications to allow for integrated simulation coupled with new technology embodying the majority of the simulation functionality. The deviation from existing end-user functionality is therefore relatively small. In contrast to SoSs that include autonomous equipment, there is significant opportunity for human review in this SoS domain. As additional motivation, we note that the hazard assessment and safety case production for an individual training scenario must be as streamlined as possible.

The approach for hazard assessment and safety case development is outlined in Figure 1. We propose to analyse safety from two perspectives, 'pre-deployment' and 'post-deployment' (discussed in more detail later). We model the limited, well-defined variations between training scenarios as a feature model. The configuration process automatically suggests the corresponding safety case structure, hazard log, derived safety requirements and mitigations, as traceable, validatable links from the configuration specification to explicitly-defined reusable artefacts. At each stage, the automated suggestions are validated using a validation guide that is specific to the type of training scenario being configured. Where mitigating actions alter the configuration, the process is iterated to assess any remaining hazards. To ensure that this process terminates, we impose a constraint that all mitigating actions correspond to a move from one configuration to another that is no less constrained.

To set up the artefacts for this process, we also base our up-front processes on the feature model, as shown in Figure 1. The initial data for each system or agent involved in IAT is derived from a differential analysis, looking in detail at the way the use of IAT influences a particular task or system. For example, when the IAT SoS is active, cockpit display systems will represent data pertaining to both Live and synthetic agents, also the briefing process may need to include participants who are to 'fly' as Virtuals as well as those who are to fly as Live platforms in the training scenario. A high-level preliminary assessment is performed on the general training scenario scope at a suitable configuration stage. This is chosen so that the groupings correspond to distinct training scenario types, as determined by domain experts. The assessment is based on HAZOP and HAZAN (Hazard Analysis) with customised guidewords for specific flow types. A low-level analysis is performed on exemplars of each training scenario type, to investigate detailed training scenario characteristics. This is generalised into the scope of the preliminary analysis. Where there are mismatches or other issues from generalisation, we perform a specific interaction analysis based on both nominal and abnormal behaviours, and we generalise from all such analyses to inform the overall hazard assessment approach. Finally, where there are specific translations or mappings from one representation or medium to another, we explicitly assess the gap to determine whether it contributes additional deviations that need to be addressed. We recognise throughout this approach that system hazards, SoS hazards, likelihood and severity may all be contingent on the particular configuration options that are selected.

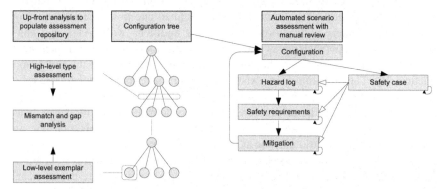

Fig. 1. Configuration-directed hazard assessment and safety-case production

Our initial process definitions have highlighted a number of specific characteristics of the assessment approach, as detailed in the following sections.

2.1 Feature modelling

A typical feature modelling approach represents features – aspects of a product that are interesting to particular stakeholders – and the available combinations of features (Czarnecki and Eisenecker 2000). The original feature modelling approach (Kang et al. 1990) is based on binary features and logical feature dependencies; we are using an extended feature modelling approach with:

- cardinalities, representing replication of a feature, to handle the variation in the number of participants in a training scenario
- staged configuration, allowing for partial customisation of the feature model
- uncertainty, to represent approximate configurations
- explicit binding processes, to structure the configuration stages and uncertainties into a manageable sequence of decisions.

It is recognised that feature models provide a very useful representation of features and dependencies for a particular product, however care needs to be taken as some types of product feature might be more appropriately represented using a different modelling technique. Typical examples include N×N dependency matrices (Stephenson et al. 2004) or parameter envelopes.

One final concern with the use of the feature model is its central role in deciding what reusable artefacts are included. If the feature model is incorrect, it has consequences for the validity of the hazard assessment, the safety claims and the entire safety case. To offset this concern, we note our assumptions that:

- Many issues with appropriateness of scope and with validity will be uncovered as the safety assessment process explores the configuration space.
- We are able to set up and maintain appropriate feedback paths within the development process to allow any member of the development team to report problems with the feature model.
- We are able to assign appropriate responsibility and authority to control the evolution of the feature model, with associated traceability and change history.
- We are able to set up and maintain similar feedback paths between the customer and the development process to catch any remaining problems that occur.
- We are able to budget for, set up and conduct periodic reviews of the scope and validity of the model.

2.2 Configuration space structure

In our development approach, there is an assumption that the different binding processes are able to communicate the scope of the intended use of the system using a customised feature model. For this to work in practice, it must be able to represent:

- the changes to the configuration over time – as decisions are made, as feasibility studies are conducted, as work is completed to integrate component systems
- the different versions of the product – as new features are developed and enabled for successive releases of the product

- the different customers – each installation will have different equipment available, different subsets of the training needs and so on.

Moreover, these aspects must be managed in the binding processes (the processes that make decisions about the configuration of the model) and the configuration stages as well as in the dependency structure of the feature model. For example, if a later version of the product for a particular customer needs to enable a new type of training scenario, it must be possible to create the appropriate configuration stage within the binding process associated with that deployment; this configuration stage is a rebinding of the configuration that was used for the previous version. There is nothing inherent in this process that ensures that neither of these versions undoes a commitment made in the previous configuration stage, within the development process. Indeed, it may be necessary to unbind internal development commitments in order to produce a product release with the desired features.

Propagating unbinding through previous development stages is especially costly when the feature model and the configuration approach are the basis for the safety assessment and safety case. To limit the effects of these issues, we take the traditional step of aligning feature model structure to business goals (Bayer et al. 1999) – a step well-supported by the use of MODAF (Ministry of Defence Architectural Framework) as it covers both managerial and technical activities –but we also aim to provide specific validation criteria such as measurements of the distances between scenarios with similar objectives, that report on the healthiness of the feature model. We expect that this will be especially valuable when dealing with feature models that carry uncertainty information.

2.3 Pre-deployment hazard assessment

The pre-deployment hazard assessment must take into account the presence of hazards across all of the different agreed possible uses of the deployed system. The assessment is divided into two parts:

- assessment of the non-variable elements of the SoS: the training devices, the network infrastructure, the set of training needs and the process structure
- assessment of variable elements of the SoS: particular objectives for a training scenario, particular training needs, particular equipment used for a training scenario.

We expect the former to be relatively straightforward. For the latter, the goal is to set up appropriate reusable data for the post-deployment assessment process. This includes reusable artefacts such as hazard entries and derived safety requirements, but also specific versions of the assessment process for particular types of training scenario.

2.4 Post-deployment hazard assessment

The suggested hazards from the previous step provide a 'head start' in the hazard assessment of the training scenario and the production of the safety case, augmented by manual review. Particular issues of concern here are:

Incompleteness. There may be hazards in the training scenario that were not associated with the feature model, but which would have been found in a conventional assessment approach. This is a serious concern with any approach that tries to automatically identify hazards in a system. Our aim with the post-deployment assessment is to show that we have supplied appropriate artefacts for reuse and that there are sufficient opportunities for manual review and operational activity to uncover and mitigate additional hazards.

Pessimism. The up-front analysis is likely to be conservative. In certain configurations it will highlight potential hazards that will not be manifest in practice. Similarly, the likelihood of an event may be overestimated or the severity of the consequences may be overstated. We expect to discover these problems during the validation stage and to devise specific guidance on the reduction of pessimism. It is likely that we will introduce mechanisms to measure pessimism in the analysis for particular training scenarios as part of the overall evaluation of safety assessment effectiveness.

System Interactions. The presence of unintended interactions between nominal behaviours complicates the assessment approach. We expect that the constrained scope will lead to a small set of interaction classes to analyse for any given training scenario, generalised from the results of particular assessments. For example, the presence of 'fictional' elements in training scenarios is expected to give rise to a general class of interactions as well as specific issues for particular elements. As part of the analysis of the effectiveness of the safety assessment approach, we intend to provide for feedback and review of interaction analyses.

Multiple Versions. It is desirable to be able to meet a particular training need in a number of different ways, to avoid learning by rote. At the same time, it is important to be able to compare similar training scenarios to ensure that large variations in the safety assessment results are catered for. This naturally leads to the idea of comparing training scenarios for similarity; we are particularly concerned with the possibility that configuration similarity may be quite different from training scenario similarity, and that this may lead to training scenarios that are superficially similar being assessed in similar ways without properly investigating the details of the training scenarios such as the varying demands on human participants.

2.5 Safety case

A number of standards require a system to be accompanied by a safety case, and a SoS should be no different. The safety case communicates an argument, supported by evidence, that a system is acceptably safe in a given operational context. The safety case captures the underlying reasoning and evidence that support claims made about the safety of a system. We believe that the hazard assessment process we have proposed is compatible with the creation of a safety case. We also believe that it will be possible to produce a manageable SoS safety case which takes account of SoS specific issues and which conforms to relevant standards.

Process-based standards such as IEC 61508, DEFSTAN 00-55 and DO-178B list predetermined activities, which when followed by system developers are considered to result in an acceptably safe system. All three standards use a risk-based approach according to which – depending on the consequences of the risk (i.e. catastrophic, major etc.) – the system is assigned a 'safety' level such as Safety Integrity Levels. Safety levels represent quantified risk targets that a system has to meet, based on probability for the occurrence of an accident and/or the severity of that accident. According to the safety level a system is required to achieve, standards specify the means with which the developers will acquire assurance about the system's operation. This also applies to evidence collection, for which there are tables prescribing the testing techniques and methods required (or recommended) for each safety level. By and large, higher assurance levels involve more thorough examination of a system. This can involve additional testing techniques 'cross-checking' the system behaviour, as well as more advanced techniques (such as formal methods) contributing to the overall assurance of claims regarding the system's safe operation.

Use of prescriptive standards provides a specific and easily interpreted way of acquiring assurance about the safe operation of the system. In contrast, goal-based standards such as DEFSTAN 00-56 (Issue 4) require the developer to assure the safety of the delivered system through structured reasoning, with the provision of a safety case. This includes reasoning about using the right (system development) techniques at the right time during system development to support the safety case. This allows potentially greater flexibility, as developers are not instructed to use a specific set of techniques. Although the two categories of standards adopt different philosophies, it is generally recognised that the higher the involved risk is, the more evidence and scrutiny are required. This is a default position in prescriptive standards. In evidence-based standards this principle appears in the form of quantity and quality of evidence required to support a position. DEFSTAN 00-56 (Issue 4) recognises that: 'The quantity and quality of the evidence shall be commensurate with the potential risk posed by the system and the complexity of the system'.

It has thus been identified that there is a requirement for SoSs to be accompanied by a goal-based SoS safety case. One 'fiction' relating to SoS safety cases is that producing and maintaining an SoS safety case for a large, very complex and changeable SoS will be in all cases an onerous task that borders on the impossible. However, we believe that a maintainable SoS safety case should be achievable through the development of a SoS safety case with a modular design.

The main advantage of adopting a modular approach to the safety case is in its maintainability. Developers can create coherent arguments about an aspect of the system, which can then be integrated into the system safety case. This can be particularly useful for incremental development of the safety case, in parallel with the system. Adopting a modular approach can be useful in the management of change, which is inevitable in development of an incremental safety case. Packaging the safety case in cohesive modules can help in isolating the change and understanding its impact. The effectiveness of a modular safety case (with respect to managing change) depends on the type of change. However, adoption of a modular approach is recommended as it exhibits the following advantages (Despotou and Kelly 2008):

- will contain some of the changes
- does not add any technical overhead when compared to a monolithic safety case
- improves the clarity of the safety case
- allows different stakeholders to isolate the arguments that are most relevant to them.

Furthermore, a modular design will allow isolation of claims about scenarios and the evidence that will need to be produced to support scenario related claims.

In the case of our exemplar, IAT, preliminary safety activities have started to identify the types of evidence that will be considered suitable to support the claims made in the safety case to an acceptable degree of confidence. The identified types of evidence include evidence that are produced by processes common in systems adhering to older standards (such as 00-55) as well as more novel safety analysis methods. Part of the novelty of IAT derives from its SoS characteristics, and therefore novel safety analysis techniques are required.

Another 'fiction' relating to SoS safety cases is that the adoption of Def Stan 00-56 Issue 4 will make it difficult to construct a safety case because the onus is on the designers to argue that the right evidence has been produced in support of the safety case. However, the 'fact' is that Def Stan 00-56 Issue 4, being a goal-based rather than a prescriptive standard, allows potentially greater flexibility in the types of evidence that can be presented in order to support the safety case and demonstrate that the system of systems is acceptably safe. Therefore the outputs of novel safety analysis techniques can be used as evidence to support the SoS safety case.

All of the safety analysis techniques that have been discussed in this paper will support the SoS safety case by providing evidence that we have identified all IAT hazards, both hazards at traditional system boundaries and from system interactions, and that the streamlined safety analysis process for training scenarios provides a similar hazard assessment capability.

3 Analysis of the human element

The close connections between human 'error', safety and accident prevention are well appreciated in the aviation domain. BAE Systems routinely employs usability assessment, Human Error Prediction (HEP) and Human Reliability Analysis (HRA) techniques in the design and clearance of its complex system aircraft products. Assessment techniques and processes have been established for these purposes, but SoS style products are likely to present new challenges in this area. Endeavouring in a practical way to respect a contextual view on human performance during hazard assessment (see for example Dekker 2002, Hollnagel 1998) brings the need to anticipate and account for circumstances surrounding situations of system use. As we have already described, the defining characteristics of SoSs have the potential to increase complexity in this area but we believe that it is possible to acknowledge and take account of this complexity without making analysis unmanageable. We describe a human factors oriented approach to differential analysis which aims to supplement more traditional human factors analysis methods. This is seen as a key driver for the early stages of SoS hazard identification in a SoS where the human element is considered significant. We briefly show how taking account of 'differences' from the human factors perspective in the case of IAT has led us to recognise that augmented-reality training brings with it both novel sources and consequences of human 'error'.

3.1 Towards human factors methods for SoS hazard identification

Taking into account the significance of human factors to SoS safety, we have identified important roles for human factors analysis in both the IAT SoS hazard identification and hazard analysis processes.

The paper has already introduced the concept of differential analysis and its role in the SoS hazard assessment approach being used for IAT. Considering human users as some of the 'systems' in a SoS architecture, effort has been directed to the development of a human factors oriented approach to differential analysis. This way forward strikes a pragmatic balance with regard to the 'contextual human performance' problem for the purposes of hazard identification, limiting the re-analysis of existing SoS elements but maintaining an appreciation that the interaction of these elements in the novel context of a SoS may lead to hazard.

To be successful, a human factors approach to differential analysis must identify the SoS related 'differences' that may affect humans operating within the SoS but it must also be able to articulate how these differences might influence them. Work is ongoing in this area but in general terms, the 'differences' to which SoS users will be exposed may be conceptualised by taking elements of to-be-performed work and situating these against contributors such as system (software/hardware/procedural) requirements or other factors of relevance. These 'differences' are then passed through a model (or models) of human performance to consider influences on human mental and physical behaviour in a traceable, methodical and consistent way (Figure 2). The influences that are identified may then be subjected to deviation analysis by way of HAZOP or similar approaches. Returning to points made earlier in the paper, in the case of IAT it is recognised that we will need to apply this method to take account of work which takes place before, during and also after training in order to take a suitably comprehensive view.

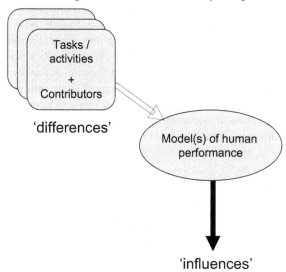

Fig. 2. Human factors oriented differential analysis for hazard identification

3.2 Human factors differential analysis for IAT

The application of a human factors oriented differential analysis to the IAT SoS is helping us to systematically explore the significance of the human element in the processes of configuring the IAT training system for use, using the system within a single training intervention and using the system across multiple training interventions. We are also looking further ahead, where factors such as 'negative training' could conceivably lead to hazard even when the IAT system itself is no longer active. We aim to account for these factors by including explicit modelling of training phases and configuration options, including the 'real mission' phases that occur outside of the training process. The differential approach is in particular helping us to systematically 'unpack' the potentially widespread implications of introducing synthetic elements into a Live training context.

In terms of configuring the IAT system for use, much of the work involved in the authoring of training scenarios will relate to the construction of the augmented reality in which Live and Virtual participants will operate. Where Constructive elements or synthetic objects are included they must be represented to an appropriate level of fidelity and accuracy. The realism and appropriateness of Constructive entity behaviour must be sufficient both to satisfy training requirements but also to adhere to important real-world rules. Incongruous Constructive entity behaviour may distract other scenario participants away from crucial tasks or perhaps lead them into hazardous situations in more direct ways. Where real-world objects are re-represented in the synthetic elements of a training scenario this must be done reliably. In addition to the reliable composition of training scenarios, scenario authors must also be equipped to understand and verify how a training scenario might evolve or progress over time, taking into account various contingencies. There may be a need to constrain the ways in which a specific training scenario is able to evolve, in effect safeguarding the circumstances in which Live and Virtual participants may be allowed to operate. Taking into account the synthetic 'difference' and its influence across a broad range of human inputs to training system configuration it becomes apparent that quite ordinary or mundane breakdowns in human performance have the potential to translate into significant hazard. For example, slips or mistakes with a keyboard and mouse during training scenario construction might have the power to translate into the incorrect positioning of a real world physical object (high terrain or a tall building) in the synthetic environment. This would influence the behaviour of Constructive entities and Virtual participants at the time of scenario execution. While this type of latent failure may not be a safety critical issue in a simulator, in an augmented reality training system there would be the potential for consequences to propagate across the SoS and for Constructive or Virtual behaviours to also influence the actions of Live participants.

Use of the IAT SoS during a training intervention is ultimately concerned with the participation of human actors in an augmented reality 'gameplay' scenario. There are of course many senses in which human performance should be analysed in this context, but exploring the synthetic 'difference' and its influence on training scenario participants reveals how aircrew behaviour may be affected by a potentially powerful cognitive phenomenon. 'Immersion' is a term commonly used by those working in the domains of gaming and virtual reality. It is colloquially understood as the sense of being 'lost' in the game or virtual environment where players become highly involved in the synthetic elements of their environment and lose awareness of their real world surroundings (Brown and Cairns 2004). In trying to conceptualise this area further, researchers have proposed that immersion is a continuum (Brown and Cairns 2004) and qualitatively distinct notional 'levels' of immersion have been distinguished. In a state of moderate immersion ('Engrossment') a participant is said to become less aware of their surroundings and less self aware. They have started to 'suspend disbelief' in the game. The 'Total' immersive state is said to be achieved if a participant loses awareness of physical reality and in effect becomes 'bought in' to the synthetic elements of their experience, treating them as if they were real. The concept of immersion has close links with other areas of literature including 'Cognitive Absorption' (Agarwal and Karahanna 2000), 'Flow' (Csikszentmihalyi 1990) and of course human attention.

Although it is fair to say that immersion and other related concepts still require some clarification, these notions have attracted the interest of the IAT project and are being borne in mind for safety assessment. The differential analysis approach is helping us to take immersion seriously. Importantly, we take the position that it is not the introduction of augmented reality training that suddenly makes immersion relevant to aircrew safety. After all, training related 'role-play' with aircrew assuming the role of hostile adversaries is commonplace in current training practices and must already invite a certain 'fact versus fiction' partition from a cognitive perspective. We do argue, however, that the introduction of LVC technology has the potential to make immersion a much more significant issue. The participation of ground based Virtual participants purporting to be airborne during a training scenario when they are not and the inclusion of 'fictional' computer generated Constructive entities must serve to increase complexity in this area.

During hazard analysis, much more detailed HRA/HEP work is expected to be required. In the case of IAT we intend to pursue research of the immersion topic in more depth. We aim to understand more about what immersion-related 'error' might look like and the conditions under which immersion should be accounted for in hazard analysis. In turn we aim to appreciate how we might mitigate immersion related routes to hazard and make the IAT SoS tolerant to this phenomenon. We envisage a need to take account of the ways in which Live and Virtual participants may come to hold false hypotheses regarding what is real and what is not during IAT training scenario performance. We need to recognise if or where this could increase risk. Our analyses will also need to appreciate the cognitive work faced by Live participants who must rapidly emerge from augmented reality. We aim to design to support immersive training where this is of benefit, but at the same time we intend to design for graceful emergence from immersion, so that aircrew needing to deal with in-flight emergencies have the attentional capacity to do so without unnecessarily expending resources to determine fact from fiction in a time critical situation.

4 Validation

It should be noted that the process presented here is the subject of ongoing research and as such is not yet formally recognised. We expect its validation to be iterative and content-driven, feeding back information from every use of the process to challenge assumptions and provide further guidance. Our validation of the hazard assessment approach is structured into a number of stages:

- Validation of the underlying models (particularly the feature models) by populating the models with example data. This provides insight into the models for multiple stakeholders, provides a way of generating test-cases that reveal flaws in the models, and ensures that the model definitions match with the specific uses encountered in this domain.

- Validation of the preparatory processes, investigating coverage and estimating effort, particularly where collaboration is needed. The analysis processes are intended to cover humans, technological systems and infrastructure and to set up reusable analysis artefacts, and so the validity of these processes, both in concept and in execution, is especially important.
- Identification of a representative part of the IAT product, covering IAT development, IAT deployment, training scenario development and post-training activity. This ensures that the validation assesses processes that involve a number of different human agents and different levels of 'fiction' – aspects of augmented reality.
- Validation of hazard assessment processes on the identified IAT processes, logging effort data. This covers the complete run of processes from initial scoping through asset generation to streamlined training scenario analysis and feedback.
- Estimation of overall IAT hazard analysis effort, covering up-front processes, per-delivery effort and effort per training scenario.
- Estimation of hazard assessment effectiveness. This will involve feedback from validation stages as well as the post-deployment assessment and safety case construction processes.

It is our intention to document the case for validity of the process: one option is to provide a goal-structured argument to organise the evidence from the validation processes. We are mindful of the need to control complexity, however, and will consider the most manageable alternative. It is recognised that further validation, formalisation and standardisation must take place before this process can be used for certification purposes.

5 Summary and future work

Given that SoSs are not the same as complex systems and that complex systems such as aircraft are not SoSs, this paper sets out a vision for hazard assessment of a complex integrated SoS that involves human elements and a variety of engineered systems. From an analytical perspective, we recognise that it would be 'fiction' to treat a SoS as 'just another complex system'. The defining properties of a SoS mean that traditional analysis methods may fall short if applied without additional support. On the other hand, we also argue that the structured and comprehensive analysis of a SoS need not be so complex as to be impractical. We identify feature modelling as a potential approach to manage the complexity of hazard assessment, and structure the assessment approach so that it may be driven by configurations in the feature model, at least in the abstract. We pay particular attention to the link between the hazard assessment and the safety case, and we investigate some of the human factors issues that arise in the IAT SoS, particularly the issue of immersion and the 'fact'/'fiction' differential that an augmented reality training SoS brings from a user perspective.

Our future work on this project can be viewed as three complementary strands:

- validation of the approach, particularly its basis in feature modelling and its avoidance of analysis approaches that are targeted only at understanding interactions in systems of systems
- exploration of immersion and its impact on both system design and hazard assessment
- automation of analysis and configuration processes. Candidate processes for automation include the mapping from training scenario setup to features; the mapping of features to hazards, derived requirements and mitigations; the assessment of particular aspects of training scenarios such as network usage; and the assessment of training scenarios using agent-based simulation to discover novel interactions.

References

Agarwal R, Karahanna E (2000) Time flies when you're having fun: cognitive absorption and beliefs about information technology usage. MIS Quarterly 24:665−694

Alexander RD (2007) Using simulation for systems of systems safety analysis. PhD Thesis, University of York

Alexander R, Hall-May M, Kelly T (2004) Characterisation of systems of systems failures. Proceedings of the 22nd International System Safety Conference (ISSC '04)

Bayer J, Flege O, Knauber P et al (1999) PuLSE: a methodology to develop software product lines. Proceedings of the Fifth Symposium on Software Reusability

Brown E, Cairns P (2004) A grounded investigation of game immersion. Proc CHI. ACM Press

Csikszentmihalyi M (1990) Flow: the psychology of optimal experience. Harper and Row, New York

Czarnecki K, Eisenecker U (2000) Generative programming. Addison-Wesley, Reading MA

Dehlinger J, Lutz RR (2005) Software fault tree analysis for product lines. Proceedings Eighth IEEE International Symposium on High Assurance System Engineering.

Dekker S (2002) The field guide to human error investigations. Ashgate, Aldershot, UK

Despotou G, Kelly T (2008) Investigating the use of argument modularity to optimise through-life system safety assurance. Proc 3rd IET Int Conf on System Safety (ICSS). IET

Despotou G, Kelly T (2010) Understanding the safety lifecycle of systems of systems. To appear in: Proc 28th International System Safety Conference (ISSC), Minneapolis

Despotou G, Bennett M, Kelly T (2009) Supporting through life safety assurance of COTS based upgrades. Proc 27th International System Safety Conference (ISSC), System Safety Society

Habli IM (2009) Model-based assurance of safety-critical product lines. PhD Thesis, University of York

Hollnagel E (1998) Cognitive reliability and error analysis method (CREAM). Elsevier, Oxford, UK

Kang KC, Cohen S, Hess J et al (1990) Feature-Oriented Domain Analysis (FODA) feasibility study. Technical report CMU/SEI-90-TR-21

Kletz T (1992) HAZOP and HAZAN: identifying and assessing process industry hazards. Hemisphere Publishing Corporation, Washington

Leveson N, Dulac N (2005) Safety and risk-driven design in complex systems-of-systems. 1st NASA/AIAA Space Exploration Conference

Maier M W (1998) Architecting principles for system of systems. Syst Eng 1:267-284

Raheja D, Moriarty B (2006) New paradigms in system safety. J Syst Saf 42(6)

SAE (1996) ARP-4761 Aerospace recommended practice: guidelines and methods for conducting the safety assessment process on civil airborne systems and equipment, 12th edn. Society of Automotive Engineers

Stephenson Z, de Souza S, McDermid J (2004) Product line analysis and the system safety process. Proceedings of the International System Safety Conference

Villemeur A (1992) Reliability, availability maintainability and safety assessment. John Wiley and Sons, New York

Wallace M (2005) Modular architectural representation and analysis of fault propagation and transformation. Electronic Notes in Theoretical Computer Science 141(3)

Weiss DM, Lai CTR (1999) Software product-line engineering: a family-based software development process. Addison-Wesley, Reading MA

A Project Manager's View of Safety-Critical Systems

Thomas Docker

CITI Limited
Newport Pagnell, UK

Abstract   This paper presents a project manager's view that safety-critical systems are not a special case or category of product development, but is one dimension that is a requirement in increasingly more systems. As with any product development, the degree to which a safety-critical product is tested or proved should be based on 'cost of failure' that, in the final analysis, is a commercial decision based on benefits and business risk. It is argued that with the emphasis on cost of failure, project teams can be more effective in producing safer products, particularly in terms of focusing testing. With effectiveness in mind, an approach to linking benefits to products is described, along with how this relates to requirements and acceptance criteria. Possible impacts of the use of standards in a project are also discussed. Case studies are used to reinforce concepts and highlight concerns.

1 Introduction

I remember reading an account in the late 1970s of a traffic incident in the United States, where a traffic officer stopped a motorist who had a defective light on his car. Within a few minutes the driver was dead; shot by the officer, who had been informed by Central Command that the driver's license was invalid. The upshot was that there was an error in the computer data that led to a very nervous officer accidentally killing a very nervous, innocent driver.

This was my first conscious experience of a safety-critical system. Arguably, this doesn't quite fit the Oxford Dictionary's (OUP 2010) view of safety-critical as

'designed or needing to be fail-safe for safety purposes'

but does fit with Wikipedia's (Wikipedia 2010) definition of life-critical or safety-critical being

'a system whose failure or malfunction may result in:

- death or serious injury to people, or
- loss or severe damage to equipment, or

C. Dale, T. Anderson (eds.), *Advances in Systems Safety*, DOI 10.1007/978-0-85729-133-2_5,
© Springer-Verlag London Limited 2011

- environmental harm.'

At the time, and I guess in many cases since, this system was probably seen as just a computerized data base with human operators and a traffic officer doing a challenging job.

If we fast-forward to now, how safety-critical is a number plate recognition system? I guess it depends on circumstances, but current security scenarios indicate that it is becoming increasingly so. I feel sure that the first implementers of such a system did not see it as such.

As a project manager, the idea of safety-critical is interesting, but I am not convinced that there is a specialized category. I am of the view that many, if not all, systems have a degree of safety-criticality to them, so we are more dealing with a spectrum than distinct categories; a safety dimension. If this is the case, how should decisions be made regarding what processes, checks and balances should be put in place when developing systems that are recognized as significantly safety-critical? This paper proposes that, to be commercially manageable, the implementation of safety-critical aspects should be managed in the same way as for other developments and should be based on the *cost of failure*. What are the consequences, financial and otherwise of the system not performing as required? At the time of writing, recovery from the Deepwater Horizon oil spill is still in progress and BP has suffered much more than financial penalties. However, the overriding tragedy is the loss of life of eleven workers on the rig.

2 The commercial reality

There is a phrase that suppliers used in contracts – hopefully no more – that stated, 'As time is of the essence, we will use our best endeavours to satisfy your requirements.' In the UK, a loose legal interpretation of this is that, 'As time is the most critical consideration, we will do anything we can, including bankrupting our company, to satisfy your requirements.'

As well as being a useful reminder that writing and entering into contracts should be left to the professionals, this example illustrates a fundamental question that should be central to all product developments; namely, 'How much business risk are we willing to take to obtain the product?'

This question is typically addressed through the creation of a business case that includes options analysis. Hopefully, the business case is meaningful and provides a firm foundation for a business commitment to either do nothing or push ahead with one of the options. If the choice is to go on, the typical delivery vehicle for a new product is a project with a defined Project Life Cycle (PjLC).

In software development, one of the oldest and most well known life cycles is the waterfall model (Royce 1970), which has its most useful incarnation as the V-model and, arguably, this became the de facto standard that is still widely used today (Tschürtz and Schedl 2010).

As time has moved on, a project management profession has developed with its own views on PjLCs. The UK Association for Project Management (APM) describes a four-phase life cycle comprising *concept, definition, implementation*, and *handover and closeout* (APM 2006). The APM also provides an extended life cycle that is described as a *product lifecycle*; a through-life structuring where product improvements and maintenance, such as mid-life updates, can be run as enhancement projects within the operations phase of the PjLC.

The commercial reality of product development is more complicated than that outlined by the APM. Figure 1 provides a fuller view, but is still a simplification (Docker 2007).

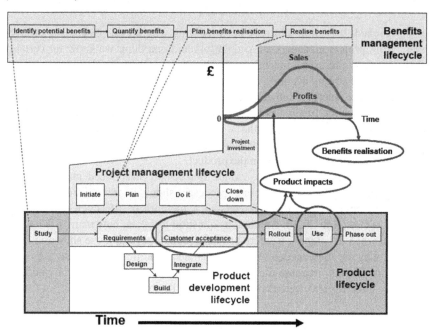

Fig. 1. Life cycles, life cycles

The Benefits Management Life Cycle (BMLC) was developed in the 1990s as an attempt to address the reality that benefits claimed for IT investments rarely materialized (Ward et al. 1996; Ward and Daniel 2005). Also worth noting in Figure 1, is that the PjLC has become a Project Management Life Cycle (PMLC) with phases *initiate, plan, do it* and *closedown*. This is to emphasize the life cycle's importance in the management of a project.

A highlight interpretation of Figure 1 is that, to get to a commercial product, three fundamental life cycles have to be managed:

Benefits management. Typically this is managed by the sponsor or Senior Responsible Owner (SRO) in PRINCE2™ terms (OGC 2009), who sits in the business and is responsible for ensuring the business impacts are made and exploited to deliver the claimed benefits.

Project management. This is managed by the project manager and, ideally, is divorced from any specific product development life cycles (PDLCs).

Product development or product acquisition. There may be a significant number of PDLCs in a project, ideally each managed by a team leader who is a domain expert for that product or process type (e.g., software development, training, marketing and procurement). The IT example we have already discussed is the waterfall life cycle and its variant V-model, a version of which is shown in Figure 1. What is clear is that the V-model is not a PMLC.

Having reached this point, you may be wondering why all this discussion on life cycles. Well, project managers are simple folk and one thing we know for certain is that life cycles are useful management tools, but they are also defect generating processes. To be strictly accurate, the people we let loose on the life cycles are the defect generators, such as Subject Matter Experts (SMEs) like software developers. It's just that some life cycles make it easier than others. The reason the classic waterfall model was replaced by the V-model was to stress the relationship between the early phases of product development and the later phases, and hopefully reduce the introduction of defects in the product.

If processes are the medium by which defects are introduced into products, there is an argument that says the use of processes should be minimized. However, in the safety environment there appears to a plethora of life cycles, including safety life cycles (Bell 2010). An obvious question to ask is, how many life cycles are needed when developing a safety-critical product, beyond those shown in Figure 1, and why are they needed? I believe that each additional life cycle is a two-edged sword that can increase the risk to the development of a product by adding yet another dimension as well as providing a specific focus (e.g., safety).

3 Doing what has to be done

Projects should do what needs to be done rather than what could be done and, to this end, a project manager needs a clear understanding of what the scope is that can be shared with the team and any third party suppliers.

If we refer back to Figure 1, there is a link between customer acceptance (measured against the acceptance criteria for the product) and benefits to the business. This link is impacts. Impacts are beneficial changes in the business caused by the introduction of the product (or set of products). Within the operational environment, these impacts should lead to benefits to the business. A useful way of mapping this is a Benefits-Impact-Product map (a BIP map), and an example is provided in Figure 2. The example is imaginary and has been placed in the context of the upgrading of the West Coast main line in the UK. On the left of the figure are two categories of financial benefits, new income (e.g., from new services) and additional income (e.g., from increased numbers of passengers on existing services).

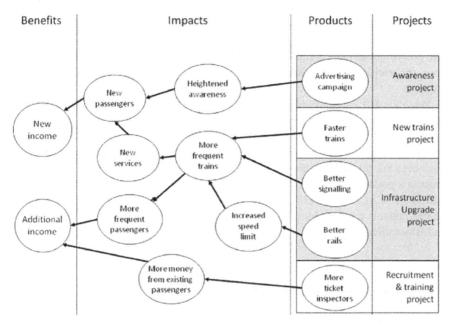

Fig. 2. BIP map for West Coast main line

If these benefits are to be realized, they are dependent on a number of impacts being made in the business, and some of these impacts depend on other impacts (e.g., new services depending on more frequent trains), while some impacts are shared (e.g., more frequent trains contributing to new services and more frequent passengers).

Towards the right are the products that are expected to make the impacts. In the figure, faster trains and better signalling are both required to make the impact of more frequent trains. Often, a single product can contribute to more than one impact, but there is not an example of this in Figure 2.

From a business perspective, a BIP map should always be developed from the benefits, a type of demand-driven system, and should be a primary concern of the sponsor or SRO. The lengths of the paths can be significant. If getting from a benefit to a product requires more than three levels of impacts, there is a good chance that something will detrimentally impact on the benefits, unless getting to the impacts is managed carefully within the project.

On the right of Figure 2, the desired products have been grouped into projects. Of particular note, better signalling and better rails have been placed in a single infrastructure upgrade project.

It should be apparent that there is a wide spectrum of safety-criticality across this programme of projects. It would be reasonable to assume, e.g., that the recruitment and training project has no safety-critical concerns, but this would be wrong. As well as ensuring ticket inspectors can be effective in emergencies to ensure passenger safety, there is the need to ensure the safety of the ticket inspectors when dealing with unhelpful passengers who do not want to pay for their journey!

A major component of the linking between the right-most impacts and the products are the acceptance criteria. Having a train travel at 125 miles per hour will contribute to more frequent trains. If the acceptance criterion was 80 miles an hour, the trickle through effect is clear: no (or seriously below expectations) new income.

What the BIP map provides includes a context for defining the acceptance criteria. The impacts should highlight what is required to realize the benefits and therefore partially what should be considered when specifying the acceptance criteria. Once this is understood, the safety implications can be assessed and the business case reviewed. Although it would be good to assess the safety considerations in a positive way, the reality is that they are likely to be assessed in terms of cost and risk to the business (Parsons and Hunter 2010). Having said this, the required impacts can provide a focus for testing, through safety cases (e.g. Bishop and Bloomfield 1998).

4 Requirements, acceptance criteria and constraints

To better understand the relationships between impacts, acceptance criteria and products, it is useful to remove requirements from the discussion. Requirements should be viewed as positive statements of the need (or problem) that we want addressed, whereas impacts and acceptance criteria, in particular, are measurable characteristics that are wanted in the solution – the products – and the business environment in which they are to operate; it is providing acceptable products that a project is concerned with.

Separating out requirements (problem space) from acceptance criteria (solution space) is central to having the right focus for product development (Docker 2007, 1998). It is nonsense when specifying the requirements for a traffic flow system, e.g., to have a requirement that 'There will be no more than five minor accidents in the first year of operation.' The requirement should be 'There will be no accidents as a consequence of malfunctions in the system' with an acceptance criterion that 'There will be no more than five minor accidents in the first year of operation attributable to malfunctions.'

In basic commercial terms, if a product satisfies its acceptance criteria, exercised through acceptance testing, then the SRO (or that person's representative) should accept the product. Destructive testing focused on process (which includes tools) and SME perceived weaknesses can be further sharpened by what is deemed acceptable through the acceptance criteria[1].

A model I developed a number of years ago that I use to explain, in particular, differences between requirements and acceptance criteria is shown in Figure 3 (Docker 1998).

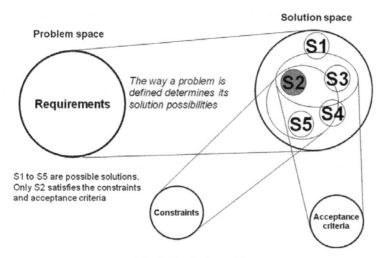

Fig. 3. Floodlight model

It is called the floodlight model as it is based on the concept of floodlights in a theatre being directed onto the stage. The primary light is requirements and the pool of light it casts defines the solution space. The second light is acceptance criteria and this reduces the solution space to a subset of the possible solutions highlighted by the requirements. The third light is constraints and this highlights a subset as well. The intersection between all these three lights, describing the brightest area, contains acceptable business solutions.

To keep the diagram simple, only one solution, S2, is so highlighted. Important characteristics of the three lights are:

- Requirements

    - describe the problem (or opportunity) as a set of positive statements
    - are non-negotiable (i.e., if we change the requirements, we change the problem we wish to address).

- Acceptance criteria

    - specify measurable characteristics required in a solution

---

[1] Unfortunately, it has too often been the case that the customer (SRO, senior user or their representatives) has been bad at specifying acceptance criteria and this mantle has been taken on by the developers or testing team. Needless to say, this approach is not commended here!

   – are negotiable (i.e., we can trade acceptable levels of functionality against
     costs and risks).

- Constraints

   – limit what is an acceptable business solution
   – in simple terms, can only be removed or relaxed with the authority of the
     SRO.

Emphasis does need to be placed on the acceptance criteria being 'measurable'.
An acceptance criterion (originally specified as a requirement!) for a frigate was
that 'It remains 50% operational after a direct hit [by a weapon of a defined type
and size]'. Leaving aside questions such as 'Which 50%?' how could this acceptance criterion be measured? The answer, of course, is that it couldn't be measured, not without causing significant damage to the ship! The solution in such
cases is to develop surrogate measures based, for example, on ruggedness tests for
component products or simulations. However, there is a problem with simula-
tors/emulators: they are abstractions and may not be that accurate (Docker 1979),
so is 40% acceptable in a simulation as a representation of 50% in the real thing?
This is starting to look like a good candidate for the Emperor's New Clothes
award. A simple rule for an acceptance criterion is: if you can't measure it, don't
ask for it, because you won't know if you got it or not.

The classic triple constraints of time, cost and functionality are well known in
projects, but other constraints can be imposed. One interesting class that is particularly relevant in safety-critical systems development is standards. Quite often the
use of a standard is described as a requirement; but it isn't. What a standard does
is constrain a project, possibly in multiple ways. The types of things standards impose on projects include process, tools, resourcing, product characteristics and
governance activities, and essentially impact on the product produced.

As already noted, standards are two-edged swords: in the current context they
limit choice and ... they limit choice. In the positive case, by restricting choice
they may reduce the temptation to do things wrong. In the negative case, they
might discourage innovation and optimization. Worse, they may impose pro-
tracted processes and handovers that invite defect generation. A good project
manager would seek to limit process activity. Having convoluted gating processes
that are not robust is more or less guaranteed to produce inferior products.

The standards that have most value are those that will benefit the project in
some way, e.g., by defining development processes that are known to be good and
will lead to well engineered products. Unfortunately, these are few and far between and I struggle to think of one. Most standards, I believe, are unnecessarily
onerous, to the extent that they are often not complied with sufficiently. Worse, an
impression might be engineered that they are being complied with. What is worth
recognizing is that many standards are compromises, often satisfying political
agendas, and are unlikely to represent best practice.

5 Testing in a smart way

If we have the following in place for a project:

- a clear mission, specified in the project initiation document
- a BIP map
- a clear statement of the requirements, acceptance criteria and associated constraints (including standards)
- the processes by which the product is to be developed or procured
- the resources to be used to produce or acquire the product

we can make sensible decisions on how we will test throughout the project to deliver a product that is fit for purpose.

We know that defects will be introduced into the product as we progress through the PDLCs. A level of maturity was reached by the 1980s when software development projects included the use of charts showing the expected number of defects that had been introduced against those that had been closed – successfully. As you have been told or discovered, there is a significant difference between knowing where a defect is and knowing that it has been successfully removed. As already stated, project managers are simple folk and most prefer the first situation: knowing where a defect is can usually be managed (unless it's an absolute show stopper), whereas removing defects is fraught with worries, as being informed by SMEs that a defect has been removed successfully leads to sleepless nights with demons that include:

- Did we test the product in the right way?
- Did we introduce other defects that were not found?

5.1 Did we test the product in the right way?

Most testing can be described as defect finding; that is, we are looking for defects in the product. We describe this as destructive testing. The notable exception to this is acceptance testing, which should be confirmatory testing – the product does what it is supposed to do (and hopefully, doesn't do what it's not supposed to do). In general, safety cases can be interpreted as confirmatory testing (Kelly 2003, Bishop and Bloomfield 1998).

In all practical product developments exhaustive testing is not feasible or desirable (e.g., we have a deadline to meet), so what should we base destructive testing on? If we are being sensible, we base it on an analysis of where the biggest weaknesses are in the life cycle, and its underlying processes, when used by the SMEs we have in the project team. We may, e.g., have different defects being generated by each of two software developers who are using the same processes, simply due to their individual knowledge and experience. Figure 4 shows such an analysis, as a Data Flow Diagram (DFD), for a technical engineering specification that was over 300 pages long and had been written by SMEs and brought together by a two-person editing team.

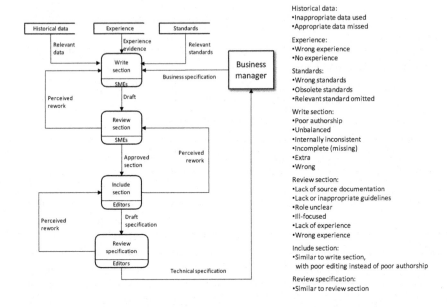

Fig. 4. Technical specification production process

On the left of Figure 4 is the DFD representation of the specification production process. On the right is a representation of some of the defect generators that could exist in the process lozenges. These lists were used in Fagan inspections (Fagan 1986) as checklists for finding defects, with the understanding that these were not the only defects to look for! Shortly before running the series of Fagan inspections (which took a month), the specification had gone through the then normal review cycle, followed by sign-off and was viewed as one of the best specifications of its kind in the industry. In fact, experts visited from overseas to discuss this exceptional specification. The formal reviewing, with its focus on looking for defects introduced by SMEs using an identifiable process, identified over 900 major defects; an average of three per page. A significant number of the defects were due to the undoubted knowledge and experience of the SMEs. Unfortunately, the project was concerned with an innovative product and their experience often was inappropriate: something they didn't spot.

Many of the defects were show-stoppers as they were injury, if not life, threatening. A post analysis estimated that the reviewing saved a potential £125m of rework costs on a £500m project.

Fundamental questions were asked, post-reviewing, on how these major defects were missed in the normal reviewing process and how the specification could have been seen as exceptional in the first place. The simple answer was that the original reviewers were focusing on success rather than failure. Interestingly, nearly half of all references to standards – and there were many – were to out-of-date versions, redundant standards or inappropriate standards. Cut-and-paste was a major tool – and process weakness.

What the normal reviewing process demonstrated is that if testing is not focusing on the probable places in the processes where defects can be introduced, the likelihood is that rich veins of significant defects would be missed. Without the right focus, the defects found may not be that harmful to the product and significant time and money can be wasted.

5.2 Did we introduce other defects that were not found?

It is important to understand that the process by which a defect is removed is different to the process by which it was introduced. Therefore, it can be sloppy to apply the test suite that was applied in the original case to the modified product. If the same test suite is to be applied (e.g., regression tests), because that is what we always do, then specific new tests should also be used. One question that the project manager needs answering is, 'What defects did we introduce as a consequence of removing the original defect and have we tested successfully for them?' Unfortunately, this can be relatively expensive in both logistical and money terms to answer; hence the sleepless nights.

With the engineering specification, no one was allowed to correct a defect in the meeting. Each defect had to be assessed outside and traceability needed to exist to ensure any corrective action was tested for success and for how other defects could have been created. This is something that should be fundamental to any product development, but essential where there is a significant safety-critical bias.

6 Project management of product defects

Project managers typically have limited resource and limited time available in a project. Therefore, two basic considerations for a project manager are:

- How much time do we need to allow for finding defects?
- How much time for rework?

These are not unrelated questions, but it is worth observing that too many project plans and schedules do not include adequate rework activities, so either the project manager sees testing as demonstrating the product will work or the project manager is happy to waste money (i.e., if the expectation is that the product will not need rework, why bother to test). Having these two considerations in mind, the project manager should look to each product development team (e.g., IT, Marketing, and Training and Development) to produce charts showing the number of defects expected to be found, the number of defects actually found, and those that are expected to be open at each reporting period. From these charts, it should be possible to estimate testing costs, time and resource needs.

How these charts are used varies across projects, but at the minimum they need to form part of an informed decision of when to stop testing. I was advising a consultant project manager who was overseeing the development of an IT product for a building society. A release point was fast approaching and they were putting all their efforts into testing, with the result that the number of open defects was growing. What should he do? The simple answer I gave him, which he followed, was to stop testing and put all his team's efforts into clearing defects correctly (i.e., minimizing the likelihood of introducing new, unknown defects). I know; the very next test might have found the most humungous defect; or perhaps the one after that; or the one after that …

Such business decisions do occur in safety-critical systems as well. An example comes to mind of an upgraded railway line (not the West Coast line!), where the head of state of the country involved was due to 'cut the ribbon' on a specified date. As the date rapidly approached, it became clear that not all signals, points and interlockings could be tested in time. The alternatives identified were to slip the date or make choices on what could be tested; effectively prioritizing safety concerns. The second alternative was chosen.

How had the rail organization got into this position? Simple. It had not gone through the numbers. Until pushed, it did not know the numbers of signals, points and interlockings (and how complicated each was). Nor did they know how long it took to test each of these, as an average or as a range. Lastly, they had no easily accessible data on how many tests failed, requiring rework, or how much rework was required for each failure, by type. Instead, it had adopted the approach that if they started testing as early as they could (and we all know that testing is the first thing to get squeezed), they will finish all required testing by the deadline. They had no defect modelling graphs and were 'managing' blind.

6.1 The fundamental question

The position my consultant project manager was in was not the right position and so the decision to stop testing was the best of a bad set of choices. As the manager, he should have been able to make the best of a good set of choices. How could he have done that?

What should have driven his testing was a strategy based on the fundamental question: 'What is the cost of failure?' That is, what are the consequences of not removing a specific defect, measured in one or more dimensions that are useful to the business, such as money and public credibility. A number of years ago, one government department spent a considerable amount of money testing to ensure that a woman recently widowed did not have a letter arrive from the department addressed to her husband. One cost of failure that particularly concerned them was the likelihood of the widow's Member of Parliament raising questions in the House on how this could have occurred. Was this a wise spend of money? Who is to say?

6.2 Relating cost of failure to cost of testing

Determining the cost of failure for most products within a project can be done using qualitative 'What-if?' considerations. Others will benefit from quantitative methods, such as Monte Carlo analysis. In identifiably safety-critical developments, attempting to demonstrate that safety cases are invalid and assessing the outcome is an obvious mechanism (Bishop and Bloomfield 1998). However it is done, it is useful to have an agreed categorization for products based on the cost of failure, which should drive the approach to destructive testing. The scheme I have used for many years, based on keeping it simple, is:

Scratch. The product is typically tested through a desk check or its equivalent; example products would be the agenda for a project progress meeting and an initial software module design.

Development. The product is typically tested through a peer review process; examples would be a project plan and a product design document.

Production. The product is typically tested through a formal review process; examples would be a user manual for the customer and the company standard for a test plan.

Business critical. The product is typically tested through a formal review process, such as Fagan inspections, using highly professional SMEs; examples would be the engineering specification, a new or upgraded industry standard (e.g., DO-178C), and the design for a life monitoring system.

The examples given are for documents. Types of destructive testing carried out on production software products (typically described as deliverables) are well known and include module, integration and system testing. Specialized types of testing are common in specific environments, but all should have the same focus – cost of failure.

A question to consider is how do significantly safety-critical systems differ from other systems in terms of the cost of failure? One might think, e.g., that such systems require all products to be business critical, but this is not the case. Projects to develop safety-critical systems would have a mix of products across the four categories, like any other project. However, if it can be demonstrated that a safety-critical system is business-critical then the profile across the categories should be appropriately skewed towards business-critical. Apart from that, there is a common objective that all products should be fit for purpose.

6.3 Benefit, cost and risk

There is a set of constraints that operate within projects that, by definition, restrict what is achievable. These are time, cost and functionality – the triple constraints identified by Martin Barnes[2] over forty years ago that he described using a triangle. The relationships between these are complex and, as a basic heuristic, only two can be set within a single project; the third defines itself. Applying theory of constraints concepts (Goldratt 1984), it would be reasonable to expect that functionality will become the overriding constraint in demonstrably safety-critical systems.

Operating within the triple constraints, a project manager has a far more interesting triangular relationship to manage against. This is the relationship between benefit, cost and risk. Unless a project is mandatory, or there is an altruistic motive, the primary driver should be the benefits that can be derived from the deliverables of the project and the risks to those benefits. The cost – or better still, price – that a sponsor is willing to pay for the deliverables is important, as is the risk to that price (or cost). It would be reasonable for a sponsor to invest up to £0.8m to have delivered a product with a 10% chance of returning £10m in the market. The question is can a project be put in place to produce an adequate product within the £0.8m?

Part of determining whether this can be achieved within the price requires planning the development, and a component of this is planning the testing and rework and retesting. To provide realistic estimates of these requires some understanding of the product set, how it is going to be produced, by whom and with what. Most important of all though, is knowing that the product is amenable to testing; the best way of developing this confidence is to design for testing.

6.4 Design for testing

A number of things contribute to determining the right level to test at, but all of them should be *ex ante* factors. They can be collected together under the concept of 'design for testing'. Using the V-model in Figure 1 as an example, during the design phase consideration should be given to how components are to be integrated and this should determine the integration and system testing; even to the extent of changing the design to ensure effective and efficient testing can take place. It is at the design stage that we would determine, e.g., that we do not need to test a specific component, but a sub-assembly of which it is part. The driver is, only test what you have to.

If we took a simplistic approach and tested every component, there might be reachable unsafe states that a component can be in that will not be reachable when

---

[2] Martin Barnes is President of the Association for Project Management in the UK.

incorporated into a larger component. It would be foolish to waste money testing and trying to rectify that component in isolation, particularly as we might introduce other defects in doing so, and possibly leave them undiscovered. Knowing the right level to test at is fundamental to the efficient and effective use of the testing budget and time.

Leveson uses the example of the loss of the Mars Polar Lander to highlight that although the landing legs and onboard software each worked correctly, together they resulted in the premature shutdown of the engines (Leveson 2010).

What informs the testing strategy at the design phase, in order of importance, are:

- the benefits, impacts and acceptance criteria for the products
- the cost of failure
- the development or acquisition processes to be used to obtain the products
- the SMEs that will be used in obtaining the products
- the product design (when known)
- historical quality records for product developments of this type.

This is done within the constraints of the quality policy for the organisation or project. Note that this list is applicable to all product developments or acquisitions and there is no special case for significantly safety-critical systems.

7 Concluding remarks

I have presented a project manager's viewpoint that safety-critical systems development is not a special category of product development, but is one dimension. This is partially based on the realization that more and more systems can be given a safety-critical interpretation so, instead, I suggest a spectrum of safety-criticality. I have proposed that the focus for product development should be on commercial benefit and the risks to those benefits, plus the cost of implementation. At a practical level, I have demonstrated how benefits can be linked to products through impacts, and how impacts relate to acceptance criteria, which define what is desirable in a product.

Although the focus of a project is to deliver fit for purpose products, through its processes the project offers opportunities to put defects into products. A sobering thought is that for every defect there is in a product, somebody has been paid to put it there! In recognition of this, I suggest that the focus for testing within the project should be on cost of failure with destructive testing significantly based on the analysis of weak spots in the development processes, within the context of the benefits, impacts and acceptance criteria. The safety focus can be on where, in particular, product development life cycles allow defects to be introduced into the products. Techniques that include safety cases can be used to do this, directed at the impacts that need to be made to deliver the desired benefits.

Almost paradoxically, the constraints placed on safety-critical intensive projects by standards may increase the process and tool requirements, which could potentially increase the chance of introducing defects.

References

APM (2006) Body of knowledge, 5th edn. Association for Project Management, High Wycombe, UK

Bell R (2010) Introduction and revision of IEC 61508. SIAS 2010, Tampere, Finland

Bishop P, Bloomfield R (1998) A methodology for safety case development. In: Redmill F, Anderson T (eds) Industrial perspectives of safety-critical systems. Springer

Docker TWG (1979) Some aspects of computer simulation modelling. In: Computer performance evaluation – a professional development seminar. New Zealand Computer Society, Hamilton

Docker TWG (1998) Successful requirements management. Requir Eng 3:66-68

Docker TWG (2007) Here's to the next 50 years! In: BCS at 50 IT past, present and future. British Computer Society, London

Fagan ME (1986) Advances in software inspections. IEEE Trans Softw Eng-12:744-751

Goldratt EM (1984) The goal. North River Press

Kelly T (2003) A systematic approach to safety case management. Proc SAE World Congress

Leveson NG (2009) The need for new paradigms in safety engineering. In: Dale C, Anderson T (eds) Safety-critical systems: problems, process and practice. Springer

OGC (2009) Managing successful projects with PRINCE2, 2009 edn. Office of Government Commerce, London

OUP (2010) Safety-critical. Oxford Dictionaries. http://oxforddictionaries.com. Accessed 10 September 2010

Parsons M, Hunter C (2010) Patterns in safety-related projects. In: Dale C, Anderson T (eds) Making systems safer. Springer

Royce WW (1970) Managing the development of large software systems: concepts and techniques. In: Technical papers of western electronic show and convention (IEEE WesCon), Los Angeles, USA

Tschürtz H, Schedl G (2010) An integrated project management life cycle supporting system safety. In: Dale C, Anderson T (eds) Making systems safer. Springer

Ward J, Daniel E (2005) Benefits management: delivering value from IS and IT investments. John Wiley and Sons, Chichester, UK

Ward J, Taylor P, Bond P (1996) Evaluation and realization of IS/IT benefits: an empirical study of current practice. Eur J Inf Syst 4:214-225

Wikipedia (2010) Life-critical systems. http://en.wikipedia.org/wiki/Life-critical. Accessed 10 September 2010

System Safety in an IT Service Organization

Mike Parsons and Simon Scutt

Logica UK

Leatherhead, Surrey, UK

Abstract Within Logica UK, over 30 IT service projects are considered safety-related. These include operational IT services for airports, railway infrastructure asset management, nationwide radiation monitoring and hospital medical records services. A recent internal audit examined the processes and documents used to manage system safety on these services and made a series of recommendations for improvement. This paper looks at the changes and the challenges to introducing them, especially where the service is provided by multiple units supporting both safety and non-safety related services from multiple locations around the world. The recommendations include improvements to service agreements, improved process definitions, routine safety assessment of changes, enhanced call logging, improved staff competency and training, and increased safety awareness. Progress is reported as of today, together with a road map for implementation of the improvements to the service safety management system. A proposal for service assurance levels (SALs) is discussed as a way forward to cover the wide variety of services and associated safety risks.

1 Introduction

1.1 About Logica

Logica is a business and technology service company, employing 39,000 people across 36 countries. The company delivers business consulting, systems integration and outsourcing across all industries and business functions. Logica creates value by successfully integrating people, business and technology to create effective, sustainable business ecosystems. Employees apply insight to create innovative answers to help with business needs (Logica 2010a).

C. Dale, T. Anderson (eds.), *Advances in Systems Safety*, DOI 10.1007/978-0-85729-133-2_6,
© Springer-Verlag London Limited 2011

1.2 About Logica in the UK

The UK business operates in all the key Logica sectors. There are about 5,500 staff working in the UK at client locations, in Logica offices or from home. UK staff can be doing anything from helping place satellites into outer space to supporting the armed forces or protecting the population and managing people through the court systems.

1.3 Logica services

Logica Global Outsourcing Services has operations in nine European countries, and production centres in four offshore countries. It comprises three *service lines*:

1. Applications Management (AM) (Logica 2010b)
2. Business Process Outsourcing (BPO) (Logica 2010c)
3. Infrastructure Management (IM) (Logica 2010d).

Each client is provided with the business and technology service they need, based on the relevant set of component services and blended delivery from the most appropriate set of production centres based in the UK or offshore centres.

1.3.1 Safety-related services

There are about 30 safety-related service projects running in Logica UK today, including the following:

- airport management applications
- health records systems
- hospital clinical data presentation systems
- country-wide radiation monitoring
- water supply management
- railway infrastructure applications
- power generation management and maintenance systems
- tracking of personnel on offshore platforms
- managing health and safety incidents for the armed forces.

Although these services are based around IT systems, there is generally little software *development* activity within the contract. Instead the focus is on delivering the service to a contracted level, usually involving maintenance, support and enhancements. Typically none of the software in these services is developed to a safety integrity level (SIL) (Wikipedia 2010) – all mitigations required to reduce the safety risks to acceptable levels are placed in the overall processes and procedures in the service, or are otherwise handled by the client or operations staff.

1.4 Service model description

A service delivery usually implies some or all of the following:

- responsibility for delivering an IT service to the customer, in support of their business, usually over a long period (e.g. 5 or 10 years)
- responsibilities typically defined and success measured by a service level agreement rather than a controlling specification
- taking over an existing service (including possibly staff and other assets) from another (often in-house) supplier; the main deliverable is not a system.

The main differentiators between the delivery of a project and a service are often articulated as the service's additional need for:

- service level management
- knowledge management
- service improvement.

Another differentiator is that the applications management components of service delivery are concerned with providing user support, e.g. advising users, fixing software defects, and creating minor enhancements, rather than delivering complete systems or major enhancements.

1.4.1 Service delivery lifecycle

Figure 1 shows the overall lifecycle for service delivery, and a brief description of its key stages is given below.

1.4.1.1 Bid

Bidding in Logica for all opportunities (including services) follows the existing internal process, Bid Smart. The purpose of this process is to ensure that the resources necessary to win business are mobilized, whilst ensuring that appropriate steps are taken to mitigate risks (including safety risks). The process is also intended to ensure that the appropriate internal stakeholders (including safety experts) are engaged early enough in the process to add real value and to create a competitive advantage. At the outset of an opportunity a Bid Smart analysis is performed to determine the mandatory and discretionary reviews applicable to a given bid. All safety projects require a mandatory safety review, supported by guidance materials and checklists to help with hazard identification.

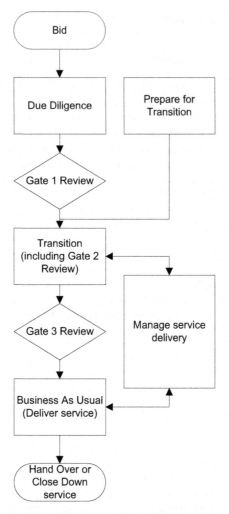

Fig. 1. Simplified Logica service delivery lifecycle

1.4.1.2 Due diligence

The aim of due diligence is to confirm the understanding of the basis upon which the service is to be delivered, and the risks associated with undertaking the services requested by the customer. It is completed when a successful Gate 1 review has been carried out, in which it is confirmed that the due diligence has achieved the necessary scope and depth of coverage, that the findings are understood, and the resulting consequences have been recognised and mitigated in the proposal.

1.4.1.3 Transition

The transition stage moves the service delivery from the current basis onto the agreed outsourced basis in line with the agreed transition and quality plan, and in doing so, assures continuity of service and minimises potential concerns of staff. The cut-over from the existing delivery basis to the Logica delivery starts when a successful Gate 2 review (service readiness) has been carried out. At this time all necessary plans, schedules and resources are in place for Logica to begin the process of taking over operation of the service.

Transition is considered complete when a Gate 3 review (transition complete) has been carried out, in which it is confirmed that the agreed service transfer criteria have been met, that the service is established and reporting regularly to the customer, and that all staff, assets and infrastructure have been transferred successfully.

1.4.1.4 Business as usual

The aim of this stage is to deliver the service in accordance with the agreed service level agreement (SLA) and service delivery plan. As such it begins with a successful Gate 2 review and therefore partially overlaps the transition stage.

1.4.1.5 Hand over or close down service

This stage takes place at the end of the service contract, although the process begins sufficiently in advance of the contract end date for the service to be handed over or closed down without disruption. Where the service is handed over, it may either be handed back to the customer or to a new third-party incumbent.

1.4.2 Service lines

The service lines provide capability into each service project. Each has a primary area of focus, and they collaborate to provide a seamless range of services to customers. Service lines cover AM, IM and BPO. Some example services lines are:

- problem management
- desktop hardware management
- license management
- datacentre hosting
- network management
- network security
- database administration
- availability management

- continuity management
- international payroll
- workforce administration
- expense management.

1.5 Origins of work

Historically Logica has focused on design and build projects with relatively few service projects undertaken. Today the situation is reversed with major design-build-operate contracts, and many applications management / infrastructure management projects (where the development work has already been completed by another contractor or by the client, and the contract is largely for maintenance/evolution).

For Logica today, the major safety risks clearly lie in service operations rather than development projects.

1.6 Existing safety guidance

In general today's established system safety standards tend to be focused on development activities, or maintenance of particular products or specific items. Typical safety standards in widespread use such as IEC 61508 (IEC 2010), Def Stan 00-56 (MoD 2007a) and DO-178B (RTCA 1992) generally cover service only in terms of maintenance or evolution of a system originally developed to the standard.

The latest MoD Def Stan 00-56 issue 4 does mention service aspects including change control, analysis of failures and maintenance of the safety case (and balancing of operational imperatives against safety risk), but not in the context of running a large scale, ongoing mixed IT service.

There is a through-life safety course module run by York University (York 2010) which covers the safety issues that arise after system deployment including:

- managing operational risk
- safety policies for system operation and management
- safety aspects of operational procedures
- system monitoring and fault management
- maintenance and modification
- configuration management
- hazards associated with maintenance and modification activities
- effects on the safety case and recertification issues
- regression and acceptance testing.

However this course doesn't really address the complex IT service issues considered here.

An MoD guide to in-service safety management (MoD 2007b) covers service aspects of safety *'concerned with ensuring that the in-service arrangements for sustaining the Safety performance of equipment introduced to service, are recognised, put in place and operated'*, but makes little reference to software.

2 Systems safety in a service organization

This section describes the origin of the business changes and gives the details of the updates required.

2.1 Internal functional audit

A wide-ranging internal safety functional audit was conducted at the end of 2009 on the Logica UK Outsourcing Services (OS) part of the business where the majority of the service work is undertaken. The report with findings was published in early 2010. In summary the main findings were:

- Systems safety needs to be better embedded within the OS organization. General awareness of safety issues and safety culture throughout staff and services could be improved.
- Safety management is complex in some services due to service implementation being spread over diverse teams and locations. Offshoring requires that knowledge and appreciation of systems safety concepts and UK legislation is placed in offshore units (e.g. in India).
- Applications management or framework contracts have risks as often little is known about safety aspects of the applications or work orders at bid time. Once such a contract is won there is a need to assess the supported applications for safety in a systematic way.
- The way services are specified and documented via Operational Level Agreements (OLAs, internal agreements between part of Logica providing an element of a service and the service project itself), SLAs, Call Logging Instructions (CLIs), etc. should explicitly address systems safety aspects.
- The due diligence process requires strengthening to highlight any safety aspects early during the bid process.
- Traceability from the hazard log to the controlling documents needs to be improved. In particular CLIs and OLAs should contain guidance on the identification, management and verification of hazards.
- Contracts may need to include clauses to ensure that appropriate action is taken by both the client and Logica if a safety problem is found.

- The safety alert and escalation processes need to be formalized.
- Internal communication within Logica of safety issues and problems which may require senior management visibility needs improvement.
- Any significant changes to the way a service is implemented (e.g. offshored) may require a specific safety assessment.

2.2 Road map for implementation

The findings were wide ranging and would take time to implement so an overall strategy or road map was developed. In summary this covered:

1. identification of all existing services with a safety element
2. identification of the service processes affecting safety and their controlling documents; and updates to the documents to include appropriate safety references, checklists, reviews, etc.
3. roll-out of the updated processes to existing services, including the necessary changes to processes and procedures; operator and service staff training (for both onshore and offshore resources); competency management; addressing any cultural issues, etc.
4. bedding in changes and ongoing improvements, including analysis of trends, monitoring changes in culture, performing safety audits, safety metrics, etc.
5. resolution of any conflicts, international or cross-service issues.

This paper concentrates on the work to date which has been largely focused on parts (1) and (2) of the road map.

2.3 Identification of safety services

It was realized that this task was not as easy as it might first appear – there were several hundred operational services run by OS UK, some of which had limited information available and most of which were not safety-related.

A review of project documents was undertaken together with a joint examination of the full list of service projects to identify possible candidate services which could be considered safety-related. This review was conducted with the business safety manager of OS UK and one of the authors (Simon Scutt).

This activity concluded that a further 15 service projects should be considered safety-related, taking the total to 30. Services added to the list included:

- application management projects for county councils (added as they include maintenance functions)
- power generation applications management
- hospital projects.

2.4 Identification of service processes and controlling documents

2.4.1 Process and template changes

The required changes were split into three phases of the service lifecycle: due diligence, transition and business as usual.

2.4.1.1 Due diligence

During the due diligence phase it is important that any safety aspects of the proposed service are identified and clarified. This is particularly relevant if the initial bid activities did not initially identify the service as being safety-related. The documents updated were:

Due diligence process. This document provides a background and framework for conducting due diligence activities, including the required inputs and outputs. The changes made were to include the new safety management checklist, clarify the use of the Safety Briefing Memorandum (SBM, an internal brief to Logica management on the safety risks of a bid), and to highlight that the due diligence manager has a duty to ensure that any system safety issues are properly considered.

Due diligence Gate 1 checklist. This is a template agenda for the due diligence confirmation review meeting. It details all of the deliverables required to determine whether the activities have been completed and the service is in a suitable state for transition to commence. The changes made were to clarify that the safety briefing memorandum needs to be updated with the results of the due diligence activities.

Due diligence safety management checklist. This was a new document that provides a structured list of questions to be answered as part of due diligence and is intended to be used by people without a background in system safety. As such it provides key phrases to search for within the original ITT documentation, questions to determine the operational context of the service, and key documentation that should be available if the development or current operation of the service includes system safety management. If the answers to the questions posed by the checklist indicate that the service is safety-related and, either it has not been acknowledged as such in the ITT, or there is insufficient evidence that it has been managed appropriately, then that is added to the RAID Log (Risks, Assumptions, Issues, Dependencies Log) as a risk on the successful delivery of the service.

Logica

Process Definition: Due Diligence

- **Service Management** stream to address company wide business SLA and continuity, together with the Service Desk Performance and Service Processes.
- The **Projects** stream will be concerned with any in-flight and planned projects. Most of these will be identified by the Applications and Infrastructure streams but this stream needs to collate their findings and identify the process for project approval and resourcing, etc.
- The **Transition** stream must gather information that will feed into the Transition (and Transformation) activity and ensure that the Solution document is updated (finalised).

Other areas for consideration by the Due Diligence Manager are:

- Facilities (Physical Building Access for on site service, the customer locations and facilities from which Logica will be delivering the service).
- Health and Safety related Issues.
- Compliance to other statutory bodies, e.g. audit.
- System Safety issues, e.g. the project would be operating within a safety-related business sector (such as Rail, Health, Aviation, Child Protection, Police, etc.).[ii]

Whilst the accumulation and assessment will take place in streams the key to success is the communication and corroboration of information across streams. For example, the Service Stream will discover information about call volumes to a central help desk, but the applications stream can ask the user population whether they report all problems to the help desk or not? Similarly a business SLA that is operated by one part of the customer business may not be operable or desirable in all user departments or across the supporting infrastructure.

Fig. 2. Change to the due diligence process document

2.4.1.2 Transition

The changes made to transition processes and templates ensure that the activities carried out and the documentation produced during the transition phase are done in such a way that the safety aspects are taken into account. The documents updated were:

Transition process. This document details the services transition process. It provides a background and framework for conducting transition activities, including the required inputs and outputs. The changes made were to highlight the need for a safety engineer within the service team and a safety management plan in the process outputs, to highlight that safety mitigation activity must be suitably covered in the testing approach, and to highlight that the transition manager and the future service delivery manager have a duty to ensure that any system safety issues are properly considered.

Transition application management process. This document describes the applications management element of the transition process. The change made to this document was to highlight that it is necessary to identify any safety-related applications within those that are to be supported, and to assess their criticality so that they can be handled appropriately.

Process Definition: Transition Service

4.1.1   Appoint Transition Management

The following roles will be appointed by Service Delivery Management (unless continuous from bid and/or due diligence phases:

- Transition Manager(s)
- Country Service Delivery Manager(s)
- Project Officer(s)
- Service Architect
- Technical Architect
- Project Safety Engineer (if a safety-related project)

Process	Appoint Transition Management
Frequency	Once, at Initiate Transition
Purpose	• To appoint Global and/or Country Transition Manager(s) who will manage the overall Transition Programme • To appoint Global and/or Country Service Delivery Manager (s) to work on Transition team and manage the Steady State Service (post Cutover) • To appoint Project Officer(s) to support Transition and Service Delivery

Fig. 3. Example change to the transition process

Service operations manual templates. These templates document the aspects of the process defining the service to be provided to the customer by Logica, including availability management, change management and incident management.

The changes to these templates were to include a safety engineer within the team and to ensure that the various aspects of the process address safety. As an example, the changes specific to the change management template were as follows:

- highlighting the necessity of documenting how safety considerations are to be remotely managed
- documenting the role of the safety engineer within the Change Control Board (CCB)
- highlighting that one of the duties of the CCB is to ensure that the change being considered does not adversely affect system safety.

Transition Gate 2 checklist. This is a template agenda for the service readiness review meeting, which is called to determine the level of confidence and risk associated with proceeding to the cut-over stage of transition. It also details all of the deliverables required. The changes made were to clarify that a safety management plan and safety justification report are required deliverables, and to check that any requirements relating to system safety have been factored into the delivery and the appropriate budget has been allocated.

- To participate in the acceptance of, and confirm closure of the Change Control Note, as appropriate to the nature of the change.

4.5   Project Safety Engineer

The Project Safety Engineer is responsible for:

- To ensure that each change is properly assessed for safety impact

- To update the safety documentation (including the Hazard Log) after each change is implemented

- To advise both Logica and the customer on any change process or procedures with regards to the safety aspects

4.6   Change Advisory Board (CAB)

The Change Advisory Board is the Logica forum that will review information presented to them in support of Change Control Notes and approve, reject or hold in abeyance for further information as they see fit. The CAB will work to ensure that where the change has dependencies on other projects/services that these will receive due attention so as not to hold up the review or implementation of the change.

The specific responsibilities of the CAB are:

- To review and approve/reject/defer the CCNs as appropriate

- To resolve scheduling conflicts and prioritise CCNs as necessary

- To ensure that any dependencies outside the Logica supply are properly managed

- To ensure that the CCN does not adversely affect system safety

- To receive reports on Fast Track and Urgent changes.

OS-SOM - Change Management.doc
© Logica plc   page 18 of 21

Fig. 4. Example change to the change management service operations manual

Transition Gate 3 checklist (transition complete review). This is a template agenda for the transition complete review meeting, which is called to confirm that all of the required transition activities have been completed and the service can progress to business as usual. It also details all of the deliverables required. The changes made were to clarify that a safety management plan, hazard log and safety justification report are required deliverables.

2.11   Document Check

The following documents must all be complete at the completion of Transition and many of them should have been completed by Gate 2 Review. Confirm that all documents are now complete. (N.B. this document checklist should be completed during the review meeting – comments and date of lodgement added to each line as required)

	Outputs	Responsibility	Comment	Issue no.	Location of Document
1	Transition and Quality Plan	Transition Manager	Reviewed at Kick Off		
2	Transition Manager Terms of Reference	Vertical Operations	Reviewed at Kick Off		
3	Safety Management Plan	Transition Manager	If Applicable		
4	Hazard Log	Transition Manager	If Applicable		
5	Safety Justification Report	Transition Manager	If Applicable		
6	Up to date Risk Register	Transition Manager	Updated for closure of Transition.		
7	Up to date Issue	Transition	Updated for closure of		

Fig. 5. Example change to the Gate 3 checklist

2.4.1.3 Business as usual

The focus of the changes made to business as usual templates was to ensure that the activities carried out, and the documentation produced, for or during business as usual are done in such a way that the safety aspects are taken into account. The documents updated were:

Call logging instructions. This document is used to detail the actions to be taken in order to log a support call to the helpdesk. The changes made were to clarify that safety-related calls must always be considered as a critical priority.

Operational level agreement. This document describes all of the operational details of the service to be provided, such as which Logica sites are involved, response times, required system availability, and technologies used. The changes made were to add sections for system safety aspects, staff competencies, and whether a safety standard is mandated in the contract.

Hours of Service:	*\<Insert hours of support\>*
'Out of Hours' Support:	*\<Insert 'out of hours' support times and links to escalation procedure if necessary\>*

Priority	Key Contacts	Notified
\<Insert priority i.e. Critical, High, etc.	*\< Insert name and contact number of person to be contacted for this type of priority\>* *\<If this is a safety related service all safety related incidents will be prioritised as Critical. If there are additional contacts (e.g. Project Safety Engineer) for safety related incidents they should also be inserted here\>* You can insert extra rows if required	*\<Insert how the person should be notified, i.e., phone or e-mail\>*

Fig. 6. Example change to the call logging instructions

Quality plan. This document describes the objectives, structure, schedule, organisation, resources and costs of delivering the service, together with the approach, processes, controls and procedures that will be applied by team members to their work, in order to accomplish the objectives. The only change was to highlight that safety indicators should be included in the regular status reporting and the required escalation of safety-related issues must be defined.

> - *[SUP.P190] Manage measurements collation.*
>
> 4.2.6   Status reporting
>
> *Define the status reporting procedures for the service delivery, both internally and to the client and other stakeholders, as necessary.*
>
> *For safety-related projects this must include a minimum of monthly reporting of safety indicators to the BSM and SSO, and the escalation of safety related issues.*
>
> *Default process and guidance references:*
>
> - *[MSV.P80.30] Service delivery control and reporting*
> - *[MPJ.P60] PT-PD Project tracking process*
> - *CSM-LCG022 Client reporting.*
>
> 4.2.7   Financial processes

Fig. 7. Example change to the quality plan

Status report. This is a template document for regularly reporting various aspects of the service status up the management chain. The change to this template was to include sections for safety indicators and safety issues, in accordance with the changes to the quality plan.

Safety management plan (SMP). This document describes the approach, processes, controls and procedures that will be applied in order to accomplish the safety objectives of the service. It also details the review and approval mechanisms. This document was based on the existing SMP template for development projects, and was modified to use OS terminology and OS-specific documentation that requires review and approval (e.g. CLI and OLA documents).

2.4.1.4 Close down or transfer service process

This is a section of Logica's business management system which is concerned with the process for closing down or transferring a service being operated by OS.

The changes made were to clarify that in all cases the safety documentation must be updated and archived, and handed over to the client or new incumbent. In addition, if the service is being transferred to a new incumbent then it may be necessary to brief them on the safety aspects of the service.

2.5 What happens next?

2.5.1 Roll-out of updates to existing services

Now that the processes and document templates have been updated the next stage is to roll-out the modifications to existing services, and to ensure that any new services in the due diligence or transition phases follow the new processes and use the updated templates. This roll-out must be carried out in a pragmatic way: while there are advantages to having a consistent approach to safety management across all projects, where a given project already has a suitable safety management system in place then updating the project documentation set simply to apply new templates is not of immediate benefit. Therefore the focus will be on those projects where there is little existing safety management activity.

This phase will require some operator and service staff safety awareness training (for both onshore and offshore resources). It will also ultimately require competency management and addressing of any cultural issues, especially with offshore resources. One way forward is to ask key staff on the services to join the active Logica safety community[1] to gain exposure to safety activities and network with staff who are already active participants.

---

[1] The Logica safety community currently has over 70 members, mainly from the UK but also the Netherlands. It meets bi-monthly and discusses a wide range of topics relevant to safety bids, development projects and services.

2.5.2 Monitoring and ongoing improvements

As with any business improvement activity, the next stage of the implementation will be to bed in the changes, monitor the effectiveness of the new processes and instigate further updates where necessary. This will be achieved by means of regular collection of metrics and audits as part of the standard delivery assurance activities but focused on the safety management aspects of the projects.

2.5.3 Resolution of Issues

The final phase will be to look at longer-term potential conflicts or cross-service issues. These are possible because services are increasingly being provided by shared service centres and in more generic ways (e.g. some shared resources may be asked to work on both UK and French contracts with different legal approaches: ALARP vs GALE (Boulton 2010) and some safety services may be hosted on virtualized servers running both safety and non-safety services).

3 Future work

In looking at the services run by Logica it is clear that not all services are the same: not only in their safety risk levels but also in the way they are implemented and operated. It is clear that a 'one size fits all' approach may not be appropriate. The concept of *Service Assurance Level* is proposed as a way to implement the appropriate level of assurance on each service provision.

A Service Assurance Level (SAL) concept may be useful when all or part of the safety mitigation required to produce a sufficiently safe service is placed *within the service operation itself*, rather than within the software or systems (as is usual with a Development Assurance Level or Safety Integrity Level (SIL)).

By this we mean that the way the IT service is implemented and operated provides the safety risk reduction required. The updates to the controlling documents mentioned earlier are an example of this: when combined with suitably trained and experienced staff they perform a mitigating function, reducing the safety risks in the service.[2]

There are many possible ways of defining a service assurance level methodology. One proposal is given here, with four levels of SAL, corresponding to the safety risk level associated with the service operation:

---

[2] It should be mentioned that, in most cases, developing the software to a SIL is not a realistic option as often there is extensive use of COTS and the functions provided by the software are not defined or documented well enough.

1. **Very low risk.** The IT service is very unlikely to cause an accident; any consequences are mild and short-lived, affecting few people.
2. **Low risk.** The service is unlikely to cause an accident; consequences are not serious and not permanent, affecting at most a small number of people.
3. **Medium risk.** The service may cause an accident; consequences are significant and may be permanent, including major injury, and may affect a number of people.
4. **High risk.** The service may cause a major accident; consequences are severe (including death) and may affect a large number of people.

Given a range of risks such as those above, a simple mapping to the components of the service gives us a useful starting point. For this proposal we consider process, procedure and people aspects of the service, as shown in Tables 1, 2 and 3.

Table 1. Service assurance levels for processes

SAL	Name	Description
1	Informal safety management system (SMS)	Informal or combined service SMP. Simple project-level hazard log (HL) created, occasionally updated. Some informal safety justification but spread over multiple documents. Project safety engineer (PSE) appointed but may be very part-time across many projects.
2	Operational SMS	Service SMP produced and maintained. HL actively maintained in specific tool. Client involved in regular hazard review meetings. HL and safety analyses updated regularly from variety of inputs. Single safety justification document produced (e.g. safety case report) and occasionally updated. Regular safety briefings to staff. PSE is more than half time on project.
3	Embedded and proactive SMS	Complete service SMP formally reviewed and signed off. HL and safety analyses updated as matter of routine from variety of inputs (i.e. HL process integral to observation report (OR) process). Unit-level tools used consistently. Some formal safety analyses. Safety justification production partly automated. All staff aware of safety issues and responsibilities. PSE fully embedded in project and influential on all key staff. Full higher management support. A formal service model used.
4	Institutional and improving SMS	Company level tools and training applied consistently to service. HL and multiple independent safety analyses used to predict and proactively address safety risks before any warnings or reports received. Safety justification simply and consistently produced as outputs from tooling used to hold all data. Formalised and continuously improving. Formal service models used extensively.

Table 2. Service assurance levels for procedures

SAL	Name	Description
1	Informal	Informal safety instruction and guidance split over several documents, shares, workspaces, web pages, etc. Occasionally maintained. No specific references to hazards or mitigations. Procedures defined informally for OR and change assessment.
2	Defined	Instructions and procedures managed. Most procedures and definitions derived from single or small set of sources (e.g. HL). Procedures defined for call logging, escalation, OR assessment, risk assessment, change assessment. Tools used for managing ORs, changes and risks. Regression testing used after change made.
3	Controlled	Guidance and clear instructions controlled, managed and approved. All documents under formal configuration management using suitable tool. All procedures and definitions derived and traceable to/from single or small set of sources (e.g. HL). Procedures defined for call logging, escalation, OR assessment, risk assessment, change assessment. Suitable tools used. Impact assessment and regression testing used after all changes. Some metrication.
4	Fully integrated	Safety risk assessment used to drive all activities. All problem reports, documentation and changes managed and approved using formal processes and stored in an integrated management tool. Hazard management fully integrated with all other service activities. Traceability automatically maintained across safety and design and test documents. Safety justification inputs produced automatically. Process metrics collected automatically and used to optimize and improve.

Table 3. Service assurance levels for people

SAL	Name	Description
1	Informal	Some knowledge of safety among one or two service staff. Safety awareness briefing held in last year.
2	Supervised	Most staff working to terms of reference (ToRs), some of which include safety aspects. Safety briefings held regularly. PSE has attended a safety training course. PSE is competent to supervised level on IET safety competency criteria (IET 2006).
3	Practicing	All key service staff have attended formal safety training. ToRs include formal safety responsibilities and are signed. PSE is demonstrably competent to practitioner level on IET safety competency criteria.
4	Professional	All key service staff have attended formal safety training and refresher. PSE is demonstrably competent to expert level on IET safety competency criteria; other key staff are also assessed at practitioner level.

The mitigation achieved by implementing these SALs on the three aspects above has not yet been assessed – this is left as a starting point for further work.

4 Conclusions

This paper reports on work in progress within Logica to improve the safety management of IT services which have complex implementations, including some with offshore elements. An overall strategy has been outlined and significant progress has been demonstrated in identification of safety services and updating of the numerous controlling documents. Work is continuing and the next phase will involve the roll-out of the updated documents to live services.

The concept of service assurance level is introduced and may prove to be useful when there is significant mitigation within the service to manage the wide variety of services within Logica.

References

IEC (2010) IEC 61508 Functional safety of electrical/electronic/programmable electronic safety-related systems, edition 2.0. International Electrotechnical Commission

IET (2006) Competence criteria for safety – related system practitioners. Guidance provided by the IET in collaboration with the HSE and BCS

Logica (2010a) About Logica. http://www.logica.co.uk/we-are-logica/about-logica/. Accessed 13 September 2010

Logica (2010b) Application management. http://www.logica.com/we-do/outsourcing/application -management/. Accessed 13 September 2010

Logica (2010c) Business process outsourcing. http://www.logica.com/we-do/outsourcing/busi ness%20process%20outsourcing/. Accessed 13 September 2010

Logica (2010d) Infrastructure management. http://www.logica.com/we-do/outsourcing/infra structure-management/. Accessed 13 September 2010

MoD (2007a) DEF STAN 00-56 Safety management requirements for defence systems, issue 4. Ministry of Defence

MoD (2007) SMP13 In-service safety management system. http://www.mod.uk/NR/rdonlyres/ BF8B98F0-DBA9-4E56-A386-7334D77AEF77/0/SMP13v22final.pdf. Accessed 13 September 2010

RTCA (1992) RTCA/DO-178B Software considerations in airborne systems and equipment certification

Boulton D (2010) GALE or ALARP: which to choose? Safety Systems 20:1:1-3. Safety-Critical Systems Club

Wikipedia (2010) Safety Integrity Level (SIL). http://en.wikipedia.org/wiki/Safety_Integrity_ Level. Accessed 13 September 2010

York (2010) Through Life Safety (TLS) course notes from MSc in safety critical systems engineering. York University Department of Computer Science

Systems Safety in Healthcare

Integrating a Risk-based Approach and ISO 62304 into a Quality System for Medical Devices

Celestina Bianco

Systelab Technologies

Barcelona, Spain

Abstract   A recent standard for medical device software lifecycle processes, ISO/IEC 62304 (ISO 2006), assumes and specifies a software safety classification scheme, where documentation, verification and validation tasks to be carried out depend on the safety classification. This means that a risk-driven approach has become an accepted standard for medical devices.

This paper describes how Systelab have progressively defined a quality system that integrates as core processes those specified by ISO 62304, and that applies a risk-driven approach also supporting processes such as contract and supplier management.

1 Introduction

To assure safety for the protection of public health, regulatory bodies have issued requirements and guidelines. The requirements relevant to a product depend on the *risk level*.

Validation that provides confidence that the quality of the software is appropriate to support public health is expected from the manufacturer.

To be able to certify that software can be commercialized because it is safe and fulfils its mission for public health, an inspector needs to know what the software does, that it works properly and that it does not imply risks. Validation of safety is a broad concept for medical devices; in 'software speak' it means the assurance that the process of software design, construction and verification is planned and controlled.

With the increasing role and complexity of medical software, manufacturers started to adopt risk control management as a basis for project planning and management, introducing a practical approach to optimizing safety with effects that are as low as possible on costs and time-to-market.

Recently, a standard for medical device software lifecycle processes, ISO/IEC 62304 (ISO 2006), has been released by a commission representing regulatory bo-

C. Dale, T. Anderson (eds.), *Advances in Systems Safety*, DOI 10.1007/978-0-85729-133-2_7,
© Springer-Verlag London Limited 2011

dies. The standard assumes and specifies a software safety classification scheme, where documentation, verification and validation tasks to be carried out depend on the safety classification. This means that a risk-driven approach has become an accepted standard for medical devices.

2 Risk management to assure safety

The first rule that software for medical devices must respect is to be safe, which means be reliable, appropriate, robust and easy-to-use. Residual risks can be assumed only if the clinical relevance is high, meaning the probability of beneficial effects highly outweighs the likelihood and importance of harm. Risks to be considered are for example incorrect diagnosis, incorrect therapy, injury to patients, and injuries to user. Among the causes we must investigate are the intrinsic characteristics and features of the medical system, technical problems, software defects, and also misuse or under-use. Software, either as part of a medical system or stand alone, has the final responsibility to protect against hardware faults and incorrect use.

Risk management is the continuous process of minimizing the risks through a device's lifecycle, to avoid, prevent, or reduce the probability of risks in the use of software and/or to mitigate the severity of the consequences.

The risks shall be reduced to the lowest practicable level: the ALARP principle. The principle considers also that the complexity of any mitigation can result in an additional source of risk because it can cause defects or misuse; or it can imply a delay in availability, with a potentially serious impact on public health. Risk management progressively and iteratively identifies mitigation, verifies the efficacy, and assures the balance between protections and their complexity or inconvenience for design and use.

2.1 Risk-driven approach

At Systelab, in order to be compliant with safety and customer requirements, we have progressively defined a quality system that integrates as core processes those specified by ISO 62304 (ISO 2006) and that applies a risk-driven approach also to supporting process such as contract and supplier management.

The risk-driven approach can be summarized as follows:

- in the definition of an offer, identify the areas of risk, and regulatory requirements
- during requirements definition with the customer, identify the risks and discuss controls
- define the document tree based on the class of risk of the product

- define a modular architecture that justifies different levels of validation for modules of different classes of risk
- detail design and verification according to the class of risks
- prioritize development, verification and validation based on risk classification
- assign responsibility and evaluate changes considering risks class
- quality controls and activities requested before releasing a version depend on class of risk and on the purpose of the version.

This approach allows us to focus on really critical safety areas, and always to be able to justify the choices. We have defined procedures and instructions that make use of tables and decision trees, to provide guidelines of easy application.

3 ISO 62304

ISO 62304 (ISO 2006) is a standard about requirements for software development life cycles aimed at guaranteeing the safety and effectiveness expected from a medical device.

The introduction of ISO 62304 states[1]:

> Software is often an integral part of MEDICAL DEVICE technology. Establishing the SAFETY and effectiveness of a MEDICAL DEVICE containing software requires knowledge of what the software is intended to do and demonstration that the use of the software fulfils those intentions without causing any unacceptable RISKS. This standard provides a framework of life cycle PROCESSES with ACTIVITIES and TASKS necessary for the safe design and maintenance of MEDICAL DEVICE SOFTWARE. This standard provides requirements for each life cycle PROCESS.

3.1 Outline of the standard

62304 *does*

- specify a framework: processes, that include activities, further divided into tasks
- identify what has to be done and what needs to be documented
- specify a *software safety classification scheme* (request application of risk management reference standard, 14971 (ISO 2007)
- assign responsibility for tasks and for documents to be issued and approved.

62304 *does not* prescribe how to implement details of the tasks, and procedures and documents can be split up many different ways The processes identified are:

---

[1] In ISO 62304, CAPITAL refers to subjects which are further defined inside the standard.

- software development[2]
- software maintenance
- software risk management
- software configuration management
- software problem resolution.

3.2 Integration with risk processes

ISO 62304 cannot be followed without strict control of risks; the introduction continues:

> As a basic foundation it is assumed that MEDICAL DEVICE SOFTWARE is developed and maintained within a RISK MANAGEMENT system. The MANUFACTURER shall apply a RISK MANAGEMENT PROCESS complying with ISO 14971.

3.2.1 Software life cycle and classification issues

The software is to be designed, documented, tested and validated according to its safety classification; this is obvious to engineers in safety critical fields; a classification scheme is introduced by the standard to allow lower control on less critical parts, focusing on full safety measures for most critical parts.

> … The software safety classes shall initially be assigned based on severity as follows:
>
> - Class A: No injury or damage to health is possible
> - Class B: Non-SERIOUS INJURY is possible
> - Class C: Death or SERIOUS INJURY is possible
>
> … The MANUFACTURER shall assign to each SOFTWARE SYSTEM that contributes to the implementation of a RISK CONTROL measure a software safety class based on the possible effects of the HAZARD that the RISK CONTROL measure is controlling. …
> … When a SOFTWARE SYSTEM is decomposed into SOFTWARE ITEMS, …
> … The MANUFACTURER shall document the software safety class of each SOFTWARE ITEM if that class is different from the class of the SOFTWARE ITEM from which it was created by decomposition.

---

[2] The software development process includes
- software development planning
- software requirement analysis
- software architectural design
- software detailed design
- software unit implementation and verification
- software integration and integration testing
- software system testing
- software release.

> ... For each SOFTWARE SYSTEM, until a software safety class is assigned, Class C requirements shall apply.

In spite of the attempt to avoid procedural, documentational and inspectional overloads that are not useful, the inputs required for the classification scheme imply that in most cases the safety classification of components cannot be done until architecture and design are completed. For this reason compliance requires the application of the strictest process to the initial phases of the design for all items.

3.3 Comparison with other known standards

Differences in standards depend on the differences of the field of application.

Analyzing the differences between 8110.49 (FAA 2003) and DO178B (RTCA 1992), adopted in aircraft certification, and standards for medical device software, one can see that they depend on the characteristics of the software to be controlled.

For examples, in aircraft, software is one critical component, and there is wide reuse of legacy software; in medical applications, software is the last control against potential damage to the user, patient, environment, and reuse is applied rarely. Configurability is broad in medical systems, much narrower for flying systems.

Field loadable makes another difference although most of the medical software is in fact field loadable as new versions are installed in field, it is quite unusual to replace and integrate it in redundant parts, as redundancy is not a common safety mechanism in medical devices.

Characteristics that most of the critical software have in common are:

- use of third party software, dedicated or commercial
- possibility of chain of risks that alone are minor, whilst in a chain can result in a final consequence of life harm
- need of strict control of changes
- need of reviews of the design.

The list of commonalities and differences can grow considering further details and specific devices; if we focus on the ones listed above and analyze the standard defined and enforced, one can see consequent correspondences and emphasis.

For example, about User Modifiable Software, we find in Chapter 7 of FAA Order 8110.49:

> Applicants should identify in the PSAC their intention to develop an airborne system that will contain a UMS component(s) ... Any changes to UMS that affect the following items warrant rescinding the classification of the software as user-modifiable, and requires design approval under the applicable regulations:
>
> 1. Safety margins, operational capabilities, flight crew workload, any non-modifiable software components, protection mechanisms, and software boundaries.
> 2. Pre-approved range of data, parameters, or equipment performance characteristics.

In medical software configuration of parameters is normally requested for its use; the risk control that applies is based on human factors and access level. Restrictions cannot be severe as the operator would not be able to operate, or he would operate with an overhead that may cause other risks to appear: tiredness, drop of attention, etc.

Both have a strong emphasis on the evaluation and validation of third party software, the design of which is not under the critical software manufacturer's control.

3.4 Integration with the quality system

> The MANUFACTURER of MEDICAL DEVICE SOFTWARE shall demonstrate the ability to provide MEDICAL DEVICE SOFTWARE that consistently meets customer requirements and applicable regulatory requirements. Demonstration of this ability can be by the use of a quality management system in compliance with …

This states the fact that to guarantee safety the software life cycle process needs to be supported and complemented by other processes that generate the conditions for such processes (e.g. resource control, vendor control) to be carried out with efficacy and efficiency, and recognizes that other complementary process are needed for correct business development (sales, marketing, etc.).

3.4.1 Processes within scope – full match or mapping

In a medical device company, whether software is designed as a component of a large system or is a system standing alone, most of the quality system processes are within the scope of design, verification, maintenance, etc., meaning that the processes included in ISO 62304 cover a great part of the company processes. The core of the quality system will be modeled on 62304: some of the processes will match almost exactly in scope, purpose, activities and maybe name, others will need mapping. The alternative chosen often depends on the organization of the company before the establishment of ISO 62304 and risk management processes.

3.4.2 Processes out of scope – compatible and complementary

Supporting processes, more needed the more complex is the product and the company, must be complementary and not in conflict with the safety requirements; this means for example that the sales department must consider the results of risk management and regulatory constraints, and administration and human resources need to budget for training in safety technologies.

4 Map of processes

Our map of processes is based on the ISO 62304 set of processes. It is not possible to have a complete matching for both legacy reasons and because of the need for long term projects to be consistent with processes applied so far, or for the need of sharing part of the process with customers. Furthermore, the quality system will include activities which are not part of the life cycle, also if related to software. There are therefore processes which are an exact match with the standard, or that can be easily mapped – mainly in project control – and others which are relevant for the company and the quality of its products and services but are not included in the ISO 62304 process set.

From responsibility charts one can detect that all the roles in the company are affected and involved in risk related tasks.

Internal audit check that all the flow, starting with definition of an offer and ending with maintenance and customer support, implement appropriate measures for safety control.

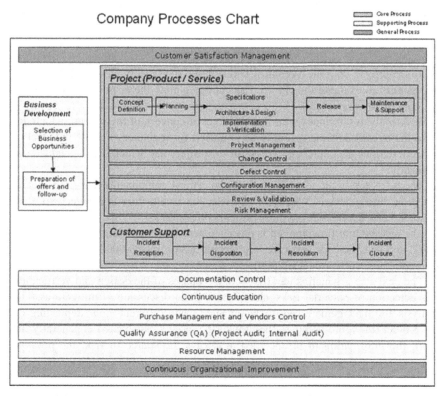

Fig. 1. Map of processes in Systelab Technologies quality system

In the following sections the main processes will be described with their relationships to the standard and safety control; sections of the quality procedures used in the company are presented in *italics*.

4.1 Risk management

Risk management[3] is formally carried out in all phases of an approved project. Review of the concept definition document includes analysis of clinical risks, both derived from functionality and from technology. As soon as concept definition phase has been concluded, a risk analysis document is drafted.

In fact, risk management is also carried out before, and during the review of a proposal to customers. The procedure in place for the management of proposals reads:

> *The purpose of this procedure is to define activities common in the process of preparing and negotiating a proposal for a customer ... It must be assured that:*

> - *Both technical, functional and regulatory aspects are defined*
> - *...*
> - *functional and technical risks are known, classified and controlled.*

Before approval, both the Technical Director and the Quality Director have the responsibility to evaluate the clinical risks and negotiate the responsibility for mitigation with the customer.

Risk analysis continues with first the level of concern of the system, which defines the overall documentation to be produced for regulatory bodies; the level of concern defines the content expected for the project file, which will be audited periodically.

The next step is the identification of the critical components that need special attention during design. Whenever possible, the architecture is designed so as to define precise boundaries for those critical components.

The process and flow applied is designed around the standard ISO 14971 (ISO 2007) and specified for software in a technical report TR 80002 for guidance on the application software (IEC 2009).

The next step – which is iterative with the phases of the design and verification – is detection of potential risks, classification, and discussion of mitigations. The analysis and management can be documented using different tools, depending on the project (the more complex the project the more sophisticated is generally the tool); the information to be included is always the source of risk, the possible

---

[3] 'Risk' in the context of this paper is used to mean *'safety risk for the patient, the operator or the environment'*.

mode of failure, the consequences, the rating of the risk, the mitigation and the rating when mitigated. Table 1 is a simple decision table used for this purpose[4].

Table 1. Risk management decision table

		Severity		
		High	Medium	Low
	High	Intolerable	Intolerable	Clinical evaluation
Probability	Medium	Intolerable	Clinical evaluation	Acceptable
	Low	Clinical evaluation	Acceptable	Acceptable

The table is used to state the need of a mitigation, and the risk zone after the mitigation is applied. The goal is to have all the risks in the acceptable zone; when the identification of a mitigation is difficult or expansive, when it can lead to additional risks or when the protection does not move the risk in the acceptable zone, the residual risk is evaluated against the clinical benefits of the functionality.

Mitigations of risks are identified by a team, and their development has priority. The software project plan takes into account the results of risk analysis and the level of design and code review of mitigations is higher.

Risk analysis may also require additional evaluation before adopting new techniques or tools.

4.2 Reviews

Reviews play an important role in verification; risk analysis is an input of a review meeting; issues found in a review, either of documentation, architecture, code or other, are classified and to the risk.

Each action item will be evaluated, depending on its risks and priority.

4.3 Verification and validation

Mitigation of risks is the highest priority in testing each version to be released.

Regression testing must always include the 'risk related test', which is a nickname, a short definition, for the set of tests that verify the efficacy of the mitigations. The V&V process is made of eight sub-processes, each of which has risk analysis as an input. The process is defined to comply with ISO 62304 (ISO 2006), ISO 14971 (ISO 2007) and also guidelines issued by FDA (FDA 2002) to

---

[4] The decision table shown is the simplest possible; it can be made more complex if an higher level of detail is used in the classification of a risk in terms of severity and probability; we tend to keep for each project the classification of risks as detailed as the classification of defects.

take into account the final stages of validation, to guarantee safety and effectiveness of mitigations.

The verification and validation procedures state:

> *In planning, identify verification activities to be performed and the items to be and not to be verified based on risks and other project needs ... identify the testing platforms needed for test of mitigations ...*
>
> *Risk analysis is the key to determine the minimum amount of test cases needed in order to release a new version to the field. This evaluation shall be executed when the project or phase is initiated but also when a new functionality or change is considered risky. ... Determine the items that require inspection taking into account risk analysis, changes introduced, number of defects found ... Functional test execution is mandatory only for new functionalities or changes, and to cover risk mitigation ... Test report analyzes severity of potential risks associated to open known defects ...*
>
> *As part of the preventive validation, include verification of embedded OTS to avoid possible environmental incompatibilities and problems as part of the development process ...*

4.4 Defect control

Defect Management is another risk-driven task process. Defects are classified with same classes of risk used in risk analysis, and fixing is prioritized according to the risk level:

> *During evaluation, the defect manager determines the difficulty of the fix, the risk involved and the amount of time necessary to make and test the fix. If a defect is set to 'onHold', the reason/justification to accept the open defect in the released version will be documented.*

4.5 Change control

Evaluation of change requests, both functional and technical, is risk-driven. The change management procedure states:

> *Analysis of the change request includes the evaluation to determine how it affects the safety of the software product in terms of introduction of additional potential causes contributing to a hazardous situation and therefore the need of additional software mitigations. It also evaluates the impact of software changes on existing mitigations. ... The change manager evaluates change request information (including risk) and disposes it, the reviewer reviews the documented proposal of the change request, analyzing the risk, and approves or rejects it. ...*
>
> *Risk evaluation and mitigations update will be carried out before the final approval. Tasks are derived from here in case of need (this is for adding new risks to the RAM document, adding new mitigations or reviewing the existing mitigations) ... The*

verification includes Test Cases that assure that risk mitigations are implemented correctly and that they are effective.

4.6 Release process

In order to release a product – and all its updates – for clinical use, it is mandatory to re-evaluate all the open defects for their level of risk; none with severe safety risks can be left open, all those remaining have to be formally evaluated and accepted, documenting the reasons for the acceptance and/or the workaround to be applied. The formal defect disposition is the last step of the validation process and an input to release process. Defect list, risk evaluation, disposition and justification are part of the validation records. In special cases a version can be approved for release if the validation documents are not formally completed; in no case can a version be approved if the risk evaluation is not completed.

> *... NOTE: Defect disposition list may be included in software release notes or test summary report documents. If the TSR document is formalized after the release, the defect disposition can be an appendix of the release readiness checklist.*

The release procedure is defined following almost exactly the correspondence process of ISO 62304; in case the version is an official main release, and especially if it is to be submitted for approval of a regulatory body (typical FDA 510(k) clearance or CE mark), the overall residual risk is to be evaluated and documenting; it takes into account the verification and validation of risk mitigations and the remaining open risks.

4.7 Supporting processes

Also the supporting general processes that are carried out in parallel with the project life cycle deal with safety risks. Starting with the input to a software development project, that is the contract upon an accepted *offer*. The process of offering and negotiations takes into account safety and regulatory requirements. A preliminary estimation of the risk level is done to determine the test effort and the set and level of detail of the documentation to be generated and delivered. The contract also states the responsibility and/or disclaimers for safety issues should they occur[5].

All the projects are then supported by the process of *documentation control*; the set of documentation to be maintained, the level of revisions and the rigor of the reviews depend on the project risk level. We have defined three main groups: the

---

[5] Details about the risk management during the offering process have been discussed in previous sections.

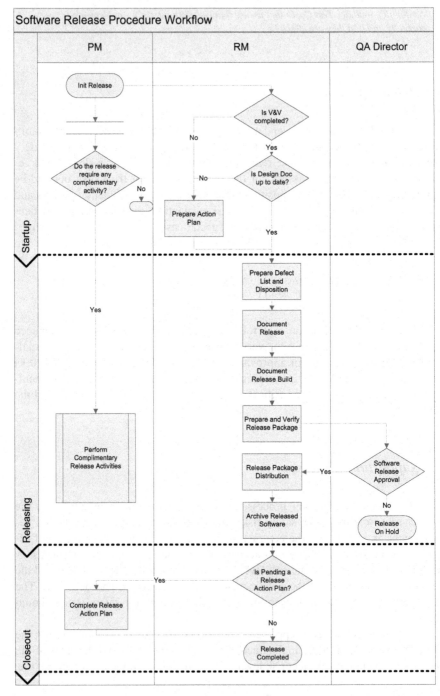

Fig. 2. Release process flow

projects that are in the scope of medical devices for FDA and/or CE mark, and those outside the scope of medical devices. Those in scope generally fall in the moderate level-of-concern classification; our process is focused on this class and includes description of exception were the project high or low level risk.

During the planning phase of the project the project manager should:

1. *Evaluate for the project the standards and/or regulations applicable to the project. For this task the project manager should determine the intended use and the market distribution. In this task it will be helpful to review the compilation of regulatory information on previous projects and Systelab's QA assessment.*
2. *Define the documentation items needed according to the required document list and the previous assessment.*
3. *Customize the project documentation plan based on the project file document responsibilities.*

Figure 3 shows the required documents and the review, approval and project file archive necessities for each document type.

SOURCE	RECORD	FDA			CE			SYSTELAB			NOTES
		App lic.	Rev.	Sig n.	App lic.	Rev.	Sig n.	App lic.	Rev.	Sig n.	
SW Design Plan(s)	SW Project Plan	✓	⟳	✎	✓	⟳	✎	✓	⟳	✎	
	SW Schedule	-	-	.	-	-	-	✓	-	-	
	SW Quality Plan	(draft)	⟳	✎	-	-	-	(draft)	⟳	✎	Can be included in Project Plan
	SW Requirements / Specifications	✓	⟳	✎	✓	⟳	✎	✓	⟳	✎	
	SW Architecture	✓	⟳	✎	✓	⟳	✎	✓	⟳	-	
	SW Design	(draft)	⟳	✎	(draft)	-	-	Prj.	-	-	Mandatory only for critical parts
SW Verification and Validation	SW Test Plan	✓	⟳	✎	✓	⟳	✎	✓	⟳	✎	
	SW Risk Analysis	✓	⟳	✎	✓	⟳	✎	✓	⟳	✎	
	Test Design	-	.	.	-	-	-	Prj.	-	.	
	Test Cases – Unit	(draft)	⟳	-	-	-	-	Prj.			Mandatory for critical parts
	Test Cases – Functional	✓	⟳	✎	✓	⟳	✎	✓	-	-	
	Test Case Report – Unit	✓	-	✎	-	-	-	Prj.	-	-	Mandatory for critical parts
	Test Case Reports – Functional	✓	-	✎	✓	-	-	✓	-	-	Full last version
	Test Summary Report	✓	⟳	✎	✓	⟳	✎	✓	⟳	✎	
	Traceability	✓	⟳	✎	✓	⟳	✎	✓	-	-	Full and signed last version
	Review minutes (technical)	✓	-	✎	-	-	-	-	-	-	
	OTS documentation	(draft)	-	.	-	-	-	(draft)	-	-	Can be reference to SYSTELAB -OTS Library (that is TBD)
	Acceptance Test Protocol	(draft)	⟳	✎	(draft)	⟳	✎	Prj.	⟳	✎	Can be customer responsibility
	Usability Test Protocol	(draft)	⟳	✎	-	-	-	Prj.	⟳	-	If Human Factors compliance is required.

Fig. 3. Project file requirements table

Another supporting process parallel to projects life cycle is *quality assurance*. All projects are submitted to internal audit periodically, once or twice a year. The scope of the processes and activities audited differs depending on the characteristics and on the risk level of the project.

A plan of audit is defined yearly; the plan includes all projects developed and/or tested under Systelab responsibility. The plan is defined according to the following guidelines:

- *each project will be audited once a year, with one follow up to verify the implementation of corrective actions described in the action plan*
- *each project will be audited against the SOPs relevant depending on its phase an against those that have open no conformities from past audit*
- *if the project will have to pass through a submission or external inspection during the year, the CSD audit will be focused on that external event (e.g. 510(k) or CE submission, FDA inspection).*

The plan will detail for each project date of audit, scope of the audit (SOPs) and expected follow-up date.

Table 2. Example of audit plan

Audits	2009								
	May	Jun	Jul	Aug	Sept	Oct	Nov	Dec	SOPs
Prj1	14					*10*			Requirements + Release + Project File
Prj2	20		*21*						Defects + Requirements + Project File
Prj5					25				Defects + Requirements + Project File
Prj6		16					*10*		Audit checklist (FDA 820.30)
...					17		*16*		Defects +Release+ Project File
Prj11					N.A.				Requirements + Defects + Project File

Among the supporting processes, the *vendor control* process is also risk based: the tasks requested for vendor and product classification depend on the purpose of the product to be acquired; the more critical for the development process or the final product is the purchased part, the more the checks and frequency. A software component to be embedded or used in conjunction with medical software may affect safety; they are pre-validated and follow a strict configuration control process. Whenever possible, the vendor development process is audited.

For critical packages, potential risks will be included in software risk analysis and the coverage matrix will link some specific test cases with specific third party software features they exercise.

Table 3. Documentation and validation criteria of third party software

Third party software	Documentation	Validation criteria
OTS embedded	Basic description Selection process* Maintenance	Include all potential hazards from OTS in 'Software risk analysis and management' process
Installable platform	Description Selection process* Maintenance Operations	Mitigation of risks is installation test and qualification test with any platform combination
Development and test platform	Description Selection process* Maintenance	

* Vendor and product

5 Conclusions

Writing this paper has given me the opportunity to study similarities and differences with quality and safety rules and processes in medical software compared to other kinds of life-critical software. In summary, if we consider for example requirements from FAA and FDA we can see that they strictly depend on the intended use of the system and above all on the intended use of the software inside the system. An analysis of the differences in use and structure of the software in the two environments has been done in details above.

We can remark that the analysis of characteristics is done to define the class of risks. Once that is done, the process is the same in the different environments. Once the risk analysis is made, the safety requirement is to mitigate, with appropriate techniques and methodologies. Once the critical categories are identified, a strict process of software engineering is established, focused on mitigations. Like a good meal, that is cooked to perfection once the menu is established and the appropriate way to cook the dish is applied.

References

FAA (2003) US. Department of Transportation Federal Aviation Administration – Order 8110.49 software approval guidelines
FDA (2002) General principles of software validation. US Food and Drug Administration
IEC (2009) IEC/TR 80002. Guidance on the application of ISO 14971 to medical device software
ISO (2006) ISO/IEC 62304 – Medical device software – Software life cycle processes. Edition 1.0
ISO (2007) ISO 14971 – Medical devices – Application of risk management to medical devices
RTCA (1992) DO-178B Software considerations in airborne systems and equipment certification

Maintaining the Safety of Operational Health ICT Systems

Alan Debenham

Logica, in partnership with UCL Hospitals[1]

Staines, UK

Abstract In the context of increasing complexity and scope of computer systems used in the UK National Health Service, this paper describes the response a Foundation Trust hospital has made to the challenge. From a set of ICT activities which were founded on informal but capable principles, the expansion of the computer systems identified the need for improvements. This increasing awareness was present in the wider NHS, resulting in the publication of standards for applying safety management principles to health related software. This paper summarises the improvement measures taken across a number of areas, taking the safety case report as the focus for safety management activities.

1 Introduction

The University College of London Hospitals Foundation Trust ('the Trust') provides a range of services through a group of hospitals. Within the Trust, computer services and associated infrastructure are provided by the ICT department.

Logica provides outsourcing services to the Trust ICT department. This service originally, and contractually, had a certain amount of safety management of a parochial nature.

The Trust ICT department, with Logica, is responsible for supporting the computer network, connections to it, most of the servers and clients attached to it, and many applications including patient records. The separate medical physics department oversees medical devices and works closely with the ICT department to ensure continuity of safety management activities. The scope of ICT has increased

---

[1] UCL Hospitals is an NHS Foundation Trust comprising the Eastman Dental Hospital, the Heart Hospital, Hospital for Tropical Diseases, National Hospital for Neurology and Neurosurgery, the Royal London Hospital for Integrated Medicine and University College Hospital (incorporating the former Middlesex and Elizabeth Garrett Anderson Hospitals).

C. Dale, T. Anderson (eds.), *Advances in Systems Safety*, DOI 10.1007/978-0-85729-133-2_8,
© Springer-Verlag London Limited 2011

over the years as the contribution of computer systems to healthcare has expanded. Safety management is expanding to match.

Safety management methods for ICT were originally introduced as part of the outsourcing service provided by Logica. To start with, these were limited in scope to the deliverables of the contract. In consequence, the original safety management plan, safety board and associated activities had a limited impact on the overall operations of the ICT department. In 2009, when DSCN 14 and DSCN 18 (ISB 2009a and 2009b) were being promulgated, there was already a realisation within the Trust that the scope and formality of safety management activities should be improved.

Since then, a significant set of work has been carried out to implement these improvements. The publication of the standards provided additional motivation and focus to enable the work. The Trust continues to improve its safety management methods, through adopting and managing a strategy which addresses the safety culture of ICT and infuses safety into development, procurement and maintenance of its computer systems.

This paper describes examples of what can be done, but without necessarily claiming that they would be appropriate in all circumstances.

2 Regulatory framework

Regulations for ICT in the healthcare sector are presented in this section, with their impact on managing safety within the Trust's ICT department, for development and operational use. The impact is in the area of formal and evidenced management of safety; the safety case report is identified as a key artefact to be planned, produced and maintained. The updates to EC directives for stand-alone software as a medical device are discussed.

The need for effective safety management is recognised in order to:

- avoid doing harm through negligence or inactivity
- minimise the risk of accidents and consequent claims, litigation and publicity.

This should be done in the context of legislation, regulations, and standards. In some situations, criminal law applies which can result in prison term or fines.

The risks are that IT failures may cause harm or deaths and subsequent investigations and litigation. Experience with incidents would indicate that this is a real possibility to be taken seriously. There is an ever increasing dependence on IT and its infrastructure. The more successful it is the more it will be trusted, and the more responsibility there is on us to perform effective safety management on our IT systems.

2.1 Legislation and case law

Applicable legislation includes the following:

- The Health and Safety at Work Act has wide applicability, as does the Corporate Manslaughter Act.
- Under the Consumer Protection Act, medical devices regulations from the EC are imposed by Statutory Instruments (SI). The latest directive is SI 2008 No 2936, the Medical Devices (Amendment) Regulations 2008, which came into force on 21 March 2010 and include a specific change with impact on the Trust and Logica, bringing stand-alone software into the realms of medical devices. Regulations are supported by guidance from the regulator, MHRA.
- EC Directives include:

  - Directive 93/42/EEC, which covers the placing on the market and putting into service of medical devices
  - Directive 2007/47/EC, which came fully into force on 21 March 2010 and amends the medical devices directives following a review of the existing provisions by the European Commission and member states. In particular the definition of a medical device now includes standalone software used for diagnostic and therapeutic purposes.

- The term 'duty of care' was established in a test case in 1932 (Lord Atkin: Donoghue v Stevenson).
- The term 'reasonably practicable' was established in 1949 by Lord Justice Asquith, and is widely used as a criterion for sufficiency of risk reduction measures, when further resources would be 'grossly disproportionate' to the benefit gained.

2.2 NHS regulatory requirements and international standards

The National Health Service has required, via DSCN 14 and DSCN 18, that health software comply with the draft standards formerly issued as ISO/TS 29321:2008 and ISO/TR 29322:2008. These are very similar to ISO 14971, but brought into line with the manufacture, deployment and use of health software, rather than medical devices. These were published to take effect in December 2009 and March 2010 respectively. Other applicable standards include:

- ISO 14971 Medical devices – application of risk management to medical devices
- ISO 9001 Quality management systems. Requirements
- ISO 13485 Medical devices. Quality management systems. Requirements for regulatory purposes

- IEC 80001-1 Application of risk management for IT-networks incorporating medical devices.

3 Impact and response

3.1 Impact of regulation

The NHS published standards DSCN 14 and DSCN18 require more formality and governance for safety management. The production of safety cases from suppliers or manufacturers and from the healthcare organisation (i.e. the Trust) is mandated. To support the safety cases a safety management lifecycle is defined. The intended dates for implementation were a challenge. In practice, there needed to be a process in place by the time of the implementation dates to derive safety cases.

Current health software developments within the Trust are intended to comply with these NHS standards. Developments are supported with a safety case report. The strategy is to build up a set of sub-system safety cases until there is a comprehensive set covering all applicable parts of the Trust's IT.

The Trust has expanded the scope of its ICT safety management to include infrastructure so there will be no substantial change of scope when and as planned compliance with IEC 80001 be required.

As far as medical devices directives are concerned (SI 2008 No. 2936, Clause 2.h), the current understanding of 'medical devices' in the Trust context is more limited than the new EC directive definition. Most of the applications developed in-house are being provided for the Trust's own use, and are not being marketed, which reduces the Trust's need to provide formal compliance with the directives.

Duty of care extends beyond strict contract limitations and may well invalidate any dependence on the contract to limit liability.

Similarly, while the DSCN 14 and DSCN18 standards refer to software applying to patient safety, we should apply similar applicable disciplines to the infrastructure and without excluding harm to parties other than patients.

3.2 A strategy for compliance

The safety case, safety case report and supporting activities were the key to developing a safety management strategy. When the regulations were updated, some parts of the necessary response were already in place within the Trust, but not all.

Contemporary practice and records would not fulfil all the needs for a safety case. Where activities and processes were already in place, the level of formality of existing records would be unlikely to fully support a rigorous, and possibly hostile, independent scrutiny.

Templates were produced for safety case reports and hazard analyses. It is now policy that safety case reports are to be produced at an early stage in the development of any new work. Training has been provided for key staff, to achieve this.

Methods used by the Change Advisory Board (CAB) have been enhanced to fully take into account safety. In many cases, sufficient information is on the change form to provide a justification for the safety of the change, both as it is implemented and in the subsequent steady state.

Medical devices are subject to established methods which provide the evidence and safety argument without the need to introduce new procedures. As the safety management system grows in maturity, it is likely that improvements will filter across between software support and medical device controls.

4 Strategic considerations in the Trust context

A demonstrable justification that ICT is maintained in a safe operational state is the primary objective of the safety management system. In order to develop an effective safety management system, a number of considerations have been taken into account, with an impact on working practices which are explained more fully in following sections of this paper.

A *strategy* has been developed and is being maintained. With the support and commitment of ICT management, the strategy is owned by a *Safety Board* which reviews the effectiveness of safety management activities, provides advice to ICT management and records the strategy in the *Safety Management Policy* document. The strategy is prepared with contributions from key *stakeholders* within the Trust.

Commitment to, and a *culture* of, safety has been fostered, and includes the development of *capability* using internal safety briefings and more formal training for key participants in safety management activities.

A key part of the strategy is the recognition of the central role of *safety cases.* They provide a focus for the activities which are needed to prepare and support them and set expectations of achievement of safety across the team. The need for the safety case to be and remain valid has influence on methods and processes for:

- an overall approach to safety justification
- hazard analysis and risk management
- development lifecycle
- record keeping and assurance
- procurement
- change and release management

- incident management processes
- network management and medical devices.

4.1 Elements and principles of strategy

Some guiding principles have been adopted in formulating the strategies for safety management:

- Foster a safety culture across the team.
- Build on existing good practice.
- Adopt a common approach across the Trust.
- Extend beyond the strict formality of DSCN 14 and DSCN 18, e.g. beyond just patient safety, and inclusive of infrastructure (anticipating IEC 80001).
- Take retrospective action, via CAB, as old applications are updated.
- Take any retrospective action needed for mature products not seen by CAB.
- Improve key processes and monitor their effectiveness by the Safety Board.
- Take into account methods used for medical devices and other 'clinically critical' software and infrastructure.
- Keep manual processes for business continuity and risk reduction.

5 Implementation

In this section, it is shown how the strategic considerations described have led to improved working practices which aim to meet the goals.

5.1 ICT Safety Board

The ICT Safety Board has been set up as a strategic body to support and advise the Trust's ICT Director. Tactical decisions about system safety are subject to processes for detailed operation. The Safety Board oversees these, and decides on strategic issues. Membership of the ICT Safety Board has extended from the original, mainly Logica stakeholders, to a much broader base including ICT and other interested parties within the wider Trust, in particular medical physics and system managers. System safety specialists are part of the membership, including the Safety Manager and, from time to time, a contribution from the Logica UK wide System Safety Officer. The Board meets on a monthly basis and has performed an important role in obtaining commitment to system safety management of health software, developing concepts which would have taken far longer without it. The

Board has significant momentum currently; the challenge will be to maintain the contribution to continuous improvement which has been a feature of recent activity.

5.2 Safety Management Policy document

The Safety Management Plan was originally a Logica team strategy document, but has now evolved into a joint Trust and Logica document. It was already in place and being expanded before the recent tightening of formality included such a document in its list of requirements. The renamed ICT Safety Management Policy has been reviewed and agreed by the Safety Board, with support from the ICT Director and Logica management. Within the document, the requirements of the standards have been mapped to specific sections of the policy.

5.3 Coordination with stakeholders

On a Trust wide basis, the Head of Clinical Governance and Risk and her team are responsible for regulatory compliance, risk management, quality and information governance. The intention is that the ICT activities, as overseen by the Safety Board, support and complement the activities performed at the wider Trust level. They are kept informed of Safety Board activities; at a working level the ICT information governance representative at the Safety Board looks after risk management interfaces. The coupling between ICT system safety and the Trust's risk and incident management processes has been productive, and ensures that where practicable, the methods are aligned, for example in the use of a common risk matrix.

A separate department within the Trust has responsibility for the safety of medical devices. The operating practices are well established. As more software is developed to support medical devices, and wider use is made of networks by devices, then there will be scope for establishing working practices which are more closely aligned.

5.4 Safety culture, commitment and safety management

An inherent characteristic of staff in the NHS is their concern for patient safety. This has been built on for safety management by providing a set of methods and disciplines which harness and formalise the good attitudes and practices into a more formal safety management approach across the team. The approach has been taken to involve everyone in safety management and not to divorce it from routine practice by making it an 'opaque' or arcane area of practice. Routine software development, change and support activities all have their safety management component. Routine briefings are given to all staff to raise awareness. In some cases, specific training needs have been identified and training procured. Training helps them to be familiar with safety management techniques and terminology and to understand a safety case when it 'bites' them.

5.4.1 Assurance and competencies

Most safety arguments contain a set of assertions about processes and the competence of people with safety management responsibilities. The evidence to support this type of argument comes from safety assessment/audit. A review takes place, independently of the day to day incumbent, of the effectiveness and efficiency of the safety management system. It is an inherent feature of most systems that they are developed and improved within the scope of experience of a discrete set of professionals, and that it is easy for the working practices to have weaknesses which are difficult for the embedded staff to detect.

As a supplier to the Trust, Logica has a group of safety management specialists and a process for monitoring projects independently, by people without allegiance to the project. This has brought benefits in terms of improving processes.

It has been shown that unplanned absences of key personnel can prejudice achievement of safety management matters. Succession planning, with the nomination of deputies, can reduce this risk.

5.5 An overall approach to safety justification

The production of a safety argument and a safety case summarised in a safety case report is crucial to the implementation of the current safety standards, embodying as they do current good professional practice. A safety case is intended to be a compelling argument that an acceptable level of safety has been achieved, supported by objective evidence.

The Trust has had to establish a viable way ahead to deal with those parts of the system which have been made operational before the more formal safety management methods were established.

As there are many applications and pieces of equipment on the estate, an approach has been adopted of building up a set of safety cases as development, procurement and maintenance continue. The longer term aim is to have all information and infrastructure assets identified with their safety status, and for there to be an overall safety case comprising all the component parts. In the meantime, any new or updated applications are required to have a justification for acceptable levels of safety risk.

A list of information assets with safety categories was compiled some time ago, but not maintained. This has been used as an input to the activity. More recently, an information asset register has been compiled, with safety status information being captured.

The review and update of this list could be used as a mechanism for enabling changes of use to be monitored. This would be supplementary to the operation of the change board, which looks at new usage where this impacts on the validity of the safety case.

5.6 Safety management: hazard analysis; risk reduction; achievement

Hazard analysis activities have been performed for some time by the Trust. The added value of recent improvements has been to provide a formal framework and associated methods into which they fit as a major component. The analyses were founded on traditional risk management techniques. These have been reviewed and developed, resulting in a similar format for the records produced. Improvements have been made by using a team rather than an individual for carrying out the analysis. The use of a set of guide words has helped to enable a consistent approach to the examination of design representations of the system under review. The technique was heavily based on the HAZOP method advocated in Def Stan 00-58 (MoD 1986); in this, it evolved into a similar form to that promoted as SHARD (Pumfrey 1999).

As part of the records produced from the hazard analysis, risk levels and risk reduction measures were identified, keeping the previously established practice, and using a risk classification matrix already in wide use across the Trust for incident and risk management purposes. Residual risk is included, assuming that risk reduction measures proposed will have been achieved. Earlier work stopped the records at this stage; more recent work has recognised the need to record supporting evidence for achievement of risk reduction, in a form which is auditable, and in more significant cases has been subject to actual audit.

5.7 The lifecycle includes safety management

System safety activities are likely to be ineffective if they are not built into the lifecycles and processes for developing and maintaining software, systems and infrastructure. We are still refining the processes and in particular the trigger points for safety management as part of Trust ICT activity. Much of the contribution which is needed will be due to the recognition and commitment by the team to safety management. For this, a safety culture continues to be fostered, and ways and means of applying the right level of formality need to be developed, where too much bureaucracy weakens the commitment, and too little rigour provides for inadequate objective evidence.

Where there are projects for specific developments, the model is for a draft safety case report to be produced at an early stage of that project. This sets expectations for the activities and outputs which will be needed. The activities as described in the standards will follow, such that hazards are identified and analysed, risk reductions prioritised and implemented and evidence to support the safety argument derived, recorded and checked.

The scope of safety management activities is not limited to just the safety of patients, but to anyone who could be affected. The scope has also been extended to include the infrastructure: workstations, servers, network etc. This extends the formal scope of the standards into a cohesive approach which addresses the safety of all ICT activities for the Trust. Where a safety case report is issued for deployment and use of in-house developed software, then the requirements for a 'manufacture' safety case are also addressed, thus avoiding the need for the same team to produce two reports.

A specific department in the Trust, Medical Physics, is well established and takes responsibility for medical devices. For some time, it has been recognised that medical devices rely increasingly on software, and also on the general equipment provided by the ICT department. The two departments work together increasingly closely to achieve effective safety management. The improvements here are still ongoing.

5.8 Development methods and controls

How a product is specified, designed, reviewed and tested has an impact on its suitability to perform safety related tasks. There is an analogy here with PES (Programmable Electronic Systems), for which ISO 61508 asks for justification for the level of rigour applied to development activities. In that context, for sensitive applications, the need for formal methods is to be considered. Although considered, the need for formal methods has been discounted for the current range of Trust applications.

In use, some unanticipated misbehaviour of interfacing applications has been observed, and following a safety root cause analysis, the need to apply improved development methods was recognised and promulgated.

There are some areas in which best practice as currently understood has not been applied, or at least recorded, historically, and until upgrades or obsolescence come along, then currently working systems would benefit to a lesser extent than new developments.

5.9 Development file, records and configuration management

The normal good practices as defined in a mature quality management system are necessary to support a realistic safety management system. Requirements, design and test specifications should be baselined. Records are needed for all reviews and test results. The code should be subject to error reporting and tracking, and configuration management. We cannot justify the safety of an ill-defined product.

5.10 Safety records

An essential but not the only repository for evidence to support the safety case is the hazard log. This is owned by the safety specialist responsible for the area, with contributions from team members performing system safety activities. At the heart of this is a database which has been developed over a period of time, and has been shown to support a group of records which underpin system safety management activities. To date, the user interface has not been developed for ease of use by a large group of people with a passing contribution to make. The immediate developments are to make capture of hazard analysis and risk tracking easier by using a standard spreadsheet format which can be readily imported without the originator needing to learn how to operate the database and its forms. Similarly, safety arguments in GSN (goal structured notation) format should be able to be captured from a graphical application into database format. These techniques have proved to be useful, and are used to maintain change records and their safety assessment.

When data has been collected, then it needs to be assessed and reported on. Reports include hazard analyses, safety argument diagrams (GSN), assets assessed, safety incidents, change assessments, meeting records and actions. If the data is captured then a specific report or query can be generated. As the volume of data has expanded, then the value of using a database has been realised in terms of information which can be extracted.

The hazard log is supported by records of processes operated across the ICT teams, including change control, release management, incident management and problem management.

5.11 Impact on procurement from third parties

A safety management trail from suppliers to the Trust needs to be established and maintained. The suppliers' user documentation and safety case need to be sufficient to support the Trust's safety case(s).

CE marking and registration in accordance with EC directives applies for medical devices and software. There is a need for the Trust to understand the regulations so that compliance by suppliers can be checked when products are procured and supplied which fall into the medical devices definition.

Where regulations and/or directives apply then the affected product may need to be subject to CE registration. Depending on the class allocated, then this can be more or less onerous on the supplier. It involves applying the disciplines defined in ISO standards for safety management and quality management with the production of a safety case report, safety files and technical files. For Class I, this is self certifiable, with the regulator having the option of auditing for compliance. For Classes II and III, then the product with its technical and safety files is subject to audit and assessment. It is noted that when Canada introduced a similar but more rigid regulation, the heath software industry was reported to have been brought to a halt for at least nine months (the message here is that obtaining external regulation is non-trivial).

5.12 Change Advisory Board (CAB)

Not all activity is the subject of formal development projects, but the need to apply safety management techniques is just as strong. Such change is monitored through the Change Advisory Board (CAB), or through incident management processes.

The CAB is a key component of the Trust's ICT processes. It is the final stage at which all changes to the ICT system are vetted and scheduled, and includes products from third party suppliers. As well as the safety of the resulting state of the system after the change, the safety during a change is included (e.g., how temporary downtime is to be addressed, data migration activity).

A three tier safety classification for changes has been adopted:

L: Low or minimal risk. There is no realistic mechanism for the behaviour of the system under consideration to cause an accident, or a quick assessment identifies that the severity or probability of an accident are so low as to make any further risk reduction action of minimal benefit.

Y (Yes): safety related, of a simple nature. The information contained in the standard change form identifies risks, risk reductions and actions taken, in sufficient depth to need no further safety analysis.

HL (Hazard Log). The information in the change form is unable to provide a compelling argument that the change is acceptably safe. In such cases, a separate safety analysis is performed and recorded in the safety files/hazard log. A major release of an electronic patient records system would fall into this category.

5.13 Release of applications and equipment into the live environment

The addition or alteration of equipment or applications attached to the network has always been subject to control. The criteria for allowing such activities have been extended to include acceptance of associated safety risk levels. As there are a number of mechanisms for making such changes, this process needs to be monitored for ongoing effectiveness.

Of particular relevance are the checks made for connecting devices to the network:

- If the item is a medical device then is it recorded as such, so that routine updates to standard desktops do not make device environments invalid.
- Can the item operate safely when the network becomes slow or unavailable?
- Can the item adversely affect the network or other equipment connected to it?
- Is the device effectively protected against malware? In some cases the platform for a medical device might be invalidated by the presence of anti-virus software.

5.14 Incident management, root causes and after action reviews

During live operational use, the occurrence of incidents may be indicative of a threat to the existing safety case (or notional safety case for older systems). When an ICT incident occurs, several things need to happen to maintain assurance that operations are at an acceptably safe level. This is a good example of how safety management principles have been embedded into the processes established to support service management as recommended by ITIL (OGC 2007).

Recovery from an incident is an activity which itself needs to be performed safely so that the existing risk is not made worse. Part of the risk reductions for a hazard may be the existence of manual procedures to be followed in the event of an IT failure or planned outage.

When service is restored it needs to be checked for safe operations. The (operational) safety case may need to be reviewed to ensure its ongoing validity.

A root cause analysis should be considered to establish why the incident occurred, with a view to learning how to reduce the risk in future. An after action review is also useful; when the team involved with the incident can get together promptly to identify what should have happened, what actually happened and why there were any differences.

The validity of the safety case may be threatened if the incident reveals an unpredicted failure mode, or questions the likelihood of an event or the severity of that event.

Throughout the management of an incident, communications are important so that stakeholders can take appropriate action.

5.15 Network resilience, diversity and reliability

In a diverse system of systems such as exists within the Trust, as a group of hospitals, the importance of the network has become ever greater. For some years, a policy of improving the capacity and resilience of the network has had many benefits. Technological diversity, physical separation and avoidance of single points of failure have all been developed as guiding principles. The performance of network components is kept under review, with less reliable components being updated as needed.

5.16 Marketing of software as a medical device

Where services are being provided to organisations outside the Trust, clarification with the regulator (MHRA) has confirmed that the current scope of software such as clinical data records falls outside the strict scope of the medical device definition because it provides no calculation or image processing. If a computer system replaces paper without extra processing to help conduct diagnosis or treatment then it is currently deemed to fall outside the definition.

In the event that any of the Trust's health software products should fall into the category of medical devices under the new definitions, then the directives will apply only to software which is marketed as a product, and so excludes any bespoke developments for internal use. (What is currently marketed contains no diagnostic or therapeutic functionality as understood by the regulator – it will however be necessary to ensure that this proviso is not breached with future requirements or changes in use.)

6 Conclusion and way ahead

A set of process improvements and developments has been presented. Further to process definition and process improvement, the value of a safety culture has been recognised. The concept of aiming for an ongoing valid safety case has permeated the development of a safety management strategy. Significant achievements have been made, but much of the work presented is still in progress, and the role of the ICT Safety Board is key in obtaining commitment to further improvements.

Acknowledgments   The material in this paper could not have been presented without the support of the UCLH Hospitals NHS Foundation Trust. Nor would it have been as easy or as effective without the training provided by the University of York.

References

ISB (2009a) DSCN 14/2009: Application of patient safety risk management to the manufacture of health software. Information Standards Board for Health and Social Care

ISB (2009b) DSCN 18/2009: Application of patient safety risk management to the deployment and use of health software. Information Standards Board for Health and Social Care

MoD (1986) Def Stan 00-58: HAZOP studies on systems containing programmable electronics (withdrawn). Ministry of Defence

OGC (2007) ITIL v3. Office of Government Commerce: Information Technology Infrastructure Library

Pumfrey DJ (1999) The principled design of computer system safety analyses. Thesis, The University of York

Testing of Safety-Critical Software Embedded in an Artificial Heart

Sungdeok Cha[1], Sehun Jeong[1], Junbeom Yoo[2] and Young-Gab Kim[1]

[1]Korea University, Seoul, Korea

[2]Konkuk University, Seoul, Korea

Abstract   Software is being used more frequently to control medical devices such as artificial heart or robotic surgery system. While much of software safety issues in such systems are similar to other safety-critical systems (e.g., nuclear power plants), domain-specific properties may warrant development of customized techniques to demonstrate fitness of the system on patients. In this paper, we report results of a preliminary analysis done on software controlling a Hybrid Ventricular Assist Device (H-VAD) developed by Korea Artificial Organ Centre (KAOC). It is a state-of-the-art artificial heart which completed animal testing phase. We performed software testing in in-vitro experiments and animal experiments. An abnormal behaviour, never detected during extensive in-vitro analysis and animal testing, was found.

1 Introduction

The number of patients who suffer from heart-related disease is increasing rapidly. The American Heart Association estimates that about 800,000 American deaths were due to heart-related disease in 2006, exceeding casualties caused by cancer and accidents (AHA 2010). Organ transplant is only a partially effective solution because a patient's immune system may reject a transplanted heart, and because the number of heart donations simply cannot satisfy the demand. According to the Organ Procurement and Transplantation Network and Scientific Registry of Transplant Recipients, only 2,277 heart donations were made in the US in 2006 (HHS 2008, 2010).

To the vast majority of cardiac patients, an artificial heart is the only practical alternative to extend precious life. In 2004, the US Food and Drug Administration (FDA) approved clinical use of artificial hearts (FDA 2004), and nearly 850 patients received artificial hearts manufactured by SynCardia (SynCardia Systems 2010). However, to the best of our knowledge, there have been no attempts to validate the safety of software embedded in an artificial heart in a clinical environment. With active cooperation by biomedical researchers, we performed validation of software embedded in the H-VAD system (Jeong et al. 2009, Lee et al.

C. Dale, T. Anderson (eds.), *Advances in Systems Safety*, DOI 10.1007/978-0-85729-133-2_9,
© Springer-Verlag London Limited 2011

2009). After gaining an in-depth understanding of source code including its architecture, we measured code coverage using probing statements, performed in-vitro[1] testing, and discovered two abnormal behaviours previously unknown to KAOC staff despite extensive 'in-vitro system validation' and animal experiments. We recently completed the initial phase of animal testing[2] whose primary objective was to replicate newly discovered abnormal behaviours.

This paper is organized as follows. In Section 2, we briefly explain the H-VAD system with emphasis on software architecture. In Sections 3, we report results observed in software testing of artificial heart software. We describe both in-vitro and animal testing. Section 4 concludes the paper and suggests future work.

2 H-VAD artificial heart

H-VAD is a portable artificial heart which set the record of 183 days of successful operation on a calf. This record is sufficient to satisfy FDA regulations on long-term experiments. Primary features of KAOC H-VAD are:

- It is easier to carry than other portable artificial heart systems. It combines two traditional methods to drive pump: air-driven and electric motor-driven. The motor-driven actuator generates air pressure necessary to pump blood without any additional air compressor or vacuum pump.
- The system has two control parameters, pumping rates (PRs) and stroke lengths (SLs), whose values can be changed by pressing buttons. The former sets the heart beat rate while the latter controls the volume of ejected blood.

The system consists of one or two blood pumps and a control device. As depicted in Figures 1 and 2, the control device consists of the following components:

Pneumatic pump. The electric motor moves pusher plates back and forth to produce air flow to the blood pump via a closed-loop air tube. Subsequent valve movement in the blood pump complements a less than fully functional heart. Three motor hall sensors provide the input necessary to compute the current direction and speed of pusher plate movement. Another pump hall sensor captures crossing of the pusher plates over the centre of the pump.

Display. Essential information (e.g. operation mode, pump status) is shown on the LCD display.

Control panel. Six buttons, including start and stop, allow users to change the pump setting.

---

[1] A procedure performed not in a living organism but in a controlled environment.

[2] The animals were treated in accordance with *The Guide for the Care and Use of Laboratory Animals* issued by Korea University School of Medicine.

CPU. A TMS320 F2810 microprocessor, a Texas Instrument chip, executes the embedded software.

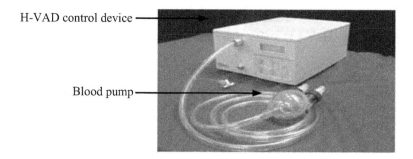

Fig. 1. KAOC H-VAD

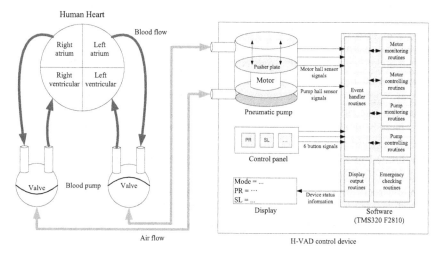

Fig. 2. Hardware context diagram of H-VAD

H-VAD software monitors and controls the motor to keep the pump's movement stable according to the current PR and SL setting. PR is calculated based on the number of pusher plate movements per minute, and SL is calculated on the distance between the two end points.

There are about 9,000 lines of C code, including vendor-supplied skeleton code, scattered in over 20 files. Logic unique to KAOC H-VAD is implemented in about 3,800 lines of code organized in an event-driven architecture, with four interrupt handlers tracking motor speed and plate movements, six routines processing button inputs, and a timer routine.

Two emergency modes of operation are built into the system. One is triggered if there is no motor hall sensor signal input for 500 milliseconds, and the other occurs when the pump actuator does not pass the centre position in 3,000 milliseconds.

3 Testing the H-VAD software

Our quality assurance effort on H-VAD software consists of two parts: code coverage measurement in in-vitro environment using blood-like liquid and 'live' animal testing conducted in close consultation with KAOC staff and in compliance to the relevant guideline.

3.1 In-Vitro environment: testing and code coverage measurement

When our project began, the H-VAD system had already been fully developed, and animal testing successfully kept a calf alive for 183 days. However, no analysis had been conducted with a particular emphasis on software. Our first task was to understand the system requirements and develop in-depth knowledge of the software logic through code review. We monitored execution, using 211 probing statements we added, in an in-vitro environment to determine which program paths have been taken. Because all branch conditions are relatively simple, no differences existed among several coverage criteria (e.g. branch or condition coverage) defined in the software testing literature. We made sure that probing statements did not alter program semantics.

While recording execution traces, we manipulated the H-VAD setting by repeatedly pressing buttons so that the software would exercise as many branches as possible. Figure 3 illustrates how we systematically prepared test cases based on the following guidelines:

- Each button, the only medium through which users may influence system behaviour, is pressed at least once.
- All permitted parameter values are covered, and an attempt was made to set the value outside the possible range. For example, stroke length may vary from 30 to 90 while the 'typical' setting is 60.
- The stop button was pressed at arbitrary and random moments to simulate as many exceptional situations as practicable and at various pump positions.
- We tried to force the system to engage in both predefined emergency modes.

Analysis of execution traces revealed that 170 of 211 probe statements (80.6%) had been executed. Further analysis of uncovered probes revealed the following:

- Some statements are logically unreachable. For example, the switch statement had true and false paths to follow, but the programmer, for some unknown reason, had implemented yet another default path to follow in case neither path is taken. Statements in the default clause could never be executed in the absence of abnormal control errors.

- The possibility of executing some statements is permanently determined by the hardware configuration. For example, execution of some *switch-case* statement is based on a control variable indicating deviation of the centre hall sensor installation position from the actual centre position of the pump. Such deviation never occurs unless one performs physical reconstruction of the pneumatic pump.

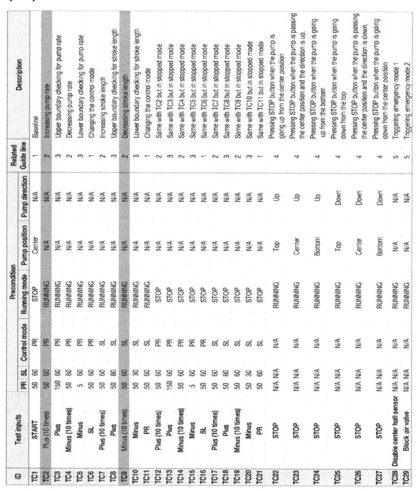

ID	Test inputs	PR	SL	Control mode	Precondition Running mode	Pump position	Pump direction	Related Guide line	Description
TC1	START	50	60	PR	STOP	Center	N/A	1	Baseline
TC2	Plus (10 times)	50	60	PR	RUNNING	N/A	N/A	2	Increasing pump rate
TC3	Plus	150	60	PR	RUNNING	N/A	N/A	3	Upper boundary checking for pump rate
TC4	Minus (10 times)	50	60	PR	RUNNING	N/A	N/A	2	Decreasing pump rate
TC5	Minus	5	60	PR	RUNNING	N/A	N/A	3	Lower boundary checking for pump rate
TC6	SL	50	60	PR	RUNNING	N/A	N/A	1	Changing the control mode
TC7	Plus (10 times)	50	60	SL	RUNNING	N/A	N/A	2	Increasing stroke length
TC8	Plus	50	80	SL	RUNNING	N/A	N/A	3	Upper boundary checking for stroke length
TC9	Minus (10 times)	50	60	SL	RUNNING	N/A	N/A	2	Decreasing stroke length
TC10	Minus	50	30	SL	RUNNING	N/A	N/A	3	Lower boundary checking for stroke length
TC11	PR	50	60	SL	RUNNING	N/A	N/A	1	Changing the control mode
TC12	Plus (10 times)	50	60	PR	STOP	N/A	N/A	2	Same with TC2 but in stopped mode
TC13	Plus	150	60	PR	STOP	N/A	N/A	3	Same with TC3 but in stopped mode
TC14	Minus (10 times)	50	60	PR	STOP	N/A	N/A	2	Same with TC4 but in stopped mode
TC15	Minus	5	60	PR	STOP	N/A	N/A	3	Same with TC5 but in stopped mode
TC16	SL	50	60	PR	STOP	N/A	N/A	1	Same with TC6 but in stopped mode
TC17	Plus (10 times)	50	60	SL	STOP	N/A	N/A	2	Same with TC7 but in stopped mode
TC18	Plus	50	80	SL	STOP	N/A	N/A	3	Same with TC8 but in stopped mode
TC19	Minus (10 times)	50	60	SL	STOP	N/A	N/A	2	Same with TC9 but in stopped mode
TC20	Minus	50	30	SL	STOP	N/A	N/A	3	Same with TC10 but in stopped mode
TC21	PR	50	60	SL	STOP	N/A	N/A	1	Same with TC11 but in stopped mode
TC22	STOP	N/A	N/A	N/A	RUNNING	Top	Up	4	Pressing STOP button when the pump is going up from the center position
TC23	STOP	N/A	N/A	N/A	RUNNING	Center	Up	4	Pressing STOP button when the pump is passing the center position and the direction is up.
TC24	STOP	N/A	N/A	N/A	RUNNING	Bottom	Up	4	Pressing STOP button when the pump is going up from the bottom
TC25	STOP	N/A	N/A	N/A	RUNNING	Top	Down	4	Pressing STOP button when the pump is going down from the top
TC26	STOP	N/A	N/A	N/A	RUNNING	Center	Down	4	Pressing STOP button when the pump is passing the center position and the direction is down.
TC27	STOP	N/A	N/A	N/A	RUNNING	Bottom	Down	4	Pressing STOP button when the pump is going down from the center position
TC28	Disable center hall sensor	N/A	N/A	N/A	RUNNING	N/A	N/A	5	Triggering emergency mode 1
TC29	Block air valve	N/A	N/A	N/A	RUNNING	N/A	N/A	5	Triggering emergency mode 2

Fig. 3. Test cases for the code coverage test

While measuring code coverage in the in-vitro environment, we found two abnormal behaviours of the H-VAD system while executing the test cases highlighted in Figure 3. Our collaborators, biomedical engineering research staff at KAOC who developed the system and conducted 'system-level testing' as well as animal experiments, were unaware of such behaviour. They agreed that the H-VAD system appeared to be malfunctioning.

First, we noticed an unintended excessive pumping, as illustrated in Figure 4, while executing the test case TC9 shown in Figure 3. The monitored PR value is abruptly increased when Ref_Left_MAX_Velocity, one of several variables used in computing motor speed, is set to a negative value. This change flipped the shape of the curve used in motor speed decision. Sudden and excessive pumping may yield critical, if not fatal, consequences to a ventricular system in clinical use due to the increased blood flow and tension.

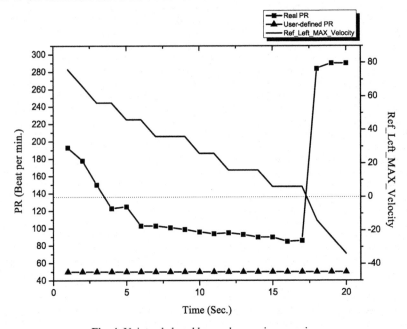

Fig. 4. Unintended, sudden, and excessive pumping

The other anomaly, shown in Figure 5, involves recurrent oscillation of pump speed where actual pump rate is simply unable to match the specified rate. Test case TC2 from Figure 3 uncovered this anomaly. This pattern was 'audibly' apparent as the pump kept trying to meet but ended up exceeding the target value and repeated a similar effort in the reverse direction. It appears that the H-VAD control algorithms failed properly to deal with subtle and exceptional scenarios in sufficient detail.

However, we must not forget that these anomalies took place in a realistic but not actual environment. While the in-vitro circulatory system mimics the human body (e.g. fluid characteristics closely match those of human blood), there are fundamental gaps between the two. It is difficult, if not impossible, to accurately reproduce the dynamic and continuous physical changes occurring inside a human body using a static in-vitro system. Still, the anomaly we discovered was serious enough to warrant further investigation in a more realistic environment, and an animal test was scheduled.

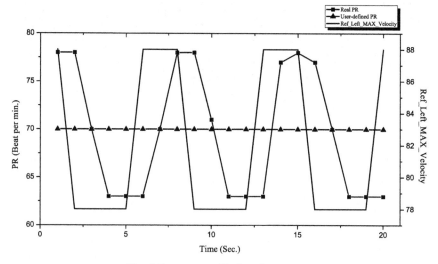

Fig. 5. Recurrent oscillation of pump rate

3.2 H-VAD software testing in an animal experiment

The primary objectives of animal testing were to compare code coverage in the clinical environment against that recorded in the in-vitro setting, and to determine if the two abnormal behaviours we uncovered in the in-vitro setting would occur in the clinical environment. Prior to the animal experiment, in addition to obtaining proper approval, we carefully developed and documented scenarios to repeat the anomalies. In addition to logging the values of critical variables used in the software, we also logged all the critical information, including vital biometric signals such as blood pressure and flows, using sensors attached to an animal. Furthermore, we used a video camera to record all relevant information during an animal experiment to enable accurate post-mortem analysis. See Figure 6.

When measuring code coverage, we tried to the best of our ability to maximize coverage while not endangering the life of the testing subject (a piglet). In the in-vitro setting, we could arbitrarily change the PR and SL values, but in the animal experiment updates made to the PR and SL values could result in rapid and potentially fatal changes in the blood flow and pressure of the animal. Such constraints limited the feasible test cases we could execute in the animal experiment. Furthermore, behaviour of the H-VAD system, even in the identical setting, is different between animal and in-vitro environments. For example, an attempt to set the SL value to the permitted minimum failed in the animal experiment, as it kept triggering an emergency mode; this had not previously happened.

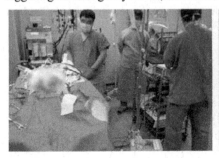

Fig. 6. Animal experiment setting

In the animal experiment, we observed that 166 out of 211probing statements (78.7%) were covered. This small difference in coverage was caused by our inability to repeat certain test cases so as not to endanger the animal's life. We therefore concluded that there was virtually no difference in code coverage between the two experimental settings.

In the animal experiment, we were unable to recreate situations where excessive pumping occurred despite our complete understanding of the software logic and the test sequences which led to the anomaly. We knew that Ref_Left_MAX_ Velocity would assume a negative value, in the software configuration we tested, if the actual pump rate was much larger than the user specified PR value. While we were able to increase the real PR value fairly rapidly in the in-vitro environment with no difficulty, such a phenomenon did not occur in the animal experiment. Figure 7 illustrates our effort. Our domain experts explained that the root cause of the difference lies in the strong blood tension in the live circulatory system and the subsequent decrease in the pump rate.

One must remember that our inability to reproduce this anomaly does not necessarily guarantee that the system is completely free from such an anomaly. However, considering the physical and fundamental differences in operational environments, it appears fairly safe to claim that such an anomaly would not occur in clinical usage.

On the other hand, we were able to recreate the other anomaly in which the H-VAD system was unable to converge to the specified setting. Figure 8 illustrates how this anomaly is revealed in the blood pressure graph. Partial success of H-VAD software validation in the animal experiment clearly reveals that further analysis of software correctness is absolutely necessary prior to clinical use.

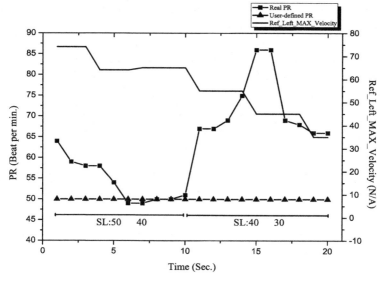

Fig. 7. An attempt to recreate the excessive pumping anomaly

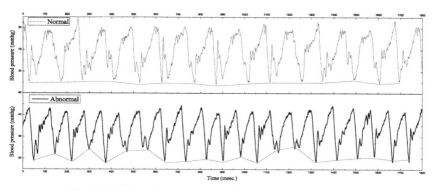

Fig. 8. Oscillation of pump rate revealed in irregular blood pressure

4 Conclusions

Use of software in medical devices, especially in life-critical and clinical settings, is beginning and will increase in the future. In practice, as well as artificial hearts, a robotic surgery system is another notable example where software has direct and immediate impact on a patient's life. Such trends, however, will surely increase and appear to be irreversible. In order to ensure the safe operation of such devices, researchers in the software engineering and software safety communities need to work more closely with domain experts. The research reported in this paper could not have been carried out without the active participation and enthusiastic support of physicians and biomedical engineers.

One must develop systematic approaches to safety-critical software validation while minimizing casualties, including animals used in clinical testing. Real world validation through deployment, like command and control systems in military war game systems, is often impossible. Yet, one must develop approaches to develop credible safety assurance.

While it is absolutely necessary, animal testing is labour-intensive and costly. In order to conduct the animal testing reported in this paper, three MDs, including a surgeon, and several assistants had to offer their expertise. The preparatory surgical operation alone took nearly six hours. Each animal used in an experiment has different and unique vital characteristics. Therefore, one must be careful not to overly generalize results from animal experiments.

Our experience proves once again how difficult it is to make a credible claim on software quality especially in a safety-critical setting. Although highly useful and essential, testing of safety-critical software embedded in medical devices in an in-vitro setting has limitations.

We are planning various activities to continue our research on software safety issues in medical systems. One possibility includes model-driven development (MDD) of software. Once a formal model is developed, test cases might be generated automatically, and model checking techniques could be applied. One might able to synthesize source code as has been accomplished in other domains (e.g. the nuclear industry).

Numerous significant challenges must be resolved to achieve technical breakthrough. Faithful and accurate modelling of the environment seems to be one of the most difficult challenges. In the case of an artificial heart, one must mathematically model all the essential details of the human circulatory system.

Acknowledgments This research was supported by the National IT Industry Promotion Agency (NIPA) under the program of Software Engineering Technologies Development. The authors would like to express thanks to research staff at the Korea Artificial Organ Center. Mr Chi-bum Ahn provided extraordinary support in our quest to understand the H-VAD system and validate its software safety.

References

AHA (2010) Heart disease and stroke statistics 2010 update at-a-glance. American Heart Association. http://www.americanheart.org/downloadable/heart/1265665152970DS-3241%20HeartStrokeUpdate_2010.pdf. Accessed 25 August 2010
Desikan S, Ramesh G (2006) Software testing: principles and practice. Pearson Education
FDA (2004) Recently-approved devices 2004 device approvals. U.S. Food and Drug Administration. http://www.fda.gov/MedicalDevices/ProductsandMedicalProcedures/DeviceApprovalsandClearances/RecentlyApprovedDevices/ucm073321.htm. Accessed 25 August 2010
HHS (2008) The 2008 annual report of the OPTN and SRTR: heart transplantation. US Department of Health and Human Services. http://www.ustransplant.org/annual_reports/current/. Accessed 25 August 2010

HHS (2010) Organ procurement and transplantation network national data. US Department of Health and Human Services. http://optn.transplant.hrsa.gov/latestData/step2.asp. Accessed 25 August 2010

Jeong G, Hwang C, Nam K, Ahn C, H Kim, Lee J, Choi J, Son H et al (2009) Development of a closed air loop electropneumatic actuator for driving a pneumatic blood pump. Artif Organs 33:657-662

Lee J, Kim B, Choi J, Choi H, Ahn C et al (2009) Optimal pressure regulation of the pneumatic ventricular assist device with bellows-type driver. Artif Organs 33:627-633

SynCardia Systems (2010) About SynCardia Systems, Inc. http://www.syncardia.com/SynCardia /about-syncardia.html. Accessed 25 August 2010

Testing Safety-Critical Systems

A Risk Driven Approach to testing Medical Device Software

Albert Farré Benet

Systelab Technologies S.A.

Barcelona, Spain

Abstract   Software for medical devices is strongly driven by regulatory requirements. Among those, safety assurance is critical. To achieve the required high levels of safety, it is essential to reliably reduce safety risks to a residual low level.
This requirement is verified and validated mostly with software testing. An approach to software testing driven by safety risks is presented and complemented
with comments from a real project where it has been applied. Specific comments
to improve test design so as to detect more safety risks and issues are also provided based on experiences from the same project.

1 Introduction

Medical device design and manufacturing comprises many aspects of science and
technology. As techniques and methods have evolved, so has the medical device
world, and it is impossible to measure the huge impact that software has had to
this field. Specifically, it would be a really hard task to find any medical device
that does not contain any software system or that has not been designed with the
aid of any software tool. Software has become a key factor on the design and
manufacturing of medical devices even to the point where a medical device may
consist solely of software.

If someone would have to name three fields of engineering where safety is
critical to the point of overcoming other concerns such as budget or schedule, it is
highly probable that medical devices would be among them. Indeed, by definition,
taking care of human life and health is a safety matter before anything else. Consequently, software for medical devices has become a strongly regulated area in
most countries. Indeed, it is easily noticeable that all regulations share a common
concern for the safety of the patient, the operator and the environment. Some regulations have a wider scope (e.g. 21 CFR Part 820 (FDA 1996) in the US or
93/42/EEC (EC 1993) in Europe) including many different medical device types,
while some others are specific for certain types of software medical device (e.g.

C. Dale, T. Anderson (eds.), *Advances in Systems Safety*, DOI 10.1007/978-0-85729-133-2_10,

98/79/EC (EC 1998)). Whatever the specific regulation applicable, some common requirements for safety will be present. Among many other requirements, as important as the quality system or labelling, those regulations ask for evidence of risk[1] management and testing. For ease of reading and to avoid extensive explanations with a relatively low interest for the purpose of this text, we shall constrain ourselves to these and avoid discussing our quality system and other regulatory requirements.

The aim of risk management in medical devices is to ensure patients, operators and the environment are not harmed by the device. Additionally, it shall also ensure that the medical device is effective for its intended use. To this end and according to most common approaches to risk management (AAMI 2004, 2001, ISO 2000), all phases of the design and manufacturing processes shall be covered. Thus, from the very first stages of the project, risk is analyzed and controlled to bring it to levels ALARP (As Low As Reasonably Practicable).

Risk Analysis takes all inputs and products to produce a list of risk items to be properly dealt with the appropriate measures. As a general rule, risks in medical devices are usually avoided or mitigated. On the contrary, direct acceptance of a risk is not an option except for cases of highly beneficial medical devices. Even in that case, it shall be possible only for the most superficial, harmless and improbable risks that can hardly be reduced or mitigated. Mitigation and avoidance can be achieved by means of additional requirements, safety checks, boundary control, labelling, etc. Furthermore, software can hardly reduce the severity of a risk, instead it can reduce its probability to happen and/or increase its visibility should it happen. In the end, all risk items should have been brought to an acceptable level of residual risk.

In order to actually obtain this residual risk level, it is imperative to assure that these measures are effective. Then, in order to monitor the risk and to demonstrate that it is controlled, it is necessary to verify and validate risk mitigations, usually through classical software testing. Indeed, verification may comprise many techniques and procedures such as plain document review, code reviews, code metrics analysis, etc. After all, testing is one of the foundations of safety and reliability.

As a consequence, regarding risk management for medical device software, maybe the bottom line could be reworded as 'The strongest requirement lies in bringing risks to tolerable residual levels in a reliable way'. Since it is not the objective of this paper to elaborate on risk identification, avoidance and mitigation we will try to skip as far as possible the details and specifics of the risk management process. Instead, we will walk through the steps that immediately follow those, i.e. we will focus on designing an approach to properly verifying that software risk mitigations are put into place and that they are actually effective.

---

[1] Since 'risk' is used in many other different contexts (safety risk, project risk, financial risk, etc.) with different meanings, let us clarify that in this document except where explicitly noted, 'risk' shall be understood always as *'safety risk for the patient, the operator or the environment'*.

2 Risk driven testing for new software

Software projects can be managed in many different ways and be developed following many different lifecycle models (waterfall, iterative, agile, etc.). Whatever the chosen approach, a set of testing tasks will eventually be required to verify and validate product requirements. The same can be stated regarding verification and validation of risk control measures. Naturally, depending on the software life cycle, testing activities will be planned and executed in different ways and with different objectives. However, it is of the uttermost importance that software testing verifies risk requirements with the proper approach and extent to ensure risk is adequately controlled.

To illustrate the aforementioned concepts and new ones, we will complement their explanations with a real case of a medical device software project that has been approached using the risk driven test model. The medical device software project we will discuss is related to the software that controls an in vitro diagnosis (IVD) instrument. This walkthrough will show how traceability among requirements, risks and test cases is maintained. It will also provide examples of test planning according to risk, plus coverage and test result reporting in terms of risk.

The first step in risk driven testing is obtaining a list of requirements related to risks. As commented before, this is usually a consequence of performing a risk analysis where risks are identified based on initial vision, user requirements and other preliminary documentation and/or customer feedback. Regarding our specific case, prior to any software specific task, a global vision of the instrument was obtained and the intended use of the instrument defined. A risk analysis at system level was also performed. Then basic sets of requirements were defined for the system and for the software. This review provided the foundations to build a consistent risk analysis. At this point we could start the risk identification part of the risk analysis. Afterwards proper assessment of risks followed. Then, a set of measures for each risk was established in order to prevent it or reduce the residual risk to an acceptable level. Although those measures may result in both risk prevention and risk mitigation, we shall label them in this text simply as 'risk mitigations' for our convenience.

Thus, the resulting risk list included a reference to all requirements related to each risk item. Those risk requirements fell into two categories:

Requirements whose application may constitute a risk. This first group of risk requirements is generally related to customer requirements and preliminary documentation (specific for each project) but also due to common risks (usually due to Off-The-Shelf (OTS) software or common PC hardware failures among others). Customer requirements shall be regularly verified in a static manner with reviews to look for undetected risks.

Requirements whose application directly or indirectly mitigates other risks. This group usually consists of a set of design, documentation or labelling requirements focused on mitigating risk from other requirements. This is usually an outcome from the aforementioned risk analysis. These requirements are the ones to be verified dynamically and which we have labelled as risk mitigations for our convenience.

Regarding the first group of requirements, it is not rare that customer requirements already contain a reasonable level of risk mitigations. It is also not unusual that unclear or misleading requirements from the user may constitute additional risks. While it is not our intention to discuss requirements engineering here, we shall establish some verification measures to detect any unforeseen risks. We will discuss this case in section 4. Obviously some requirements may mitigate and avoid risks and at the same time be possible sources of further risks. For all cases, risk mitigations shall be verified in order to ensure their action is effective.

In order to ensure proper verification for all risk mitigations, it is necessary to establish clear traceability between a risk-related requirement and the test case(s) that eventually verify its mitigation(s). Thus, requirements are to be traced to other requirements and also to the controls that verify their mitigations. An example of our traceability method can be seen in Figure 1. Note that in the figure the risk score has been simplified into high (H), medium (M) and low (L) and risk severity, probability and visibility/detectability for the original risk and residual risk have been omitted in the interests of clarity; the actual risk item description is more complex. Note that the risk score is included in the traceability matrix to act as a priority sort criteria as we will comment later. Note also that a requirement may act as a mitigation of different risks, in that case, the highest risk score shall be used to determine the criticality of the requirement.

RISK ANALYSIS

Risk Id	A001	Req. Id	XXX_1		
Req. Description	It shall be possible to validate (approve) results				
Risk Description	If a Result is validated (approved) when it is not completed may result in a wrong result and a wrong diagnosis.			Risk score	H
Mitigation Description	The "Approve" button shall be grayed out until result item is "completed" or "completed with errors"				
Mitigation Type	Req ID	YYY_1		Residual risk score	L
Control	TC ZZZ_1, TC ZZZ_2				

TRACEABILITY MATRIX FOR TEST EXECUTION

Requirement	Risk related	Risk ID	Risk Score	Test Case	Execution Result
YYY_1	YES	A001	H	TC ZZZ_1	PASS
YYY_1	YES	A001	H	TC ZZZ_2	PASS
YYY_1	YES	A002	L	TC ZZZ_3	Pending
YYY_2	NO	-	-	TC ZZZ_4	Pending
...					

Fig. 1. Requirement trace from risk analysis to test execution

As we have seen in the figure, all risk mitigations and avoidance measures are treated in fact as ordinary requirements with regard to traceability. Each risk item contained at least one mitigation which is controlled by at least one test case. First

versions of the traceability matrix contained around 10% of risk-related requirements with regard to the total number of requirements under test.

It is worth noting that risk mitigations can be defined at different levels. In
some cases a specific change in module design would suffice while in others a
change in the architecture may be required. Test cases shall be designed to verify
each requirement at the appropriate level. Traceability levels for verification and
validation activities are established following the well known 'V model' shown in
Figure 2.

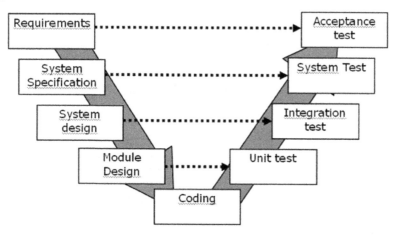

Fig. 2. The V model

Some requirements by their very nature will be tested at a unit level while others
will require a test with a global scope. Other requirements will need a user-centred
style of testing or a usability review. Thus, we cannot rely on a specific model of
test case designed specifically for risk testing, but expect a varied assortment of
techniques and methodologies depending on the type of requirement and its specification. As a matter of fact, testing is designed taking into account techniques and
methods to improve test reliability and repeatability (e.g. data driven tests and
software test automation). But other techniques and methods that include the insight of an expert tester are not uncommon. Regarding the design of test cases
well-suited for risks and beta testing, more will be explained in section 4.

Software requirements in non-critical software are usually tested with a coverage that depends on factors such as the quality system, criticality to the project, resources and schedule. Execution priority and regression execution will also depend on these factors. In the case of safety critical software it cannot be accepted
to work in the same way. Risk mitigations shall be completely and reliably tested
before releasing to the public. In other words, test coverage for risk related requirements shall be 100% in all cases. This is a very important check that ensures
that risk mitigations are put into place and effectively work.

When it comes to the time to actually run all required test cases it is important
to establish an optimal execution prioritization. In this sense, we conceive test

execution priority as a clearly risk driven classification. Tests that verify mitigations to high score risks shall be executed with higher priority than tests that have less or no relation to risk. Indeed, as described earlier, risk-related test cases shall be executed on every release of the software that is to be used for any of its intended uses. Hence, a failed test with a related high risk is very likely to include a showstopper issue, i.e. an unacceptable issue that would make key functionality useless or compromise the medical device safety. The sooner this type of issue is found, the sooner the issue can be fixed. The cost of delaying a release because of a new internal version would rarely exceed the cost of a device recall even in a beta release phase.

Finally, at the end of this process, consistent metrics shall be provided in order to assess the appropriate and sufficient verification for risks detected and mitigated. In our case, a report is delivered where all considered risks are listed, together with their risk mitigations and results of their verification outcome as seen in Figure 3. Again, risk score details have been simplified to ease reading.

RISK MANAGEMENT SUMMARY

Risk ID	Risk Score	Mitigation Requirement	Test Case	Execution Result	Residual Risk
A001	H	YYY_1	TC ZZZ_1	PASS	Acceptable
A001	H	YYY_1	TC ZZZ_2	PASS	Acceptable
A002	L	YYY_2	TC ZZZ_3	PASS	Acceptable
A003	M	YYY_3	TC ZZZ_4	PASS	Acceptable
...					

Fig. 3. Risk management summary report table

As a general rule, all risk measures shall have passed test execution with satisfactory results. Exceptionally, a failed test case can be accepted if it has a very good rationale to explain that mitigation did not actually fail and safety is not compromised[2]. Actual residual risk is then calculated and the release accepted or rejected based on the resulting residual risk and control outcome.

Naturally, other testing activities related to less risky situations shall also take place and indeed they are executed when needed as in any other software product. Since our approach relies on giving priority to risk handling, these other test cases are executed after risk related test cases. They shall be executed with the appropriate techniques and may require special attention due to project needs (such as product sales and time-to-market) or to other regulatory aspects such as privacy and data protection and security. However, this is outside the scope of our 'safety first' paradigm and is part of another discussion.

---

[2] Note that the definition of the pass/fail criteria in use may be critical for this. A cosmetic issue may not compromise safety and still fail a test case when cosmetic issues are not ruled out for test failure.

3 Risk driven testing during maintenance

So far we have considered the risk-driven approach for testing during the design of a new medical device product. Requirements have been gathered, risks have been identified and mitigations have been devised. Then, mitigations have been put into place and verified to be working efficiently leaving an overall residual risk within the acceptable level. It is assumed then that the product is ready for its first external release. Once the release part of our life cycle has been reached, the maintenance stage follows.

Maintenance can be generally described in two words: defects and changes. Whenever software goes through any change, be it of technological nature (OS, third party software, etc.), intended use or related to functionality (new functions, redesign, etc.), a risk assessment must be performed. Likewise, we can expect that once software is released new defects will be eventually detected which in turn must be corrected. If the previous risk analysis was properly performed, risks resulting from software defects would generally be dealt with by the appropriate mitigations. Still, risk assessment is also to be performed to ensure that any undetected or unforeseen risk does not slip by.

As a result of this risk assessment, risk analysis shall be updated and mitigations modified or added. Following the previously described process, traceability between mitigations and control measures shall also be updated and test cases created or updated as appropriate. Eventually, affected test cases shall become updated and rerun together with any newly designed risk-related tests.

While some extremely minor changes and fixes may not require a complete re-execution of the risk-related test suite, in most cases any new release of the software must be preceded by that execution. The object of this additional retest or risk regression testing is to ensure fixes and changes did not negatively affect any risk mitigation. In the case of software patches that introduce very small localized changes, it is acceptable to rule out part of the risk related test suite. However, in those cases a risk evaluation of the fixes shall provide positive results regarding complete insulation of fixes from other modules and areas.

Even in the case that a product is built and released without further changes to be included, risk analysis still has to be done. It is rarely the case that all user actions are effectively foreseen before the first release. Instead, user feedback will bring out unforeseen risks due to unexpected ways of using the software or the device. Those can be related to new process shortcuts, misuse, unexpected use, users deliberately working around risk controls when they become annoying, unregistered changes outside the manufacturer control, etc.

Unfortunately, it is practically impossible to predict all possible courses of action a user is capable of taking. We will always face unforeseen risk situations and risk prone features. Thus, it is necessary to constantly keep an eye open for these situations and when new risks are detected, update and improve risk control measures and related test cases at once.

4 Test definition in risk driven testing

Software test design is a knowledge field that admits different views and approaches. When software testing is focused on risk requirements, most usual design techniques keep their long-proven value. Therefore, boundary analysis, decision tables or state machine transition analysis, just to mention a few, can be used. Consequently, we have designed our test cases, both general and risk-related, following the usual guidelines for software testing. Software testing literature is abundant and full of techniques, methods and excellent applicable examples (e.g. Copeland 2003, Graham et al. 2007). With this knowledge, it is perfectly possible to design a test suite that verifies a set of risk related requirements to a point where we can be confident the software is reliably working as designed.

We do not specifically differentiate test design at unit test and integration level for risk related requirements from other tests that have no relation to risks. Still, it is true that risk related test cases will be executed more often than other tests. Taking into account the risk driven approach described in previous sections, our risk related test suite became the default regression test suite. In order to keep regression testing effectiveness high and re-execution cost low, one of the increasingly favoured techniques to consider is test automation.

We had opted for automated execution from early stages of the project since the process previously described required us to repeat risk-related test case execution with a high frequency. Naturally, test design acquires several constraints when it is to be executed automatically. We had to focus our test design for easy maintainability among other considerations too long to elaborate in this text. Software test automation is a vast and still growing field and there is already some excellent literature available on software test automation design (e.g. Dustin et al. 1999, Fewster and Graham 1999).

As commented above, testing against requirements can provide confidence that the system behaves as expected, and thus, at least the expected behaviour shall be safe. However, it cannot provide confidence that the system would be safe when working in unexpected ways. It could happen that the expectation was incomplete or even incorrect. It is possible user requirements were not properly considered at risk analysis time. Or maybe despite document reviews, requirements were just poorly worded and would not cover all possible use cases.

Therefore, having a set of specific test cases devised to verify that risk-related requirements and functionality work as defined is often not enough. Furthermore, risk related requirements do not always fit into the classical requirement specification paradigm, since they may depend on human factors that are difficult to model or quantify. A clear example is the case of an operator error. In how many ways can a user fail to communicate with the application? As a result, we designed our risk related test cases taking into account additional factors beyond boundary analysis and the like.

We shall consider users not only as passive objects for risk mitigation but also as subjects that can compromise their own safety. Safety measures can be more or less effective depending on how users behave or which protocols of use they follow. Moreover, users may follow protocols established in user manuals and approved procedures or rely on their own knowledge on similar devices. In this sense, actual use of any device is seldom the same for newcomers and expert users. While this is a matter that should have been properly dealt in the risk analysis phase, our test case design shall not ignore these variables and suppose all 'lateral' uses have been taken into account. It has proven extremely useful to us to encourage software testers to acquire knowledge of the real use of the instrument by interviewing future users or users of similar devices. A secondary source of information that provided good source material for testing were real protocols of use of IVD instruments.

As previously mentioned, one of the causes of risk to be specially considered is users acting in unexpected ways. Or at least, 'unexpected' by the design team, since users generally find their actions to be perfectly normal. This is where it is demonstrated whether the product underwent good software testing or not. Commonly, a software developer thinks 'no one would ever want to do that', but actually users tend to eventually do 'that' which 'no one' else would 'ever' do. It is the task of a good tester to verify robustness against possible ways to use the software and the device beyond the official, specified protocols. But the difference here is that the test designer shall also have enough insight about the device to be able to focus on ways that could result in safety compromise.

Special cases such as deliberate misuse and trying to work around risk mitigations to speed up or ease up repetitive and dull actions with the device shall be taken into account. This usually closes the gap between testing for safety and testing for security. Consider the case where many software mitigations rely on selective user access to different functionality (classically by user login and password). It is common to ban normal users from service functionality of the software, since use of those functions without the proper knowledge may compromise safety. Therefore, security measures act as an assurance for safety for the final user. Risk related test cases shall include enough security testing to validate those aforementioned mitigations based on the use of user privileges. Testing shall cover a degree of risk of malicious use within reasonable bounds. Nevertheless software security is a very large field where sometimes it is difficult to know when enough is enough.

One very successful measure we took was to run part of the software system test suite in the same environment as its expected final use. Hence, it proved to be an intelligent idea since we discovered many defects we would not have discovered until the instrument would have been in the field. This was because another factor to consider is the environment where the device is used, e.g. if the user works in an extremely noisy environment, then the effect of risk mitigations based on audible signals and alarms may be altered or invalidated. The same applies to visual alarms when the user is operating with other devices at the same time and not paying attention to the computer screen. Note also, as commented before, that users may interfere with the expected use. Indeed, the noisiest alarm that mitigates a safety critical situation may become useless if the user turns off the computer speakers. Consequently, it is important for risk-driven testing at a system level or higher that relevant environment conditions are reproduced or at least simulated consistently.

Finally, a concept that has become certainly important in a global world is the cultural and localization factors. By education, we are biased by our cultural clichés and commonplaces. It is difficult to foresee that some concepts that we conceive as constants beforehand are actually variable depending on culture. Some safety standards have worked at a global level (such as the bright red button for critical stop or the yellow and black wasp-like stripes in dangerous areas). Others instead, such as icons, may have different interpretations in different cultures and contexts. Test design shall also include verification for safety critical systems to take a neutral approach regarding cultural and localization factors. Any risk mitigation shall be verified to be efficient for any cultural environment and localization. In this regard it is useful to verify design against common international standards on the matter (AAMI 1993).

This user-centred design is becoming regularly an increased attention point for safety design and testing. The consideration of human factors is already required by some regulations including the fact that before releasing to the market, a medical device shall be tested within user conditions. While this was common practice from the hardware/chemistry point of view for a long time, software is catching up at a reasonable fast pace. Actually, in many contexts this pre-release can be understood as an alpha testing or a pre-beta release. While classically this beta-style test would be focused into fine tuning of hardware and precision, software would seldom be considered as a matter to test. However, we understand this user centred testing as a means to further ensure safety and quality and to validate risk mitigations efficiency, rather than an additional bureaucracy step.

All these considerations regarding the user, the user environment and cultural and localization factors are very useful for risk-driven testing. However, they often end up revealing the need to continuously amend the risk analysis. As a matter of fact, these are concepts that should have been taken into account during the software design. Testing focused on the user is performed with different techniques and methods ranging from human-machine interaction analysis to classical usability testing (Neilson 1993). Specifically, most usability testing techniques are especially good before and during design phases, with the use of prototypes, user walkthroughs, heuristics and such. They can prove useful to detect risks preventatively due to users not acting as expected. However, from the testing point of view, these may not be such good bug-catchers (at least from the safety standpoint) in the last stages of the process when the software is close to release. Therefore, other techniques shall be used to test risk-related mitigations from a user point of view in later stages. We deal with this specifically by running 'user simulation testing'.

'User simulation testing' is a mixture between a system level test focused on effective use of the software, and an expert usability test. High profile testers assume the role of end users and test the software following real protocols and procedures mimicking the real-use environment of the system. The focus of the test is to verify that high level requirements (which sometimes may lack precision and be relatively vague) are properly implemented and software fits with non-written usability requirements. Safety related risks to system requirements shall be closely examined too. By following real user protocols and procedures it is ensured that tests increase their realism and thus the software is not only tested under lab conditions.

In order to fulfil its purpose, this type of testing often requires the assistance of customers and end users to set up these protocols and procedures adequately so that it is as close to the real thing as possible. It is highly desirable that software test engineers can have contact with final users to understand the real use of the instrument and the many vices and workarounds users follow when using the device (or equivalent products) as mentioned earlier. Eventually, test execution shall take place and test engineers shall focus on user requirements but also risks, since some risks may not have been seen on the functional test detail but only when having a 'whole picture' view. Naturally use of real protocols and procedures is something that will be difficult or impossible in some cases (e.g. pacemakers) while in others, like our case for laboratory IVD analyzers, it may be easier.

It is important to note that user simulation tests shall be executed once the functional test phase is completed successfully. Otherwise, testing will be delayed by the presence of functional issues in the software. Finding those issues is not the purpose of this test. While it is reasonable to expect a few functional bugs to be found when running user simulation tests, their main purpose is to detect safety and usability flaws together with issues at the system level, and therefore it is desirable to run user simulation tests on relatively bug-free software.

5 Conclusions

Risk analysis is a live activity during the whole life cycle of the software. Risk mitigations and corrective measures are adopted and testing plays a key role verifying and validating effectiveness and correctness of those measures. A risk driven approach to medical device software testing is a comprehensive way of handling the risk verification process in order to achieve the goal of assuring overall safety of the medical device.

This approach assumes the implicit need of capable and proactive testing resources to ensure an effective and successful testing process and a safe medical device. On the other hand, risk driven testing provides a reliable methodology to ensure coverage of mitigation of risks and fast detection of safety issues which reduces the high cost of regression cycles. To reduce this cost it is required to start testing activities as soon as possible and execute them in parallel with development, not at the end of the process.

To achieve a successful outcome of this approach it is important to:

- maintain traceability between risk requirements and verification of their mitigations
- use risk related low level test cases to be executed in every regression cycle and sorted by risk score
- rethink risk related system test case design with a focus on the user as a subject in order to be able to detect leaks in user requirements and expected use of the device
- adapt test design techniques for risk-related test cases to focus on user, user environment and human factors.

We have been able to fulfil these points with systematic use of traceability matrices, automated regression tests, user simulation test cases and direct contact with the final user. Indeed, collaboration with current and future users reveals itself as an excellent source of materials and ideas to improve test cases at the system level and, ultimately, safety.

References

AAMI (1993) AAMI HE48:1993 Human factors engineering guidelines and preferred practices for the design of medical devices. Association for the Advancement of Medical Instrumentation

AAMI (2001) AAMI SW68:2001 Medical device software – software life cycle processes. Association for the Advancement of Medical Instrumentation

AAMI (2004) AAMI TIR32:2004 Medical device software risk management. Association for the Advancement of Medical Instrumentation

Copeland L (2003) A practitioner's guide to software test design. Artech House Publishers, Boston and London

Dustin E, Rashka J, Paul J (1999) Automated software testing: introduction, management and performance. Addison Wesley

EC (1993) 93/42/EEC European Council directive concerning medical devices

EC (1998) 98/79/EC European Parliament and Council directive on in vitro medical devices

FDA (1996) 21 CFR Part 820 Quality system regulation. US Food and Drug Administration

Fewster M, Graham D (1999) Software test automation. ACM Press/Addison-Wesley

Graham D, van Veenendaal E, Evans I, Black R (2007) Foundations of software testing. Thomson Learning, London

ISO (2000) ISO 14971:2000 Medical devices – application of risk management to medical devices

Nielsen J (1993) Usability engineering. Morgan Kaufmann, San Francisco

Testing Experiences of Safety-Critical Embedded Systems

Bryan Bakker

Sioux Embedded Systems

Eindhoven, The Netherlands

Abstract This paper describes the author's experiences of a test approach that has been used in the development and maintenance of a medical X-ray device used for surgical operations. It describes the activities that are performed during the preparation, execution and reporting phase of the test process, focusing on the test activities taking place in the software and the system part of the development project. Several safety related activities are executed by other disciplines, e.g. the regulatory office or hardware department, but this paper focuses on the daily work of software test engineers and system test engineers: Is their test process comparable to the process followed by other non-safety related projects? What are the specific requirements of the test process in a safety-critical environment? Are the test results documented in the same way? Is the complete system tested with maximum coverage? Are certain test-techniques preferred?

1 Introduction

Sioux Embedded Systems supplies services in the area of software development for embedded systems. Sioux aims at high quality of the systems that are delivered. One of the ways to reach this is testing. A team of testers is specialized in test design and execution as well as test consulting services. Sioux strives to provide these testing services in close cooperation with development in order to have short feedback loops to the developers.

One of Sioux's customers manufactures medical X-ray devices for patient diagnosis and patient surgery. The application described in this case study is used during all kinds of surgical operations. The system generates X-rays (called exposure) and a detector creates images of the patient based on the detected X-ray beams (called image acquisition). The image pipeline provides multiple images per second in real time, so the surgeon (for example) gets instant feedback on incision procedures performed on the patient. During an operation X-ray exposures are performed several times. The timing, the duration and the beam characteristics

C. Dale, T. Anderson (eds.), *Advances in Systems Safety*, DOI 10.1007/978-0-85729-133-2_11,
© Springer-Verlag London Limited 2011

depend on the type of operation being performed. The X-ray exposure should of course be as small as possible, but should still result in sufficient image quality.

In the Research and Development department of this specific customer, new devices are being developed, the software as well as the hardware, electronics and mechanics. Quality is of utmost importance in these applications, as failure of the system can have quite negative consequences. Testing has a lot of attention in the projects, and consumes about the same amount of effort as the development tasks, resulting in a developer tester ratio of about one to one.

2 Safety-criticality

The safety of the product described in this paper is very important. During surgical operations the patients are exposed to X-rays, which travel from the X-ray source, through the patient, and onto the detector. The detector translates the received information into images which can be viewed by the surgeon and the radiologist.

Note that this product does harm the patient, as X-ray images cannot be created without exposing the patient, and exposure is unhealthy for the patient. The main function of the system cannot be performed without harming the patient. During development of the product, but also during the operation of the product the goal is to keep the X-ray exposure as low as possible. Unfortunately, lower exposure results in decreased image quality. The surgeon on the other hand wants the best image quality for diagnosis and surgery. So a trade-off must be found between X-ray exposure and sufficient image quality.

The *ALARA principle* (As Low As Reasonably Achievable) also holds for the development of this product. Absolute safety cannot be guaranteed, but everything that is achievable must be done. An important requirement in this context is that all X-rays to which the patient is exposed must result in images that can be used for diagnosis or surgery. Consequently, it is not allowed to lose images somewhere in the internal communication of the system.

Safety requirements do not only hold for the product or its development. Also the user (the surgeon or radiologist) must take safety precautions. He needs to wear a lead apron to protect himself from X-rays. He is also responsible for the correct calibration of the system. This calibration is necessary to achieve images of sufficient quality to be used for diagnosis. These examples show that safety requirements cannot be guaranteed by the product development alone, the end user also has an important role here.

As mentioned above the safety of the product is very important. An unsafe product of course cannot be released or sold. But the testing activities within a project should not only look at these safety aspects. A perfectly safe product which lacks important functionality or provides functionality that is safe but not reliable will not be very successful.

3 The V-Model

Within the testing discipline the *V-Model* is a frequently used model to depict the different testing phases. Figure 1 shows the V-Model that has been used in this case study.

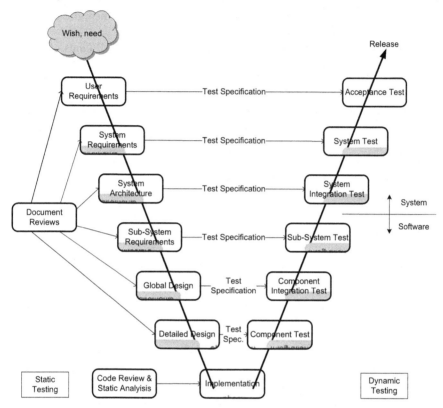

Fig. 1. The V-Model used in this case study

All starts with a wish or a need for a certain product, in the top-left part of the V-Model. This wish is translated into User Requirements, further detailed in System Requirements and a System Architecture is defined that suits the desired system. From this point on the system is divided into several Sub-Systems, e.g. a Mechanical Sub-System, an Electrical Sub-System and a Software Sub-System. Other decompositions of the systems are also possible. This case study focuses on the Software Sub-System. Requirements are defined for this (Software) Sub-System, followed by a Global Design and a Detailed Design. At the bottom of the model the software is implemented.

A lot of activities can be performed on the left-hand side to improve the quality, already early in the project. Documents are produced containing requirements, architecture and design descriptions. All these documents can and should be reviewed. In the case study, all these documents were formally reviewed in so-called inspections (IEEE 1997). The inspection technique is a very thorough way to perform a document review. Also the code implementation must be reviewed of course. Besides this code review the code has also been checked by a static analysis tool. Such a tool examines the source-code and can detect different kinds of defects, e.g. never ending loops, unreachable code or parameter type mismatches. These test activities are performed without executing the code, therefore these activities are called static testing.

Early in the project a *safety hazard analysis* is performed. All kinds of safety hazards are identified and analyzed during this activity. Actions are defined for the hazards, which can mean e.g. that the design needs to take certain precautions into account, or that the user instructions need to notify the end user of certain risks. But it is also possible that actions are defined for the test engineers, that certain test cases need to be executed, and need to pass, to cover certain items of the safety hazard list.

Another frequently used method to identify risks in the product is the *FMEA* (Failure Mode and Effects Analysis). FMEA (Haapanen and Helminen 2002) is a methodology designed:

- to identify potential failure modes and their effects for a product
- to assess the risk associated with those failure modes (not only safety risks)
- to rank the issues in terms of importance
- to identify and carry out corrective actions to address the most serious concerns.

The strength of this method is that all disciplines come together (face to face) and identify free format different kinds of risks. The test engineers are important stakeholders in these sessions, as they are good at identifying failure modes. Where the safety hazard analysis looks at safety issues, the FMEA considers possible failure modes in the product and how to tackle them; not only safety issues but also e.g. possible failures in reliability, performance and functionality.

The right-hand side of the V-Model describes the different test phases. Each development phase on the left-hand side has a corresponding test phase on the right-hand side. The different test phases have distinct sets of test cases. The definition of these test cases can start very early in the project. When the System Requirements have been defined, reviewed and accepted, which happens very early in the project, test engineers can immediately start with test designs and test specifications, before a single line of code has been written. In this way the requirements are tested in a different way than a document review does, resulting in the exposure of different defects. Later in the project when components, sub-systems or the complete system become available, the test cases belonging to the specific test phase can be executed. The right-hand side of the model shows the dynamic testing. The lower test phases have a different goal than the upper test phases. Up to and including the sub-system test the goal is mainly to find as many defects as possible, as soon as possible. Subsequently testing can also be performed on incomplete components, or an incomplete sub-system, as long as it has added value, i.e. it might find defects in the product. On these levels also several re-runs of the tests are performed.

Software testing is divided into three parts: component test, component integration test and sub-system test. All phases have their own test approach and will identify different sets of defects. The component test focuses on the specific component, the integration test focuses on the interaction between several components, and the sub-system test looks at the provided functions. Overlap should be kept to a minimum.

When the software sub-system is handed over to the systems department the testing has a different goal: testing is performed to assure that the system behaves according to its specification; this happens late in the project. Far fewer cycles are performed on these levels. It is assumed that the majority of critical defects have already been detected, resolved and verified in the previous phases. Also the responsibility is different: the lower part is the responsibility of the software test team and the upper part is the responsibility of the system test team. The system test team acts as an independent team: they are not part of the software (test) team, and also not of the other sub-system teams. The software testers on the other hand are an integral part of the software team, this way they have support and information from the software developers, needed to define test cases on these lower levels. Early testing focuses on early defect discovering, resulting in early risk reduction. Later testing is performed to increase confidence in the product.

Besides the system test team there are other important independent roles, like application testers. They have the knowledge of how the system is used in the field and what customers expect, and they are responsible for the validation of the system, which is part of the acceptance test (see the right top part of the V-Model in Figure 1). Besides that there are also roles for verifying that the system conforms to certain standards, like CE, UL, TUV and specific safety standards. This conformance is also needed to ensure the safety of the product, but is not part of this case study.

4 Risk-based testing

Early in the project when the system requirements are known (not all details need to be known), the first version of the system architecture is known and the first version of the safety hazard analysis is known, it is time for the testing lead to start with the *Master Test Plan*. In this plan the complete test approach is described. What will be tested, what will not be tested, how thoroughly the different parts will be tested, etc. Note that this plan does not contain information like test design and test case specifications. A thorough description of a (Master) Test Plan is given in (IEEE 1998).

To be able to define the test approach in the test plan, one of the first things the testing lead (test manager) should do is a *product risk analysis*. First the complete product (system or sub-system) is divided into items. The product can e.g. be divided into several logical units based on requirements which are documented in requirements specifications. Also a more technical approach can be followed by dividing the system into several architectural components. The number of items (architectural components or logical units of requirements) should not be too large, otherwise it is not workable. About thirty items is still comprehendible. The set of components should cover the system under analysis completely. It is possible to perform additional risk analysis sessions on the different sub-systems at a later stage.

The next step is to identify the relevant risk factors. Risk factors are those factors that influence the risk in our product. As we know, a risk is the combination of the likelihood and the impact. If we split up our system in several components, we should identify for each of these components the probability of containing defects which are inserted during the development process; this determines the likelihood. The complexity of the component can be a factor influencing the likelihood of defects in that component. The more complex a component is, the more defects it is likely to contain. The same goes for the size of the component. More likelihood risk factors can be identified, e.g., the number of interfaces a component has, or the inexperience of the responsible developer. The combination of all these factors defines the likelihood of defects in the different components. Note that for each product the set of factors can and will be different.

In the same way the impact can be defined. We should identify for each component the impact a possible defect could have. A possible factor for impact is e.g. the user importance. If a defect remains in a function that is very important for the end-user, the impact is high. Safety is another example of impact of a defect. Other examples are: usage intensity or visibility.

All this information can be put in one table, and a set of stakeholders should fill this table individually. It is important to take a broad set of stakeholders from the organization, not only technical people, but also people who understand the market and customer; it is even possible to include customers as stakeholders. An example of such a table is shown in Table 1. This table has been filled in by one of the stakeholders.

Table 1. Overview of components and their likelihood and impact factors

	Likelihood factors			Impact factors		
	Complexity	Size	#interfaces	Importance	Usage intensity	Safety
Component 1	5	4	5	5	3	4
Component 2	3	1	3	1	1	2
Component 3	1	5	1	4	5	1
Component 4	...	...	...	...	...	...
Component 5	...	...	...	...	...	...
...						
Component n	...	...	...	...	...	...

For each component the different factors should be rated, in this example 1 stands for low and 5 for critical. Of course other numberings are also possible. It is important that the stakeholders make choices. Not all components can be very important. The rates in each column must be evenly distributed, i.e., the same number of 5's, the same number of 4's, etc.

Not all stakeholders can estimate all factors, e.g. a marketing manager may have difficulties judging some of the likelihood factors. After all stakeholders have provided their input, a meeting is held to establish consensus. The output of this meeting is one completely filled table, which is agreed by the stakeholders. This table can be converted to a visual matrix, the so-called risk matrix. The example from Table 1 can be seen as a Risk Matrix in Figure 2. The coordinates (Impact, Likelihood) of the different components are:

- Component 1: (12,14)
- Component 2: (4,7)
- Component 3: (10,7)

The impact for component 1 equals $5 + 3 + 4 = 12$ and the likelihood equals $5 + 4 + 5 = 14$. All the components can be drawn in the risk matrix.

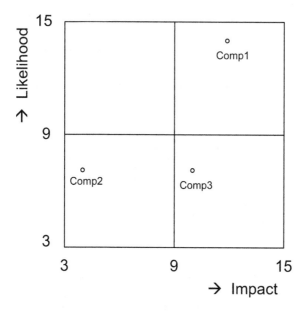

Fig. 2. Risk Matrix example

We can now see that the components can be assigned to certain quadrants in the risk matrix. It can be easily derived that Component 1 has the highest impact and the highest likelihood of all components. On the other hand Component 2 has the lowest impact and lowest likelihood (together with Component 3). As we all have limited test resources in our project we need to make choices as to what should be tested thoroughly and what should be tested less, in other words where we should dedicate our limited test effort. We can define quadrants in our risk matrix, see Figure 3.

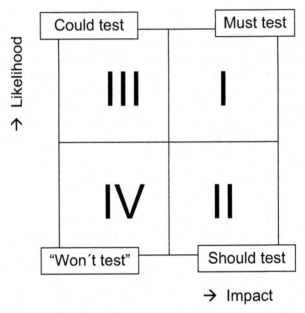

Fig. 3. Risk Matrix (MoSCoW)

Four quadrants are identified. Quadrant I is the one with highest impact and highest likelihood, and the most test effort should be spent on the components which are located in this quadrant. Quadrant IV contains the components with the lowest impact and the lowest likelihood on defects, subsequently less effort should be spent on these components. The MoSCoW naming method can be applied here:

- Quadrant I: **M**ust test
- Quadrant II: **S**hould test
- Quadrant III: **Co**uld test
- Quadrant IV: **W**on't test

Whether quadrant II or quadrant III should get more test attention depends on the test phase. Typically in lower level test phases quadrant III gets more attention, and in higher level test phases quadrant II is slightly more important.

This approach can be used as a tool to define differentiated test approaches for the components in each quadrant. Formal test techniques and extended reviews can be applied to components in quadrant I, while components in quadrant IV are tested only informally or maybe not at all (no risk – no test). It is also possible to differentiate the test approach with different code coverage criteria for the different quadrants.

In this way it is possible to guide the test resources to the high risk areas. This approach is called risk-based testing. A complete description of this process including tool support can be found in (Van Veenendaal 2006).

This process can be adapted in several ways, e.g:

- More than four risk areas can be used, when more differentiation is needed.
- In safety-critical environments it can be agreed that items that handle safety aspects are always placed in quadrant I, regardless of their estimated likelihood and impact numbers. Note that this is not needed by default, as other precautions are already taken for safety issues (results from FMEA or safety hazard analsysis).
- Items located near the center of the risk matrix can be discussed with all or several stakeholders, to decide if they are located in the correct quadrant. The location is based on estimates, and a small deviation in these estimates might put an item from category IV to category I. Best practice is to discuss the items located near the center of the risk matrix.
- If certain likelihood or impact factors are more important than others, weighting factors can be applied.

The results of the performed product risk analysis should be documented in the Master Test Plan. This analysis is one of the most important parts of this plan, since the complete test approach is based on this analysis. The goal of the Master Test Plan is to show how much test effort is needed and (more importantly) how this test effort is distributed over the different test phases and items: the test approach. This test approach is based completely on the risk matrix.

The Master Test Plan documents all test activities that need to be performed during the development and release of the product. In practice it can be seen that activities defined in the plan are often not executed because they are not needed anymore, or because of time pressure. Not performing certain activities cannot be excused by time pressure in safety-critical product development. It is important only to define activities in the plan that you are really intending to execute. Nice-to-haves should not be documented here. At the end of the project every activity needs documented results, and an incomplete activity with a rationale of 'out of time' is an unacceptable result.

Another part of the Master Test Plan in safety-critical environments is traceability. All requirements that have been defined on the left-hand side of the V-Model need one or more test cases on the right-hand side. And this relation must be documented accurately. This can be used to:

- show that all requirements have test cases
- show that the test cases have been based on requirements
- identify which test cases need to be updated when a requirement is changed (and this will happen)
- trace back to the corresponding requirements if a test case fails. Consequently these requirements are not fulfilled; it has to be decided whether or not this is acceptable.

The Master Test Plan is not the place to document this traceability, but it should define where and how this documentation is done. Note that the traceability also covers the test designs.

5 Specific test activities on high risk items

All 'normal' test activities of course also hold for projects containing safety aspects. Test designs should be documented, test cases should be derived using test design techniques, Problem Reports should be submitted for every defect encountered, etc. This chapter describes several specific attention points in safety related development that are not commonly used in other environments.

5.1 Hardware imperfections

Hardware does not always function perfectly. Hardware wears over time. Hardware may show failures directly after production (called infant mortality). Hardware can also show slightly different performance now and then, or behave differently when the environment (e.g. temperature) changes. The hardware needs to be verified to withstand these kind of conditions. This is out of the scope of this paper.

But there is more: the software that is interacting with this hardware needs to be able to handle these imperfections: failure of hardware needs to be detected and reported and acted upon, the software must be able to handle performance variations in the hardware.

Testing this at the system level can be quite difficult and time consuming. During development the hardware is based on prototypes, often these prototypes are of superior quality compared to mass-manufactured samples, as the prototypes are carefully handmade. As a result failures of the hardware do not occur that often during development. On the other hand, the prototypes may show all kinds of failures, which also adds complexity.

A possible solution to this is to simulate hardware imperfections in the lowest level of the software (or even better: in the hardware itself). In this way it is possible to test the majority of the software for this type of error handling. All hardware imperfections can be simulated and it can be shown that the software handles them correctly, and if e.g. the correct error messages are shown. Of course this might cost considerable effort. Whether or not to simulate certain imperfections is a trade-off between effort and risk reduction, as with all test activities.

This is just one example of how to make your system under test more testable, which is called *Design for testability*.

5.2 Software measures

A general rule is that as many safety precautions as possible should be covered in hardware. E.g. an emergency button switches off the complete system, this way all radiation but also all electronics stops. No software should be in charge here. But software still plays an important role. Several hardware parts cannot be stressed too much, e.g. they will get too hot. Precautions in hardware make sure the hardware is not damaged: when the part gets too hot, the system is halted without a warning. Of course it is much better to warn the user that certain procedures cannot be performed before the system has cooled down for a certain amount of time. Software is responsible for these measurements, calculations and reports to the end user. This way the actions of the user are not suddenly halted by hardware precautions.

Another example is the calculation of radiation the patient has received during a procedure (so called dose). This dose is calculated in the software. Extensive testing is needed to verify these calculations.

Software often contains so-called assertions: preconditions defined by developers in the code. If the precondition does not hold, the software will be halted. Often these assertions are only used during development and are disabled during final testing and release. In this project we decided to leave the assertions enabled. It is better to have a system that has safely halted, than to have a system running, but in an undefined state. Of course this approach is not always the best to choose. In environments where availability of the system is more important than the quality of the system, it can be decided to disable the assertions and keep the system running in case of such an assertion.

5.3 Test techniques

Several test techniques have been used during the development of the product. Below three of these techniques are described; these have been used extensively.

State transition testing is a well known test technique (BCS 2001). In embedded environments this technique is used quite often, because the design of the software generally contains multiple state machines, and errors or missed behavior in these state machines can have drastic consequences. This technique is ideally suited to test these state machine to a certain (chosen) degree. It is possible to have different coverage goals for different state machines, making it perfectly usable in risk-based testing.

Another test technique which is common in technical environments is the *Boundary Value Analysis* (BCS 2001). This technique is well known for user interface tests, but it is even more suitable for testing of the interface of software components. These tests can be executed before the component integration phase. With this technique the boundaries of an interface are tested, both the valid boundaries and the invalid boundaries. The invalid boundaries are especially important, as the correct working of the invalid interface calls drastically increase the robustness of the components.

The product described in this case study has several different configurations and options which can be bought by customers. The possible number of combinations of these variables is overwhelming and cannot be tested completely. A technique that can be used to handle this problem is called *Classification Tree Method* (Grochtmann 1994). With this technique it is possible to derive test cases in order to have a high coverage of configuration combinations. These test cases can be represented graphically, which improves the readability.

5.4 Integration testing

When large, complex and multi-disciplinary systems are developed, one of the most difficult phases is the integration phase. Developing and testing components (whether these are in software, hardware or mechanics does not matter) is well under control (at least in this case study), system testing is also well done as long as the test basis for this phase (requirements) is in place. But integration and the corresponding *integration testing* often remains a mystery. Integration testing is performed to identify defects in the interfaces and in the interactions between integrated and already tested components (ISTQB 2010). The assumption holds that these components already behave according to their component specifications; this is verified in the component tests. In the integration tests it is verified whether these components correctly communicate with each other and can perform their tasks as expected.

In this case study several parts of the system have been selected (risk based testing!) and the complete communication in the form of software messages has been verified against their specification. At the moment that these tests were performed, no user interface was available, all tests had been automated. A lot of integration issues have been identified this way very early in the project. This is a quite expensive test technique, it takes a lot of effort, and is definitely not easy, but it is very effective to integration test highly critical areas. When integration testing is neglected the next phase can be quite troublesome; the system test can be seriously delayed because of integration issues discovered late in the project.

5.5 Reliability testing

Certain requirements are very important for the system (e.g. startup, no missing images during acquisition), so extensive testing is done on these requirements. But it is not only important that these function correctly a number of times, these aspects of the system should function correctly always, although always is probably a bit too much to ask. Nevertheless the reliability of certain parts of the system is very important. We have seen that one of the safety requirements states that in the complete image chain no images may get lost. To get a profound confidence that the system indeed fulfils this requirement extensive testing is performed and the MTBF (Mean Time Between Failures) is measured.

An automated reliability test has been developed during the project in this case study. The system is triggered by external hardware interfaces (footswitches, power buttons, physical buttons on the different keyboards, etc.), and extensive system logging is available. Several different test cases that simulate user behavior have been executed at night and during the weekends. Via the logging it is possible to detect any problems during the execution of the test cases, e.g. any missing image is reported in this logging. This way numerous issues have been identified, fixed by developers and again verified with the reliability test.

In the same way other critical parts of the system have been tested and improved, e.g. the startup behavior. It is of utmost importance that the system starts within a specified time and that the startup succeeds and the system is ready for use. The system is used in different surgery rooms and is switched off and on each time, and in case of an emergency patient a successful start up is a critical requirement.

It is possible to measure the reliability while the product is still in development. In this case study the *Crow-AMSAA* model (Abernethy 2008) for reliability measurements was chosen, because the test results contain different kinds of tests on different system configurations with different software versions installed. Other models are more applicable for test results on fixed system configurations. This way it is possible to measure an increase (or decrease) in the reliability during the course of the project. Of course the system aspect that is being measured should be finished before an MTBF can be measured, but a complete system without known problems is not needed to start with MTBF measurements.

A fictitious example of a Crow-AMSAA plot can be seen in Figure 4. The x-axis represents the cumulative number of startups of the system. The y-axis shows the MTBF (Mean Time Between Failures) of the startup behavior of the system. Each triangle in the plot depicts one test run, and the straight line is the line with the best fit through all triangles. This line can be used for reliability predictions, by extrapolating it into the future. The example shows a measured MTBF of about 22, which means that in about 22 startups, one startup has failed. This is only based on the results of the executed tests with different software versions and on different configurations. The trend over time of this graph is important. Bug fixes are implemented by the development team and test cases are re-executed. The new plots show whether the reliability has indeed increased or more corrective actions are necessary.

A detailed explanation including the mathematical background of the Crow-AMSAA model can be found in (Abernethy 2008).

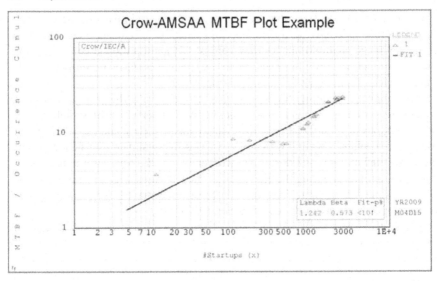

Fig. 4. Crow-AMSAA plot

6 Test reporting

Test reporting is often given low priority in projects. Lots of defects have been found and solved and the system is ready for release, so who cares about reporting? Actually this can be quite important. It should give the organization insight into how efficiently the test process has been executed. Often the test department is blamed that the project has not met its deadline, but the reporting can show that there are different reasons.

In safety-critical environments test reporting is even more important. It should always be clear what has been tested and what has still to be done. And it should be clear who has tested it, when and on what configuration. The configuration is not only the system on which the test has been executed, but also its entire configuration, and this of course includes the software version installed. This helps in analyzing defects, in fixing these defects and in verifying the solutions.

Even in safety-critical environments it is not possible (and not efficient) to execute each single test case during the project, especially not on the final (to be released) configuration. This would take much too long and is not achievable. When selecting the test cases that still need to be executed, it is a great help to know when the test cases have been executed the last time and what the corresponding result was. This implies that not only the test reporting needs to be documented and archived, it also means that this should be done in such a way that all the information can also be retrieved quite easily. It should be possible to answer questions like:

- When was this test case executed the last time, what was the result, and who executed it?
- What test cases must be re-tested when a certain defect has been solved?
- Where is the evidence that a certain test case has indeed been executed (e.g. archived log files)?
- For two weeks the configuration of a system has been invalid (e.g. an incorrect software version has been installed). Which test cases must be repeated?

This information is needed not only for the project itself, but also for internal and external audits. Regulatory bodies perform audits on a regular basis. Consistent documentation is an important precondition to pass such audits. Not passing external audits can have devastating consequences for the organization.

7 Tool support

Complex products with embedded software have a complex requirements structure. As a result the test case structure can also be quite complex. The test cases should be maintained in a test case database. To support requirements traceability the test case tool should be able to interface with the requirements management tool, where all the product requirements are maintained. Also an interface to the configuration management tooling is advised. Configuration references can be explicitly defined and maintained.

With proper tool integration it is possible to have an efficient way to document the whole test process in a consistent and reproducible way.

8 Releasing the system

When all necessary test cases have been executed, and all critical and major bugs have been resolved, it is time to release the system. But before releasing the system including the final software release, an additional test activity is executed, the so-called minimum set of test cases. This set contains test cases that show that the most critical parts of the system still work. The configuration of hardware and the mechanics are probably already fixed for weeks or even months, but the software has the flexibility to change frequently. With the final software version (this is the version that is to be delivered to customers) a set of test cases is repeated, just to make sure that no regression on critical areas has been introduced. This set of test cases is based mainly on the impact of possible defects in parts of the system. The likelihood is very small, because the software has undergone (hopefully) no drastic changes, but the impact is very high when such defects would remain in the product.

It is important that this test does not take too much effort. It is the last test performed in the project, and everyone is eager to start building and selling the new product. An extra test round of three weeks, expecting not to find anything, would just not work. In the discussed project it should not take more than two days, only the most important parts are checked. Note that all the safety checks in hardware and mechanics are already performed and need no rerun.

Another activity at the end of the project is the verification of all documentation. Everything (like test loggings, test reports, conformance statements, traceability matrices, requirements, etc.) is already documented precisely during the whole project, but a final check should be performed to make sure that indeed everything is in place and has the correct status. Ideally this verification is performed by an independent person.

9 Incremental development

During the project described in this case study an incremental approach has been chosen. Several increments have been released to selected customers before the product was complete. This has the advantage that customers can already use the system, and give early feedback to the development department. This information can lead to altered or new requirements which can immediately be implemented in the current project.

A major drawback of this approach in safety-critical developments is that the safety must of course always be secured, also for in-between deliveries. This results in an increased overhead of tests and measurements not only performed on the final product but also on all early versions which are delivered externally.

Nevertheless the advantages have outweighed the disadvantages by far. Customers were very happy that there feedback was already incorporated in the first complete version of the product.

It is also possible to follow an *agile* approach for the software part of the project, but it is not feasible to keep every version of the software releasable. The overhead would be much too high. But a lot of agile aspects can be applied with success.

10 Summary

The test approach in safety critical environments is not that different from an approach in non-safety products. The emphasis on risk analysis is much higher, it is performed at several different levels with several different goals:

- Safety Hazard Analysis:
  - Goal: identify safety risks and control (or eliminate) them

- Input for: Safety Hazard List

- FMEA:

  - Goal: identify failure modes and tackle them if necessary
  - Input for: design process

- Product Risk Analysis:

  - Goal: identify likelihood and impact of (possible) defects
  - Input for: test process (risk-based testing)

These processes may and will overlap. Risks will be identified by more than one process. This may seem inefficient, however the same mitigation can be used. On non-safety-critical development projects it is already a great advantage if only one such risk analysis is performed, while in this case study three have been performed.

Several test techniques are frequently used in safety-critical environments. This is not really related to the safety aspects but more to complex and multi-disciplinary aspects of these embedded systems.

Activities like documentation, structured testing and reporting are formally described and executed. In complex embedded environments this can be a great benefit, and can result in more predictable projects, but in safety-critical systems performing these activities in a formal way is a must.

This rather formal but still practical test approach has resulted in several releases of new and updated products. These products still have their issues, and also customers have run into issues, but no safety-related issues have ever emerged at customer sites. While the pressure from the market increases to release more functionality in a shorter time frame, this may never result in lower quality. I think we achieved exactly that, and the health of the company does not contradict this statement!

References

Abernethy R (2008) The new Weibull handbook. Robert B Abernethy, Florida

BCS (2001) Standard for software component testing. British Computer Society Specialist Interest Group in Software Testing (BCS SIGIST). http://www.testingstandards.co.uk/bs_7925-2.htm. Accessed 14 June 2010

Grochtmann M (1994) Test case design using classification trees. In Proceedings of the International Conference on Software Testing Analysis & Review (STAR), Washington DC

Haapanen P, Helminen A (2002) Failure mode and effect analysis of software-based automation systems. STUK-YTO-TR 190, STUK, Helsinki

IEEE (1998) IEEE Std 829-1998 IEEE standard for software test documentation. IEEE Standards Association

IEEE (1997) IEEE Std 1028-1997 IEEE standard for software reviews. IEEE Standards Association

ISTQB (2010) Standard glossary of terms used in software testing. Version 2.1. ISTQB Glossary Working Party

Van Veenendaal E (2006) Practical risk-based testing. http://www.improveqs.nl/files/Practical_
Risk-Based_Testing.pdf. Accessed 14 June 2010

Testing of Safety-Critical Systems – a Structural Approach to Test Case Design

Armin Beer[1] and Bernhard Peischl[2]

[1]Independent Consultant, Baden, Austria

[2]Technical University of Graz, Institute for Software Technology, Austria

Abstract In the development of many safety-critical systems, test cases are still created on the basis of experience rather than systematic methods. As a consequence, many redundant test cases are created and many aspects remain untested. One of the most important questions in testing dependable systems is: which are the right test techniques to obtain a test set that will detect critical errors in a complex system? In this paper, we provide an overview of the state-of-practice in designing test cases for dependable event-based systems regulated by the IEC 61508 and DO-178B standards. For example, the IEC 61508 standard stipulates model-based testing and systematic test-case design and generation techniques such as transition-based testing and equivalence-class partitioning for software verification. However, it often remains unclear in which situation these techniques should be applied and what information is needed to select the right technique to obtain the best set of test cases. We propose an approach that selects appropriate test techniques by considering issues such as specification techniques, failure taxonomies and quality risks. We illustrate our findings with a case study for an interlocking system for Siemens transportation systems.

1 Introduction

To build dependable systems is a major challenge for IT companies. According to the IFIP 10.4 Working Group on Dependable Computing and Fault Tolerance, *dependability* is defined as 'the trustworthiness of a computing system which allows reliance to be justifiably placed on the service it delivers'. Dependability includes the following attributes of a computing system (Avizienis et al. 2004):

- availability: readiness for correct service
- reliability: continuity of correct service (Lyu 1987)
- safety: absence of catastrophic consequences on the user(s) and the environment
- security: the concurrent existence of availability for authorized users only, confidentiality, and integrity.

C. Dale, T. Anderson (eds.), *Advances in Systems Safety*, DOI 10.1007/978-0-85729-133-2_12,
© Springer-Verlag London Limited 2011

Examples of domains in which Siemens produces dependable systems are:

- aerospace: testing of components for AIRBUS flight systems, observing the DO 178B standard
- medical solutions: computed tomography
- power generation, transmission and distribution
- transportation systems: control systems for railway stations and systems.

The following are typical for all these areas:

Growing software/hardware complexity. A railway system, for example, consists of infrastructure, logistics and interlocking blocks: these require a diverse range of different hardware and software components to interact.

Third-party integration and code reuse. Standard software, such as GUI builders or libraries, is integrated.

Certification of software. Operating systems and the software tools supporting the development process have to be certified.

In general, testing is defined according to ISTQB (ISTQB 2010) as:

> 'The process consisting of all lifecycle activities, both static and dynamic, concerned with planning, preparation and evaluation of software products and related work products to determine that they satisfy specified requirements, to demonstrate that they are fit for purpose and to detect defects.'

Several systematic test design techniques and testing approaches have been developed to assist in systematically exploring the available choices and selecting a representative sample (Beer and Heindl 2007). Criteria for selecting such a sample in safety critical systems are typically based on requirements, system models, control flow, data flow and an operational profile. Deterministic or non-deterministic models of different categories and formality are used. Relevant questions are:

- Which test design techniques are appropriate to derive test cases from these models?
- How effective are these test cases to detect potential defects?
- How much testing is enough?

2 Problems of testing safety-critical systems

In general, the various safety standards (IEC 61508, DO-178B, EN 61508; MISRA, etc.) require some kind of evidence that the safety-relevant requirements are fulfilled. Thus traceable evidence that the working products being created (in particular the software under development) conform to those requirements has to be established. Section 3 briefly discusses the requirements with respect to modelling and testing of the most important standards.

Achieving functional correctness with respect to specific safety requirements includes establishing appropriate software engineering methods as well as verification and validation techniques. In this respect, software testing, if carried out systematically and in a well-founded way, is now considered an important task during the software life-cycle. However, in a practical setting, designing appropriate test cases is regarded as a difficult, tedious and thus rather expensive task.

Model-based testing has made considerable advances in recent years and various research prototypes and industrial-strength tools are available today (Tretmans 1996, Tretmans and Brinksma 2003, Belifante et al. 2005). Moreover, various case studies report on the successful application of concrete techniques to industrial-size applications (Fernandez et al. 1997, Kahlouche et al. 1998). Because publication of the major standards such as IEC 61508 or DO178B dates back to the 1990s, they do not exhaustively cover the specific techniques for model-based software development and in particular model-based test case design and generation.

Model-based testing allows for an earlier start of test design and – in the case of formal testing models – for automated test case generation. Applying a well-defined combination of models and related test case design and generation techniques is thus an essential measure to detect errors and increase confidence in the correctness of safety-relevant software.

When it comes to the design or generation of tests from models, to cope with the combinational explosion in both the size of the model and the number of viable test cases it is of utmost importance to have means to adequately steer the test case design and generation process in terms of both the semantics of the models and its representation, and appropriate testing strategies. Therefore, the main challenges in testing safety-relevant systems are:

- the adequate representation and abstraction of the system under test (SUT) and its context
- the appropriate and goal-oriented application and adaption of the various testing strategies (e.g. testing with equivalence classes, coverage-based testing, random testing, testing with test purposes).

An important problem in safety-critical software development results from its ever increasing complexity and from the fact that software functions often interact strongly with different contexts in event-based systems. This can be a physical context (e.g. a monitored and controlled device), human users in an organizational context, or other software and hardware (e.g. a device driver). Other factors increasing the complexity of this problem are asynchronous communication with and within the system, event-driven behaviour, complex data types, timing constraints, parallel execution and non-deterministic behaviour of the system under test. Testing event-driven software thus faces special challenges. In summary, the characteristics of event-driven, safety-critical software are:

- Safety-critical software usually has a large or infinite space of possible behaviours.

- Safety-critical systems come in many variants, requiring repetitive development with numerous adaptations: this can be a possible source of non-deterministic behaviour.
- Due to the numerous dependencies, safety-critical software may deviate from its anticipated (normal) behaviour (e.g. presence of hardware faults).
- Safety-critical systems usually comprise several subsystems (software and hardware) evolving in parallel with complex interaction patterns.
- Non-deterministic behaviour, complex data types, and the fulfilment of timing requirements are the rule rather than the exception.
- Safety-critical software is often distributed over several (logical or physical) processing units (e.g. several electronic control units in the sector of embedded automotive software systems).

In order to enable test case design and generation, one has to understand the specific properties of the numerous model representations (along with their semantics) and testing strategies to choose the most adequate model/specification technique along with the approach to test case design and generation.

3 Testing requirements and standards

Certification of safety-critical systems and software relies on standards such as IEC 61508 or DO-178B. To pass the certification process successfully, an organization has to demonstrate that the development processes and resulting products conform to the relevant standard. (Stranden and Trebbien-Nielsen 2002) compared the most notable standards for safety-related applications. Among these are IEC 61508 and DO-178B. The authors conclude that although the selected standards differ in terms of focus, rigor and guidance, there are also commonalities between these standards:

a. All standards require some kind of requirements gathering.
b. All standards require a design phase and mapping from requirements to implementation.
c. All standards require hardware/software integration.
d. All standards require verification and validation processes.
e. All standards require some kind of documentation.

The requirements of a standard can be broadly categorized into two areas: process requirements and product requirements. According to (Eastaughffe et al. 1999) a standard can impose requirements on four different aspects of the safety-critical production of software or software-enabled systems:

1. the development process (e.g. project management, documentation, testing activities)
2. the development product (e.g. specific equipment, specific functions and properties such as MCDC coverage on the code)

3. the safety management process (risk assessment, hazard analysis, or FMEA – Failure Modes and Effects Analysis)
4. the safety case – the product of the safety management process (arguments that the system is safe in its intended environment).

Most notably, (Eastaughffe et al. 1999) points out that quite a lot of work and practical experience exists regarding issues 1, 3 and 4, but there is a considerable lack in understanding the detailed requirements regarding point 2, the development product. Specifically, no in-depth comparison is available that clarifies which techniques are mandatory at the highest integrity levels (e.g. SIL 4 according to IEC 61508 and DAL E in the notation of the DO-178B standard). In the following, we focus on the software parts of IEC 61508, and DO-178B, specifically considering the verification and validation processes (d) and the requirements with respect to the development product (2). Table 1 outlines the specific techniques that are listed for software verification and validation according to the IEC 61508, EN 50128, DO-178B and MISRA standards. Moreover, the table shows, for every SIL, SAS or DAL level, whether the technique is considered highly mandatory (HM), mandatory (M), recommended (R), or explicitly not recommended (NR), with respect to both testing and modelling. A dash (-) is used if the technique is not mentioned at all (HR, M, R, NR but also NR do not apply). We refer to the literature originally referred to in the standards. The DO-178B and MISRA standards do not require or recommend specific methods or techniques; therefore we interpreted the text in the standard and mapped our interpretation to Tables 1 and 2 respectively.

Table 1. Testing techniques recommended by the various standards

Testing techniques	IEC 61508				EN 50128					DO-178B	MISRA
SIL/SSAS/DAL Level	1	2	3	4	0	1	2	3	4		
Probabilistic testing (Littlewood and Stringini 1993)	-	HR	HR	M	M	-	-	-	-	-	x
Boundary value testing (Myers 1979)	R	HR	HR	HR	-	HR	HR	HR	HR	x	x
Equivalence class testing (Myers 1979)	R	HR	HR	HR	-	R	R	HR	HR	x	x
Testing by fault expectation (Voas and McGraw 1998)	R	R	R	R	R	R	R	R	R	-	x
Structural coverage testing (Howden 1976)	R	R	HR	HR	-	R	R	HR	HR	x	x
Requirements-based testing (Myers 1979)	-	-	-	-	-	-	-	-	-	x	x
Cause-failure testing (Nielsen 1971)	-	-	R	R	-	-	-	R	R	-	-
Error seeding (Voas and McGraw 1998)	-	R	R	R	-	R	R	R	R	-	x

Table 2. Modelling techniques mentioned by the various standards

Modelling techniques	IEC 61508				EN 50128					DO-178B	MISRA
SIL/SSAS/DAL Level	1	2	3	4	0	1	2	3	4		
Data flow diagrams	R	R	R	R	-	R	R	R	R	x	-
State transition diagrams	-	R	R	HR	-	HR	HR	HR	HR	-	-
Formal methods	-	R	R	HR	-	R	R	HR	HR	-	-
Performance modelling	R	HR	HR	HR	-	R	R	HR	HR	-	-
Petri nets	-	R	HR	HR	-	HR	HR	HR	HR	-	-
Prototype/animation	R	R	R	R	-	R	R	R	R	-	-
Structural diagrams	R	R	R	HR	-	R	R	HR	HR	-	-

4 A method guide for test case design

The failure of the *Mars Polar Lander* (Blackburn 2002), whose engine turned off approximately forty metres above the surface, was due to a design flaw concerning the touchdown procedure. By modelling the touchdown monitor and the sensors in a state chart and creating a test case that covers the touchdown event loops of the first and second stages, the failure would have been detected in a black-box test. The test suite detecting such a failure is required to cover the touchdown event loop of the first and second stages. Therefore it is necessary to design test cases that exactly satisfy this property. This property can be captured by modelling the behaviour of the SUT in terms of a communication process (e.g. in a notation like LOTOS (ISO 1989)) or in terms of UML state charts, for example. By covering either all state transitions or specific control flow criteria, it would have been possible to design or generate the appropriate test cases. However, given a specific test scenario, to the best of our knowledge there is no practical guidance that permits selection of the most appropriate test case design technique for this specific scenario. In this article we propose a method guide for test case design considering:

- the most relevant testing techniques
- the subject being described or modelled (e.g. the behaviour of the SUT, the data flow through the SUT, the input domains of the testing problem, the possible interactions with the environment of the user)
- the properties of the model (e.g. discrete event-driven, continuous dynamics, non-deterministic behaviour)
- the specific test selection criterion (e.g. structural model/code coverage, requirements coverage, fault-based coverage)
- the specific observable misbehaviour that is to be detected (e.g. transaction faults, erroneous functional decisions upon the input data, failures occurring in specific user scenarios).

4.1 Resolved issues and related work

(Vegas et al. 2006) present a scheme designed to promote the use of systematic test case design techniques. For each test technique, a matrix with the following sections is created:

- level (operational, historical)
- elements (technique, test cases, object, tools, agents, project, satisfaction).

The critical aspect for making a good selection is the availability of information for the 'effectiveness' and 'type of defects' parameters in the 'test cases' subsection. For the parameter effectiveness for some techniques such as BVA (Boundary Value Analysis), percentages of defects which should be detected are given. However, the source of this empirical data is not mentioned. In a study by (Kuhn and Wallace 2000) empirical data about the percentage of defects found by combinatorial testing is presented. (de Grood 2008) proposes a goal-oriented testing approach for selecting the right test-case technique. The type of description of the user and software requirements are related to a test technique. For each description of a test-case design technique, its usefulness for detecting specific defects is mentioned. For example, cause-effect graphing (C/E) is useful for 'testing small system components with a high risk'. The test strength can be varied depending on the risk estimate. It can be decided to test more or less thoroughly. For example, when using state transition or control-flow testing, the test strength is low if state/statement coverage is achieved. The next level is branch coverage and the highest level condition coverage.

Defect taxonomies are valuable for learning about the kinds of errors being made in the product development process. The general goal of defect taxonomies is to reduce the number of defects reaching the customer. Another goal is to make testing more balanced. The basis for building defect taxonomies is Boris Beizer's taxonomy described in his book on software testing techniques (Beizer 1990). The defects are partitioned into three sub-categories: functional defects in the requirements phase, structural defects in the design phase and implementation defects. (McDonald et al. 2008) organize their defect taxonomy around the stages of a defect:

- occurrence stage (where was it discovered?)
- contributing cause(s) stage (in which phase was the defect introduced?)
- change stage (how widespread is the effect of the change?)
- detection stage (what kind of test would detect it?)
- mitigation stage (how can this type of defect be reduced or eliminated in the future?).

The symptom-focused taxonomy of (Black 2009) consists of categories such as failed functionality, missing functionality, poor usability, build failed, and reliability problem, and is related to the design of test cases. In an Internet appliance case study, 46% of the defects detected were in the category 'failed functionality' and as many as 19% in the category 'missing functionality'. Whittaker's attacks (Whittaker 2003) are a focused form of testing that attempts to force specific failures to occur. It combines elements of defect taxonomies, checklist-based tests, error guessing and exploratory testing. An interesting approach is to build a taxonomy specifying the defect area, for example reliability issues such as an unexpected failure, crash or hang because of an unhandled exception (McDonald et al. 2008).

To summarize: *goal-oriented testing* is an approach which fosters the application of systematic testing. In addition, defect taxonomies are a valuable way of learning more about their origin and detection. However, for the recommendation of a *specific test technique* in a given situation, the test technique has to be related to the *specification techniques* and the *failures detected* by a specific test technique.

4.2 Analysis and design of test cases with the method guide

While each of the methods described in the last section has its benefits in promoting systematic test case design, they also have some weaknesses:

- The focus for the selection of test techniques is mainly on the parameters of effectiveness, defect type and software type and not on other parameters such as the modelling paradigm of the subject to be modelled.
- The test techniques are not related to product-specific failures derived from different defect taxonomies.
- A justification as to why a specific test technique should not be used in a situation is missing.

We thus aimed to develop a method for the selection of test-case design methods that combines the benefits of the approaches mentioned in section 4.1 with a workflow (Figure 1) that relates test techniques to the object to be modelled and to their failure detection potential. Applying a specific test design technique increases the likelihood that errors of a certain type will be found. However, errors not found by one technique are not necessarily found by another one. For example, state transition testing is useful for detecting failures:

- in process states/state machines (events on false states, false state transitions)
- in screen transitions.

The effect of such a defect may be:

- an operation produces incorrect results, hangs or crashes
- an operation is complicated or impossible to perform by a skilled user.

The method will be introduced below with a practical example from the social insurance domain. The task was to create test cases for a mid-sized project for the BVA (Versicherungsanstalt öffentlicher Bediensteter), a public insurance company for civil servants in Austria (Beer and Menzel 2008). The goal was to replace the existing host application by a Java-based web application within the time frame of about one year.

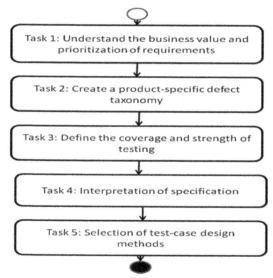

Fig. 1. Workflow of the method guide

Task 1: Understand the business value and prioritization of requirements

The tester has to analyze the tested application's specification that often exists only as plain text, enhanced with business-process diagrams, for example. The business and customer requirements are reviewed and interpreted by the test team with the aim of stipulating the clarification of requirements and their importance for the stakeholders. The product requirements are partitioned into critical and non-critical requirements. Typically, the critical requirements are the key features of a product.

Example. Test cases were derived from requirements. Testers found that some of the requirements were ambiguous, lacked details necessary for testing special and exceptional cases, and some were even incorrect. The selection criteria for the critical requirements were derived from the experience gained on how the software was actually used for managing insured persons, i.e. problematic software requirements as 'revision' or the use cases most frequently needed by call centre agents, such as 'Search for insured person'.

Result. List of requirements partitioned into critical and normal.

Task 2: Create a product-specific defect taxonomy

The potential failures which should be detected by the test cases are initially identified. The failures/defects are selected from different taxonomies and historical failure data provided by the organization.

Example. In the case of the BVA project, the taxonomy of (Beizer 1990) and historical failure data from similar projects were used as the basis for generating a product-specific taxonomy. An example of the BVA defect taxonomy is given in Table 3.

Table 3. Example of a product-specific defect taxonomy

	Failure description	Failure details	Severity
Requirements	Use-case sequence	Loop in search function	Critical
	User-interface error	Mask sequence interrupted	Critical
	Missing scenario	Use of keyboard instead of mouse not possible	Normal
	Complex	Operation too complicated to perform	Normal
Design/ functionality as implemented	Control flow and sequencing	Control initializations and states	Critical
	Exception conditions erroneous	Events in a state need error handling	Critical
Data	Default values in table	Data corruption	Critical
Implementation	User interface	Disable/enable of input fields and buttons	Normal
Integration	Interface to external component	Data are not displayed because of error in service call	Critical
Unclassified bugs	Conflicts between global and local variables	Interaction between variables leading to failure	Critical

Result. Product-specific defect taxonomy.

Task 3: Define the coverage and strength of testing

Extensive testing mitigates the quality risks associated with a product. A starting point for the choice of the technique is the test strength (de Grood 2008). The higher the coverage of the tested domain, the greater is the test strength. In safety related systems, the testing techniques and degree of coverage for example are defined in IEC 61508 according to a specific Safety Integrity Level.

Example. In the BVA example, the problematic software requirements such as 'revision' or the most frequent use case 'Search for insured person' had test strength two, which means that branch coverage and MCDC is assigned for these use cases.

Result. Product-specific failure taxonomy and an updated test plan.

Task 4: Interpretation of specification

The specifications are reviewed to determine the category of specification techniques. The models used to specify the software under test may be:

- formal notations such as finite state machines (FSMs), symbolic representations like extended FSMs or symbolic transition systems (Frantzen et al. 2006), or explicit-state models such as a labelled transition system (Tretmans 2008), temporal logics (LTL, CTL)
- semi-formal notations, for example UML (OMG 2010) state chart models (either behavioural models or – more common in practice – generalized test cases), activity diagrams, message sequence charts
- plain text.

A test-technique/specification technique table is used to determine the category of system model. The test techniques are selected depending on the modelling technique used. The test techniques in Table 4 are partitioned into four clusters.

Example. In the BVA example, the objects to be modelled and the categories are:

- the usage of the SUT – state-based notation
- the interface between components – transaction-based notation
- the static data domains – data-flow notation–and heuristic methods.

Regarding the specification techniques used in this project, a preliminary set of test techniques was selected as shown in Table 5.

Table 4. Test techniques used in the method guide

Category of test technique	Test technique	Remarks
S: Sequence oriented	S1 Use-case based testing; process cycle tests	
	S2 Design-by-contract	
	S3 State transition, control flow testing	Coverage-based testing
	S4 Control flow testing	Coverage-based testing
	S5 Transaction based (concurrency) tests	
D: Data oriented	D1 CRUD	Create, Read, Update and Delete
	D2 Classification tree method	
	D3 EP	Equivalence Partitioning
	D4 BVA	Boundary Value Analysis
	D5 Special values	
	D6 Cause-effect graphing	
	D7 Decision tree testing	
	D8 Syntax testing	
	D9 Combinational testing	
	D10 Condition testing	
O: Statistical methods	O1 Operational profiles	
	O2 Statistical testing	
	O3 Random testing	
	O4 Risk-based testing	
H: Heuristic and fault oriented methods	H1 HT	Heuristic (experience-based) testing
	H2 Fault-based testing	
	H3 Error-guessing	
	H4 ET	Exploratory testing
	H5 Fault injection	
	H6 Mutation testing	
	H7 Load/performance testing	
	H8 Stress testing	
	H9 Reliability testing	

Table 5. Preliminary set of test-case design methods

No.	Test technique	Object to be modelled	Model de-term/non determ	Paradigm/ Category	Test selection criteria	Model examples (spec.)
S1	Use-case based testing; process cycle tests	Usage of SUT	cont., discr.	State-based notation	Test paths according to test depth	UML use cases
S5	Transaction-based (concurrency) tests	Interface between components	discr.	Transaction based	Structural criteria	Message sequence charts
D3	EP: Equivalence partitioning	Static data domains	discr.	Data-flow notation	Data coverage	Diagrams, tables (2 dimensions), text
D4	BVA: Boundary value analysis	Static data domains	cont., discr.	Data-flow notation	Data coverage	Diagrams, tables (2 dimensions), text
D6	Cause-effect graphing	Static data domains	cont., discr.	Data-flow notation	Data coverage	Decision tables to model causes and effects
D8	Syntax testing	Static data domains	cont., discr.	Data-flow notation	Data coverage	BNF, text
D10	Condition testing	Static data domains	discr.	Data-flow notation	Data-flow criteria	Tables, Boolean expressions
H1	HT: Heuristic (experience-based) testing	not model based		Empirical	Experience-based criteria	
H7	Load/performance testing	Behaviour of SUT	discr., non-det.	Operational profile	Experience-based criteria	
H8	Stress testing	Behaviour of SUT	discr., non-det.	Operational profile	Experience-based criteria	

Task 5: Selection of test case design methods

The purpose of this activity is to recommend a set of test case design methods related to the product-specific failure taxonomy and regarding the test plan. The selected test case design methods are reviewed and a set of test case design methods is created which fits the methodical skills of the tester. These methods are edited in the test plan.

Example. The test case design methods shown in Table 5 are now related to the potential failures to be detected. The 'S5 transaction-based testing' technique was not used, because these tests were performed by developers rather than system testers.

Table 6. Failure detection potential depending on test technique for BVA example – part 1

No.	Test technique	Failures (qualitative)	Category of Beizer's taxonomy	Product specific taxonomy	Remarks	Literature/ Experience
S1	Use-case based testing; process cycle tests	Unsuitability of the system taking the organizational processes and procedures into account.	Requirements incorrect; functionality as implemented.	Use-case sequence User-interface error Missing scenario Bad usability	About 50% of defects found in tests originate from the requirements phase; root causes of 56% of errors introduced in the requirements phase (Mogyorodi G 2008).	Historical data recorded in the bug tracking tool of the BVA, covering three midscale and two large projects.
S5	Transaction-based (concurrency) tests	Incorrect behaviour of the system when several transactions are run simultaneously	Integration; internal interfaces	Architecture: erroneous or missing services provided by enterprise service bus	Address data of insurees are not synchronized between two authorities due to program defects.	Experience when successively adding new components to the core system
D3	EP: equivalence partitioning	Incorrect handling of the syntactic or semantic constraints of GUI.	Requirements incorrect; functionality as implemented; data	Erroneous behaviour of user interface: disable/enable of controls and input field; layout; ordering of lists.	Technique not suited for more than two dependent variables.	
D4	BVA: boundary value analysis	Incorrect boundary locations closures intersections	Functionality as implemented; data			(Tuinhout 2008)
D6	Cause-effect graphing	Logically incorrect system components	Requirements incorrect; structural bugs.	Ambiguities and gaps in decision points of process cycles.	Defects in the code due to a great variety of conditions guiding the user.	

Table 7. Failure detection potential depending on test technique for BVA example – part 2

No.	Test technique	Failures (qualitative)	Category of Beizer's taxonomy	Product specific taxonomy	Remarks	Literature/ Experience
D10	Condition testing	Expression negation fault; variable negation fault; missing variable fault; operator reference fault	Requirements incorrect; structural bugs.	Errors in checking access rights for different users; Boolean expressions to check the status of insurance.		(McDonald et al. 2008)
H1	HT: Heuristic (experience-based) testing	Errors occurring in specific usage scenarios.	Functionality as implemented.	Unspecified usage scenarios.	Test cases are designed from long-term experience of domain experts	(Beer and Ramler 2008)
H7	Load/ performance testing	Insufficient scalability of the system	Requirements incorrect; system and software architecture.	Performance bottlenecks; unacceptable processing time	Services provided by external component via an ESB are delayed.	
H8	Stress testing	Instability of the system under load.	Functionality as implemented. System and software architecture.		Insufficient stability of the system.	

Table 4.4: Failure detection potential depending on test technique for BVA example – part 2

Result. Final set of test-techniques applicable when training domain testers and used to develop concrete test cases.

To summarize, the lessons learned in the pilot project were:

- A minimal set of test cases with high error detection potential could be created.
- Training of testers in test case design is essential for success.
- Historical data are valuable for creating a product-focused failure taxonomy.
- Defect prevention measures could be applied in the maintenance phase of this project.
- New projects could benefit from the results obtained in the pilot project.

5 Case study: Testing a railway interlocking system for Siemens Transportation Systems (TS)

Case 2 looks at testing an interlocking system for the core network of the 'Deutsche Bahn'. The lifespan of the product is more than 25 years. A CENELEC EN 50128 (CENELEC 2001) compliant development process with independent validation, assessment and admittance is used.

The infrastructure represents a railway yard consisting basically of a collection of linked railway tracks equipped with features such as signals, points and level crossings. The system is characterized by a dedicated hardware/software system with triple redundancy (2-out-of-3) for automatic fault detection. All I/O interfaces are redundant. The railway control system has to guarantee safety, i.e. has to ensure that no accidents can happen. It allows the execution of commands given by a user only if they are safe; unsafe commands are rejected. The *safety integrity level (SIL)* for the critical software is SIL 3 and 4. This means that accidents of the following types, namely bounce, impact, derailment, crash of two trains caused by follow-on, frontal or slanting collisions have to be avoided. These dangerous failures may originate from:

- incorrect specifications of the system, hardware or software
- omissions in the safety requirements specification
- insufficient rigorous testing.

Testing of an interlocking system has to resolve the following issues:

- several projects for different railway organizations (specific adaptations, different types of interlocking systems) and different levels of domain knowledge
- increasing testing costs (before declaring a release as finished, for example 7,000 test cases have to be run on 12 computers with a test duration of about 28 hours and 7,000 test cases on a target system with a test duration of about 190 hours)
- requirements specifications written in a very precise way, but most still in non- or semi-formal notation, so that automated inference of test cases is not straightforward
- risk assessment: e.g. unit tests performed with 95% of all paths covered at source code level, with a non-coverage justification needed for the uncertainty in the detection of all relevant errors before production for the remaining 5% of execution paths
- unpredictability and undetectability (by humans) of side effects of a change in a complex system.

5.1 Test process

The basis for test-case design is a mature *test process* outlined in Table 8.

Table 8. Test process in a railway automation system

ID	Topic	Actual status	Remarks
1	Test process / test management	V model; agile sustainable software development with test of iterations; CMMI level 3 compliant processes.	Core functionality; many variations for different customers; IEC61508 shows a large overlap with CMMI-DEV version 1.2 (SEI 2006)
2	Testability and requirements tracing	Textual and semi-formal specifications with unique identification of high and low-level requirements and traceability.	Goal to create formal specifications e.g. state machines for automatic test case generation.
3	Test case design	TCs derived from non-formal specifications by testers with thorough domain knowledge; model-based development with SCADE (Milius and Steinke 2010).	Systematic test case design
4	Safety assessment	FMEA (Failure Mode and Effect Analyses and FTA (Fault Tree Analysis)	
5	Validation assessment	Manually with checklists.	

Requirements-based testing is mandatory in safety-critical systems according to *CENELEC EN 50128 for SIL 4*. Test cases should be generated for each high-level or low-level requirement. By careful selection, a test case written for a high-level requirement may cover some percentage of the low-level requirements as well, thus reducing the number of explicit low-level requirements-based tests needed. After testing, the level of requirements coverage and structural coverage achieved is determined. Any gaps in coverage must be determined. The order of evaluation is as follows:

1. How should the software-requirements tests be modified or augmented?
2. Should we create structure-only tests to demonstrate structural coverage of the remaining code?

To answer these questions, written specifications should be enhanced by semi-formal and formal representations such as state charts. The categories of defects detected with a specific test case design method have to be specified. In safety-critical systems, the combination of FMEA and FTA encompasses a systematic view of failures and their potential causes. In the next section, we will focus on the application of the method guide presented in Section 4 to a safety-critical system of transportation systems.

5.2 Test-case design supported by the method guide

Test cases at system and software level are designed by testers with thorough domain knowledge on the basis of the specifications written in natural language, enhanced with semi-formal specification elements. Examples of failures are:

1. signalling of a higher velocity than allowed
2. an erroneous shunt movement with the risk of a collision between two trains
3. not closing level crossings with the risk of casualties.

The prevention of these types of failures is a must. To mitigate the risks, the test cases have to be created not only by experience but also systematically to control the coverage of the software under test. In Tasks 1, 2 and 3 of the method guide, the software requirements are analyzed, the business value and critical requirements are separated and the test plan is written. Gaps and contradictions in the requirements are detected and clarified. The specifications are improved, if needed, to promote systematic testing. In Task 4 of the method guide, the tester has to select the best test techniques to cover all notations used for the specification of the system model. In Task 5, the test case design methods are selected by correlating them with the failure detection potential of the test techniques already selected in Task 4. To demonstrate the application of Tasks 4 and 5 of the method guide, the partial description of four requirements of the interlocking specification of TS is analyzed.

Example 1: Description of the shunt movement

#REQ-...# for remote-controlled shunts is valid

1. The shunts are set to the right or to the left.
2. If the shunt does not reach its final position within 8 seconds, the current will be automatically turned off (the shunt then has a supervision defect).
3. While a shunt is moving, it must be possible to reverse its movement and reset it to its original position.
4. When a train passes the shunt, the latter has to be locked so that no further movement is possible. The lock has to be opened again after the entire train has passed the shunt.

The above description has two anomalies which are detected when creating a state chart as shown in Figure 2. The following have to be clarified:

• base state after 'current on'
• assumption of the last valid state (H)
• how the 'suspension defect' state is left.

Formal diagrams lead to certainty about the consistency and completeness of test cases. The real-time movement of shunts is specified in a time-line diagram with a sequence of intervals: selection of the running track, lateral flank protection, shunt movement, signalling on the level crossing; and unblocking. The test technique for the functional test is *S3 (control flow testing)* and *H7 (load and performance testing)* because of the scheduling constraints. The result of Task 4 is shown in Table 9.

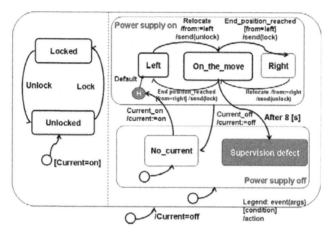

Fig. 2. Example of a state chart of an interlocking system

Table 9. Selection of test technique in relation to the modelling category

No.	Test technique	Object to be modelled	Model determ/ non-determ	Paradigm/ category	Test selection criteria	Model (spec.)
S3	State transition, control flow testing (coverage-based testing)	Behaviour of SUT	cont., discr.	Transition-based notation, operational notation	Structural criteria	UML state chart
H7	Load/ performance testing	Behaviour of SUT	discr., non-det.	Operational profile	Experience-based criteria	

In Task 5, the lines corresponding to S3 and H7 are selected (Table 10).

Table 10. Assignment of the test technique to the failure category

No.	Test technique	Failures (qualitative)	Category of Beizer's taxonomy	Product specific taxonomy	Remarks	Literature/ experience
S3	State transition (coverage-based testing)	Incorrect process states/ state machines (events on false states, false state transitions)	Requirements incorrect; functionality as implemented.	Shunt movement/lock, error in power supply, sensor malfunction.	Design flaws	
H7	Load/performance testing	Insufficient scalability of the system for different configurations	Requirements incorrect; system and software architecture.	Performance bottlenecks; unacceptable processing time	Delay in timing to unlock a shunt.	

Example 2: Requirements of flank protection

A feature of high complexity is the control of the flank protection system, because sensors and different components interact as shown in Figure 3.

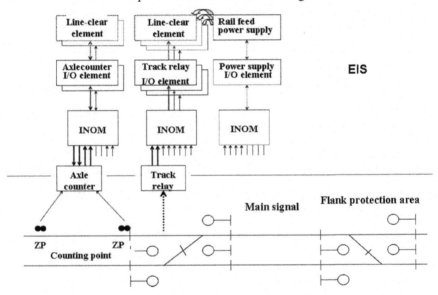

Fig. 3. Components to control the flank protection area

Elements which are monitored by about 100 commands are shunts, signals, the running track, axle counters, and track locking. Commands include reset of axle counter, repositioning of track lock, and signalling the speed limit. There is a great variation of sequences of possible commands depending on the size of the railway station. Creating test cases for every possible variation is infeasible because of the large number of test cases. Randomized testing can give at least a statistical sample of test cases for a domain. A promising approach is model-based testing with IDATG (Integrating Design and Automatic Test case Generation). A task flow model is created from the functional description. The task step represents either an atomic action or a building block with entry conditions and a sequence of several actions. IDATG generates test cases randomly if the precondition of the start step of a building block allows a connection to another one (Mohacsi and Wallner 2010). First results of a case study show that this method detects several defects or undesired behaviour of the SUT which were not found by functional tests. Randomized testing can also be used for software reliability estimation (Hamlet 1994). *S5 transaction-based tests* and *O3 randomized testing* are recommended for this example.

Table 11. Selection of the test-technique for a flank protection model

No.	Test technique	Object to be modelled	Model determ./ non determ.	Paradigm/ category	Test selection criteria	Model (spec.)
S5	Transaction-based (concurrency) tests	Interface between components	discr.	Transaction based	Structural criteria	Message sequence charts
O3	Random testing	Data flow through SUT, behaviour of SUT	cont., discr., non-det.	State-based, transition-based, operational notations	Data coverage, structural coverage	IDATG task flows

In Task 5, the lines corresponding to S5 and O3 are selected (Table 12)

Table 12. Assignment of the test techniques to the failure category for a flank protection system

No.	Test technique	Failures (qualitative)	Category of Beizer's taxonomy	Product specific taxonomy	Remarks	Literature/ experience
S5	Transaction-based (concurrency) tests	Incorrect behaviour of the system when several transactions are run simultaneously	Integration; internal interfaces	Architecture: erroneous or missing services provided by components, sensors, etc.	Commands to monitor signals, shunts and level crossings	
O3	Random testing	An operation produces incorrect results or unexpected errors, hangs or crashes.	Implementation.	Event handling, memory leakage, complex combination of events, queues.	Insufficient stability of the system, large stations.	(Mohacsi and Wallner 2010)

Example 3: Signalling velocity constraints to the train conductor

The specification is a decision table (Table 13).

Table 13. Example of decision table for signalling velocity to the train conductor

Prescription for train conductor	Signal permanent light	Signal slow blinking	Signal fast blinking	Symbol for direction
Free				
100 km/h and free		1		1
Repeating signal, expect 80 km/ h etc.			1	

The test technique selected is *D10 condition testing*. The result of Task 4 of the method guide is shown in Table 14.

Table 14. Selection of the test-technique for signal velocity constraints

No.	Test technique	Object to be modelled	Model determ./ non determ.	Paradigm/ category	Test selection criteria	Model examples (spec.)
D10	Condition testing	Static data domains	discr.	Data-flow notation	Data-flow criteria	Tables, Boolean expressions

In Task 5, the line corresponding to D10 is selected (Table 15)

Table 15. Assignment of the test techniques to the failure category for signalling

No.	Test technique	Failures (qualitative)	Category of Beizer's taxonomy	Product specific taxonomy	Remarks	Literature/ experience
D10	Condition testing	Expression negation fault; variable negation fault; missing variable fault; operator reference fault; also associative shift faults	Requirements incorrect; structural bugs.	Errors in signalling velocity constraints.		(McDonald et al. 2008)

Testers can now implement test cases efficiently using the most effective test technique. To summarize:

- A method guide for the design of test cases for an interlocking system has the advantage of focused implementation of test cases.
- Errors are detected early because the tester looks at the test object and the requirements specification in a specific way.

- The tester is forced to determine which test case design methods are suitable and which are inefficient.
- Many redundant test cases are avoided.

6 Conclusion and future work

In developing safety-critical systems, standards such as IEC 61508, DO-178B and MISRA play an important role. Although these standards differ in terms of their focus, rigor and guidance, they share common features such as the requirement for appropriate verification and validation processes. The authors of (Eastaughffe et al. 1999) point out that there is a considerable lack of understanding the detailed requirements of the development product – specifically for test and verification. However, achieving functional correctness with respect to specific safety requirements is of utmost importance in practice. Software testing – when carried out systematically and in a well-founded way – is now considered to be the major technique for increasing confidence in specific quality attributes such as functional correctness, and for detecting faults. However, the appropriate design of test cases is considered a difficult, tedious and expensive task. Thus support for the design (and automated generation) of test cases provides considerable assistance in the development of high-quality software systems, particularly for safety-relevant applications.

In this article, we introduce a method guide for test case design intended to support the systematic use of test case design techniques. This is an incremental but important step towards the automation of testing, as tool-supported automated test case generation in an industrial setting is difficult to achieve (Peischl 2007). A method guide for test case design has been the subject of research. For example, (Vegas et al. 2006) present a scheme that allows the systematic selection of testing techniques. We basically incorporate this scheme but extend it in two important respects. First, as defect taxonomies are a valuable source for learning about kinds of observable misbehaviour, we explicitly consider the product-specific fault taxonomy for the selection of testing techniques. Second, the specification and the underlying paradigm (in the case of semi-formal and formal specifications) influence the design of test cases and are thus also taken into account.

The article further illustrates the concrete application of our method guide and reports on two case studies applying the proposed method guide. Our second case study focuses on testing a railway interlocking system for Siemens Transportation Systems. Since the interlocking system is the most safety-critical layer of the railway control system, systematic testing of this layer is a key issue. In summary, the method guide supports focused implementation of test cases and early detection of errors in the design phase. Moreover, test engineers are forced to determine which test case design methods are suitable and which may be inefficient or impractical. Due to the systematic design, a method guide further supports the avoidance of redundant test cases.

Empirical insights into the strengths and weaknesses of individual test case design techniques are rare. To the best of our knowledge, no comprehensive investigation has been carried out as to which techniques could reveal certain kinds of misbehaviours. Our method guide relies on the insights gained within an expert peer group. Future research should address the creation of a comprehensive knowledge base regarding the strengths and weaknesses of individual testing techniques.

Acknowledgments The research work reported here was partially conducted within the Softnet Austria competence network (www.soft-net.at) and was funded by the Austrian Federal Ministry of Economics (bm:wa), the province of Styria, the Steirische Wirtschaftsförderungsgesellschaft mbH (SFG) and the city of Vienna within the scope of the Centre for Innovation and Technology (ZIT).

References

Avizienis A, Laprie J-C, Randell B, Landwehr C (2004) Basic concepts and taxonomy of dependable and secure computing. IEEE Trans Dependable Secur Comput 1:11-33

Beer A, Heindl M (2007) Issues in testing dependable event-based systems at a systems integration company. Proc Int Conf Availab Reliab Secur (ARES 2007), Vienna, Austria

Beer A, Menzel M (2008) Test automation patterns: closing the gap between requirements and test. Testing Experience Magazine, December 2008

Beer A, Ramler R (2008) The role of experience in software testing practice. 34th EUROMICRO conference on software engineering and advanced applications. SEAA 2008, Parma, Italy

Beizer B (1990) Software system testing and quality assurance. Van Nostrand Reinhold

Belinfante A, Frantzen L, Schallhart C (2005) Tools for test case generation. In: Model-based testing of reactive systems. LNCS 3472. Springer

Black R (2009) Advanced software testing – guide to the ISTQB advanced certification Vol1 and 2, Rockynook

Blackburn M (2002) The Mars polar lander failure. STQE Magazine, September/October 2002

SEI (2006) CMMI® for Development, Version 1.2. Carnegie Mellon University

CENELEC (2001) EN 50128 Railway applications: communications, signalling and processing systems – software for railway control and protection systems

de Grood D-J (2008) TestGoal, Result-driven testing. Collis BV, Leiden.

Eastaughffe KA, Cant A, et al (1999) A framework for assessing standards for safety critical computer-based systems. In Proc Fourth IEEE Int Symp Forum Softw Eng Stand

Fernandez J C, Jard C, Jeron T, Viho C (1997) An experiment in automatic generation of test suites for protocols with verification technology. Sci Comput Program 29:123-146

Frantzen L, Tretmans J, Willemse TAC (2006) A symbolic framework for model-based testing. In: Havelund K, Núñez M, Rosu G, Wolff B (eds), Formal approaches to software testing and runtime verification (FATES/RV) LNCS 4262. Springer

Hamlet R (1994) Random testing. In: Marciniak J (ed) Encyclopedia of software engineering. Wiley, New York

Howden W (1976) Reliability of the path analysis testing strategy. IEEE Trans Softw Eng 2:208-215

ISO (1989) ISO 8807 Information processing systems – open systems interconnection – LOTOS – A formal description technique based on the temporal ordering of observational behaviour

ISTQB (2010) Standard glossary of terms used in software testing. Version 2.1. International Software Testing Qualifications Board, Glossary Working Party

Kahlouche H, Viho C, Zendri M (1998) An industrial experiment in automatic generation of executable test suites for a cache coherency protocol. In: Proc Int Workshop Test Commun Syst

Kuhn D, Wallace D (2000) Failure modes in medical device software: an analysis of 15 years of recall data. Nat. Institute of Standards and Technology, Gaithersburg, MD USA. http://csrc.nist.gov/staff/Kuhn/final-rqse.pdf. Accessed 25 August 2010

Littlewood B, Strigini L (1993) Validation of ultrahigh dependability for software-based systems. Comm. ACM 36(11):69-80

Lyu MR (ed) (1987) Handbook of software reliability engineering. IEEE Computer Society Press

McDonald M, Musson R, Smith R (2008) The practical guide to defect prevention – techniques to meet the demand for more reliable software. Microsoft Press

Milius S, Steinke U (2010) Modellbasierte softwareentwicklung mit SCADE in der eisenbahnautomatisierung. http://www.iti.cs.tu-bs.de/~milius/research/modelbased.pdf. Accessed 24 August 2010

Mohacsi S, Wallner J (2010) A hybrid approach for model-based random testing. VALID 2010, Nice, France

Mogyorodi G (2008) Requirements-based testing – ambiguity reviews. Testing Experience Magazine

Myers G (1979) The art of software testing. Wiley & Sons

Nielsen DS (1971) The cause consequence diagram method as a basis for quantitative accident analysis. Danish Atomic Energy Commission, RISO-M-1374

OMG (2010) UML superstructure reference. http://www.omg.org/spec/UML/2.1.2/Superstructure/PDF. Accessed April 2010

Peischl B (2007) Standards for safety critical software: validation, verification, and testing requirements. SNA-TR-2007-1, Softnet-Report

Straden L, Trebbien-Nielsen C (2002) Standards for safety-related applications. Nordtest Technical Report.

Tretmans J (1996) Test generation with inputs, outputs and repetitive quiescence. Softw Concepts Tools 17(3):103-120

Tretmans J and Brinksma E (2003) Torx: automated model based testing. In: Hartman A, Dussa-Zieger K (eds) Proc First Eur Conf Model-Driven Softw Eng, Nurnburg, Germany

Tretmans J (2008) Model based testing with labelled transition systems. In: Hierons RM, Bowen JP, Harman M (eds) Formal methods and testing: an outcome of the FORTEST network. LNCS 4949. Springer-Verlag, Berlin, Heidelberg

Tuinhout R (2008) The boundary value fallacy. Testing Experience Magazine

Vegas S, Juristo N, Basili V (2006) Packaging experiences for improving testing technique selection. J Syst Softw 79:1606-1618

Voas J M, McGraw G (1998) Software fault injection. Wiley Interscience

Whittaker J (2003) How to break software. Addison-Wesley

Technological Matters

Safety, Security and Multicore

Paul Parkinson

Wind River

Swindon, UK

Abstract Historically many safety-related and security-critical systems have been developed and qualified using single-core processors. These platforms could easily meet their increases in system performance requirements through higher processor clock speeds. However, the industry is now approaching the limit of relatively simple upgrade path, and there is an increasing trend towards the adoption of multicore processor architectures in critical systems to address higher performance demands. In this paper, we will review the challenges involved in migration to multicore processor architectures and the specific challenges related to their use in safety-critical and security-sensitive systems.

1 Introduction

During the last few decades there have been a number of continuing and emerging trends in embedded systems in relation to safety, security and performance. Some of these trends have progressed independently of each other, whilst others appear to be inter-related, such as the increase in processor performance enabling multiple applications to be hosted concurrently on the same processor, which has certification implications in a safety-critical environment.

In the following sections we will review separately the trends of safety, security and the growing trend of processor development from single-core to multicore processor architectures. We will also consider the suitability of multicore processor architectures in safety-critical and security-critical systems, the specific challenges which this presents, the role of virtualization technologies, and whether there is potential for convergence between *safety, security* and *multicore* leading to a unified approach.

C. Dale, T. Anderson (eds.), *Advances in Systems Safety*, DOI 10.1007/978-0-85729-133-2_13,

2 Safety

In recent years, there has been a dramatic increase in the deployment of software in safety-related and safety-critical systems. If we consider a specific category within safety-critical systems for illustration, military aircraft, it is evident that the ongoing requirements for increased functionality and capability have resulted in dramatic growth in the number and complexity of avionics and mission systems in order to provide air superiority over potential adversaries. These mission systems include, but are not limited to, head-up displays (HUD), digital map displays, sensor systems, retina-tracking target-designation systems, and electronic counter-measures systems.

Some mission systems are now so sophisticated that they can help reduce pilot workload, for example, the Speech Recognition Module (SRM) on the Eurofighter Typhoon which provides control over non-critical functions using orally spoken commands (Wikipedia 2010a). However, as the capability of these mission systems continues to advance, there is the risk that a pilot may use (or trust) the system beyond its intended purpose, for example using a digital map display along valleys at low altitude in poor visibility or at night; thus the mission system becomes inherently safety-critical.

The result of the increased capability of these systems has been a corresponding increase in the amount of software deployed. In the 1980s, a typical military fast jet's systems contained around 100,000 source lines of code (SLOC). By the late 1990's this had increased in next-generation fighters to around one million SLOC, and one of the latest generation aircraft, the F-35 Lightning, is understood to have over five million SLOC (MAE 2010).

2.1 Federated avionics architecture

Back in the 1980s, military avionics systems used a *federated architecture*, whereby each application or function was implemented using a dedicated processor, as shown in Figure 1. This approach provides intrinsically robust separation of applications and fault isolation, but it has a number of drawbacks. It is expensive in terms of Maintenance, Repair and Overhaul (MRO), as spares for each of the Line Replaceable Units (LRUs) need to be located at each of the maintenance sites, and training is required to install, diagnose and fix each type of LRU. The federated architecture also has significant drawbacks in terms of *size, weight* and *power* (SWaP) and obsolescence.

In terms of *SWaP*, each application requires its own CPU contained in its own LRU, which consumes both volume and power. This increases interconnectivity and wiring requirements between LRUs, adding appreciably to the weight of the overall system.

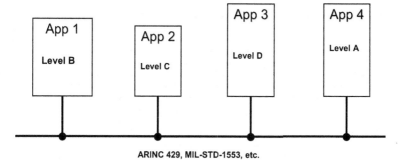

Fig. 1. Federated avionics architecture

The other notable drawback of federated architectures, which can sometimes be overlooked, is the impact of obsolescence. This is because a modern military jet is likely to contain many systems which may have been developed completely independently of each other by a number of suppliers. Therefore, the aircraft is likely to contain many different processor architectures and single-board computers (SBCs) in its federated systems. This increases the complexity and cost of spares management due to a lack of commonality of LRUs used in different applications, and also exacerbates the problem of obsolescence due to increased probability of a processor architecture reaching End-of-Life (EOL).

Obsolescence has become a more acute problem over the last decade following the US Defense Secretary's 1994 memorandum (Perry 1994) on the use of COTS in military programmes. This has enabled the defence sector to leverage the advances in commercial silicon driven by the telecommunications and industrial markets, and more recently the consumer markets, and has also provided significant cost savings for defence programmes. However, there has been a downside in the decline in the availability of military-grade processors which provided the long production lifecycles which are needed for defence programmes. Commercial and industrial-grade processors, by contrast, have tended to have shorter production lifecycles, as commercial and industrial programmes tend to want to adopt faster, high-performance and lower-power devices as they become available. This means that defence programmes have to choose processor architectures carefully. Fortunately some semiconductor companies provide extended lifetimes for some of their processor architectures, enabling them to be deployed on defence programmes in conjunction with planned obsolescence lifecycles which include periodic technology refreshes. However, even this is regarded as less than ideal, as the preference of military and safety-critical projects would be to standardize on a specific processor variant for the duration of the project, due to the cost of hardware qualification under DO-254 (RTCA 2000), including processor verification (Bate et al. 2001), and software safety-certification under DO-178B (RTCA 1992).

2.2 Integrated Modular Avionics architecture

The issues of reducing size, weight and power (SWaP) have been primary drivers for the adoption of Integrated Modular Avionics (IMA) architectures (see Figure 2) over the last decade. This IMA approach advocates the use of common computing platforms which host multiple applications concurrently, thus reducing the number of platforms required in the aircraft compared to a purely federated architecture (although some aircraft may use a combination of federated and IMA systems for efficiency and/or legacy reasons).

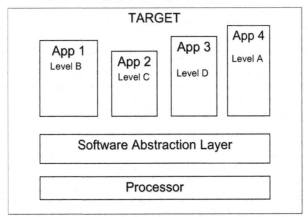

Fig. 2. Integrated Modular Avionics architecture

IMA is based upon two fundamental principles: *spatial partitioning* and *temporal partitioning*. This partitioning ensures that the individual applications do not interfere or affect each other, either inadvertently or deliberately. The enforcement of these principles is achieved through the specific implementation of the IMA software architecture (timeslot scheduling in the case of ARINC 653) and MMU-enforced separation of partitions (for details of an example implementation of an ARINC 653 architecture, see (ARINC 2003)).

In addition to separation of applications, system design needs to be undertaken carefully to ensure that applications do not interfere or interact with each other through accesses to shared resources (this is known as *coupling*, and needs to be addressed under DO-178B). In the case of shared devices, this can be mitigated through the implementation of an *I/O Partition* or a *Virtual Device Manager* which provide a software abstraction from the physical hardware devices and serialize accesses from multiple partitions.

For other shared resources, such as the Level 2 (L2) cache, the system implementation needs to ensure that system predictability and determinism is not affected by changes in the contents of the L2 cache due to application behaviour, which could lead to variations in the partition context switch time, known as jitter. This is normally addressed by invalidating and flushing the cache at the end of a partitions timeslot (known as a minor frame in ARINC 653), resulting in a consistent and predictable start-up time for the next partition.

The IMA approach has now reached maturity and acceptability in terms of Technology Readiness Level (TRL) for widespread deployment on civil and military avionics programmes, as indicated by the fact that over 200 global programmes are using ARINC 653. IMA is even being deployed to support multiple applications of differing levels of safety-criticality running on the same processor, for example the Boeing 767 tanker and Boeing 787 Dreamliner running VxWorks 653 RTOS (Wind River 2004). Normally, if a system were to host multiple applications or blocks of functionality at different levels of criticality, then the whole system would be developed and safety-certified to the level of the most critical component. However, this approach can be expensive, especially if there is a lower integrity application which has a high SLOC count (e.g. in Figure 2, Application 3 running at DO-178B Level D). Using an IMA approach, each application only needs to be tested and certified to its own level, thus greatly reducing certification effort and associated costs. However, there are two caveats, firstly the Software Abstraction Layer (which is usually an ARINC 653 or ASAAC (ASSC 2010) OS implementation) needs to be certified to the same level as the most critical application; and secondly, a robust partitioning analysis needs to be undertaken to verify that the spatial and temporal partitioning have been implemented correctly, so that, for example, the failure of the Level D Application 3 will not impact any of the other applications running on the same processor.

The IMA approach also provides the potential to enable mid-life updates or technology insertion in an affordable manner. This is an important issue, because the modification of an already certified system will require re-certification. In particular, research (Holton 2007) has shown that

the cost of change is proportional to the size of the system, not the size of the change

In a large system, this can have a disastrous effect on the incremental certification cost for an update to the system. The Integrated Modular Avionics model advocates the use of modular system components; however this alone does not provide a guarantee of modular and incremental certification. For example, if the IMA implementation combines the binary modules for individual application partitions and RTOS into a single monolithic image, then this could not support incremental certification. However, it has been shown that an ARINC 653-based IMA architecture which implements robust separation and role-based configuration under DO-297/ED-124 (RTCA 2005) can produce a platform suitable for modular and incremental certification. This approach uses XML-based configuration to define the system and partition attributes, and produces a payload stream of binary modules for the individual applications, OS and system configuration file (a.k.a. *system blueprint*).

3 Security

Before we consider the different types of security and trends, it is important that we clearly define what we mean by security and how it is different from safety, particularly as in some languages the same word can be used for both terms (e.g. *sicherheit* in German). This was concisely defined by John Barnes (Barnes 2005) as follows:

- *Safety:* the system must not harm the world.
- *Security:* the world must not harm the system.

We also want to differentiate *high security* from security in general. Traditionally, high security has been the preserve of specialized systems used in sensitive government and defence applications developed under US DoD's Rainbow Series 'Orange Book' (DoD 1985) and Common Criteria (ISO 2005), whereas the term 'security' has been used more widely for general purpose systems and applications used in the enterprise sector.

In recent years there has been a growing trend of *increased security* in systems used in critical national infrastructure (including the development and certification of high-security systems to a Common Criteria Evaluation Assurance Level, often EAL 4 and above). This is due to the perceived growing threat of cyber warfare and cyber terrorism. This potential threat was predicted by US Congressional Joint Economic Committee, which also warned back in 2002 that the extent and effects of cyber terrorism on US infrastructure were not yet understood; however, it was reported (Mann 2002) that

> the vulnerability of aviation and other key infrastructure is dramatically heightened by their indivisibility from global communications

The feasibility of cyber warfare attacks and their potential impact on critical national infrastructure has increased enormously in recent years due to the increased dependence on the Internet, which, since its evolution from the ARPANET has revolutionised global communications, leading to widespread use for personal communications as well as e-commerce, banking, and use in other business and industrial operations.

However, government and defence applications are still the main areas for *high security* applications, and this trend can be traced back in the US through government policy and legislation to Presidential Executive Order 12333 (Reagan 1981) in 1981 which stated that 'systems shall be secure'. This led to the National Security Agency (NSA) Information Assurance Directorate issuing National Security Telecommunications and Information Systems Security Policy (NSTISSP) No. 11 (NSA 2000). This policy dictates that Information Assurance (IA) is required for any system entering, processing, storing, displaying, or transmitting national security information; and from 1 July 2002, it is also required that COTS components of such systems demonstrate sufficient information assurance by evaluation and validation using an approved method.

3.1 Multiple Independent Levels of Security

Over the years, some government and defence systems need to be able to handle information with different security classifications concurrently, known as *multi-level secure (MLS)*. There has been a dramatic increase in this requirement in recent years in order to support on-going coalition operations, where systems need to handle national secret and NATO secret information concurrently whilst maintaining separation. In the past, these multilevel secure systems were built using multiple physically separated computers, networks, and displays; this required expensive equipment, which has occupied a large footprint in terms of Size, Weight and Power (SWaP). Whilst there have been efforts to address this requirement through the development of monolithic secure operating systems running on a single platform, their development and certification would have taken ten or more years.

The Multiple Independent Levels of Security (MILS) architecture (Figure 3) was originally proposed by John Rushby (Rushby 1984) as a means of overcoming these problems, but at the time the processors available on the market did not provide sufficient performance to host multiple applications concurrently or the ability to separate them in a robust manner.

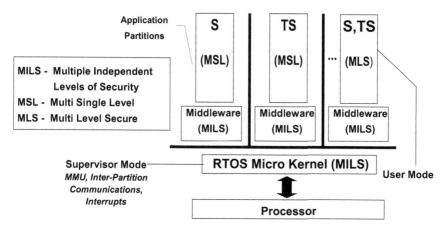

Presented by Mark Vanfleet, NSA, at Open Group Security Forum, 25th July 2002

Fig. 3. Multiple Independent Levels of Security (MILS) architecture

However, in recent years there has been a convergence between the security requirements and technical feasibility, enabling the development of MILS-based systems to become a reality. This has been due to the continuing advances in modern processor architectures which now have far greater performance than the processors of previous decades. These latest processors now provide the sufficient performance and capability to run multiple applications in completely separate domains on the same platform, and with hardware security features to provide effective isolation. The result is that the proper implementation of MILS-based systems is now not only technically possible but also economically viable. In addition to the technological advances, there have also been ongoing standardization efforts which have increased the acceptance and adoption of MILS. In the US, the National Information Assurance Partnership (NIAP) has defined the requirements for a Multiple Independent Levels of Security (MILS) separation kernel that will meet the information assurance requirements intended by the MILS architecture in the US Government Protection Profile for Separation Kernels in Environments Requiring High Robustness (NIAP 2007, known informally as the SKPP). The SKPP provides guidance to RTOS vendors in development of a COTS MILS OS, which in turn can be used to build a multi-level secure system.

Essentially, the separation kernel (SK) is built on four fundamental security policies:

- **Information Flow.** This defines the permitted information flows between partitions.
- **Data Isolation.** This ensures that a partition cannot access resources in other partitions.
- **Periods Processing.** This ensures that applications within partitions execute for the specified duration in the system schedule.
- **Fault Isolation.** This defines that a failure in one partition does not impact any other partition within the system.

These four policies create an architecture that allows the creation of additional components that are Non-Bypassable, Evaluatable, Always Invoked and Tamper Proof, which is known as *NEAT* (Parkinson and Baker 2010 give details of the implementation of a MILS Separation Kernel). In addition, system designers need to take extreme care to ensure that as well as implementing the four fundamental security policies correctly, they also need to minimize unintended implicit channels of communication between applications, known as *covert channels*.

A *covert timing channel* can occur when there is variation in the duration of a partition's execution, known as partition jitter. If the delta is large enough, it may be detected by the application which runs in the next partition, thus providing a means for the applications to communicate a binary 0 or 1 value implicitly. Similarly, a *covert storage channel* can occur when an application attempts to access a device, other shared resources or cache, and finds that is unavailable because it is used by another application, this also provides a means for the applications to communicate binary values between them (DoD 1985 discusses covert channels further).

3.2 Hypervisors and virtualization

Recent implementations of MILS separation kernels have also been able to exploit the hardware virtualization capabilities provided by the latest processor architectures. In particular this enables the *implementation of a hypervisor* which can run guest operating systems on top of the MILS separation kernel in a virtualized environment. This provides the MILS separation kernel with greater control, enabling it to enforce data isolation and control data flows to prevent covert channels from occurring.

Two approaches are often used here: *full virtualization*, where the guest operating system runs unmodified due to the presence of hardware virtualization support; and *paravirtualization*, where the guest operating system is modified to improve system performance in the absence of hardware virtualization support. In the former case, the processor's hardware virtualization support enables the MILS separation kernel to run guest operating systems in a virtual machine environment (or partition) on top of the separation kernel at a reduced processor privilege level, and also to prevent the guest operating system from accessing physical memory outside its virtual machine. This data isolation is implemented and controlled solely by the separation kernel and is not dependent on the cooperation of the partitions to achieve virtualization. In the latter case (of processors without hardware virtualization support) the separation kernel enforces data isolation using the processor's memory management unit (MMU). In addition, in order for the virtualization to be secure, the implementation of the hypervisor must be correct, otherwise there is potential for security compromise or external attack, as has been claimed by for the Blue Pill attack (Wikipedia 2010b) against the Xen Hypervisor used in Enterprise environments. For this reason, some MILS kernels are being developed using formal methods, which is necessary for systems which will undergo security evaluation by the Common Criteria at high EALs, and, in many cases EAL 6+.

A hypervisor-based MILS architecture could also be used in conjunction with a DO-297/ED-124 role-based development approach. This enables separation of configuration data and build activities by role (Platform Supplier, Application Developer, and Systems Integrator), and provides the potential for incremental modification of the system.

4 Multicore

There has been a long-term trend in processor development, described by Moore's Law (Wikipedia 2010c) whereby the transistor count that can be placed on an integrated circuit increases at an exponential rate, doubling every two years. This trend is expected to continue for a number of years yet, although there is disagreement about when the limit for miniaturization of transistors will be reached. From 1970 to 2005, performance increases were achieved by increasing the processor clock frequency from 1 MHz to several GHz, which has provided predictable performance growth for applications. However, this has approached the limits of viability because as processor clock frequencies have climbed, power consumption has soared, as it is directly proportional to the clock frequency. In addition, in order for the processor to run at higher frequencies, the voltage also needs to be increased, but this raises power consumption dramatically as it is also proportional to the square of the voltage. This compounded effect is shown in the simplified equation Power = CV^2f, where C is dynamic capacitance, V is supply voltage, and f is clock frequency.

The result has been that there has been a *disruptive change* to the processor evolutionary development trend through the introduction of multicore processor devices. Multicore processors combine two or more independent cores into a single package composed of a single integrated circuit (IC) and they can be run at lower clock frequencies, resulting in lower overall power consumption whilst still achieving increased overall performance. This is illustrated in Figure 4, where the maximum frequency for a single core processor is shown on the left, resulting in relative performance and power consumption of 1; the next pair of columns show that the impact of reducing the processor clock frequency to eighty percent of the maximum is to reduce the power consumption by fifty percent; finally, the last pair of columns show the performance of a dual core processor (effectively equivalent to two single core processors running at eighty percent of the maximum clock frequency), providing the same total power consumption as the single core processor, but providing 1.6 times the processor performance.

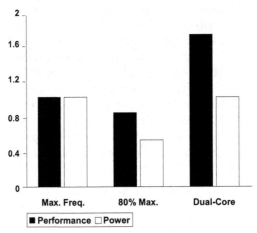

Fig. 4. Multicore performance and power consumption

However, this is not the end of the matter, because the 1.6 times increase in processor performance does not necessarily mean that an application will run 1.6 times faster. This is due to the fact that in order to exploit the performance of the dual cores, the application needs to exhibit sufficient parallelism so that different parts of the application can run concurrently on each core. In general, the parallel speedup which can be achieved with multiple processors (or cores) is determined by the portion of the application which must be executed sequentially. This is known as Amdahl's Law (Amdahl 1967), which can be expressed formally as the following equation.

$$Parallel\_speedup = \frac{1}{(\text{parallel fraction of code / number of cores}) + (1 - \text{parallel fraction of code})}$$

The degree of parallelism exhibited by different types of applications can vary enormously. For example, some numerical computations are inherently sequential, whereas applications such as radar, sonar or image processing are often inherently parallel. This variation has lead to the development of a range of multicore software configurations, as shown in Figure 5.

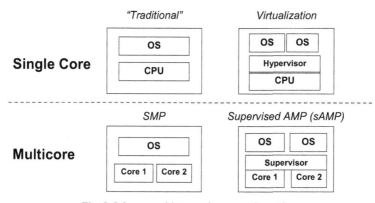

Fig. 5. Primary multicore software configurations

4.1 Symmetric Multiprocessing

Symmetric Multiprocessing (SMP) involves the use of a single instance of an operating system running across multiple processor cores. Historically, this has involved the OS running across multiple single-core processors, but the advent of multicore processors has resulted in a trend to consolidate an architecture comprising multiple single-core processors into a single multicore processor-based architecture, reducing footprint in terms of Size, Weight and Power (SWaP).

The scalability of an SMP multicore architecture will be determined by the balance between the processor cores' performance, memory performance and I/O performance. So for example, if a processor provides cores with fast instruction execution, but has limited on-chip instruction and data cache, and relatively limited bandwidth I/O to external memory, then this will be deemed to be *I/O bound*, and will limit the usable hardware performance of the system.

SMP provides a homogenous environment to applications, and the operating system kernel performs scheduling of application processes and threads across the system's multiple cores. This is usually done in a manner which is transparent to applications, but some implementations also provide the ability to tie individual processes or threads to individual cores, known as *affinity*, in order to improve real-time performance.

Significant software development effort may be required to efficiently migrate single-core architecture applications to a multicore SMP architecture, as parallelism support may not have been explicitly considered in the original software design. However, even with a balanced processor architecture design, there are practical limits to the number of cores to which SMP will scale, due to the fact that SMP applications need to explicitly protect shared data to ensure serialized access. So, whilst SMP will provide an acceptable overhead on a system involving a relatively small number of cores, this will ultimately limit the performance of the application on a system involving many cores, and in this case SMP may be combined with alternative multiprocessing architectures to optimize the use of all of the available processing units.

4.2 Asymmetric Multiprocessing

Asymmetric Multiprocessing (AMP, sometimes referred to as ASMP) uses a different approach from SMP, by treating each core as a separate processing element. This enables multiple instances of the same application to be replicated across multiple cores and to operate on separate sets of data. In addition, it is also possible to run different operating systems on different cores if required; typically, a real-time operating system (RTOS) may run on one core for real-time sensor or control, and a general-purpose operating system such as Linux on another core to provide a graphical interface.

However, in multicore AMP systems, individual cores will need to share hardware resources with other cores, usually including L2 cache, memory buses and certain peripherals. This increases system complexity and requires that careful software design and implementation is undertaken to ensure that access and control of shared resources is handled correctly. This can be quite a challenging undertaking, especially when different operating systems are running on the cores, and the consequences of incorrect software operation could result in the propagation of a fault from one core to another. For this reason, AMP is now increasingly being adopted as part of a multicore architecture which uses supervision and/or virtualization (this is discussed in section 4.3).

At the application level, the cores operate independently which can help to minimize the software development effort required to port to a multicore architecture. However, if communication with an application running on another core is required, then this will need to be explicitly implemented in the application using the appropriate inter-processor communications (IPC) mechanism which will utilize an underlying hardware IPC transport. This contrasts with SMP where inter-process communication to software running on a different core is transparent to the application.

4.3 Supervised and virtualized asymmetric multiprocessing

Multicore AMP systems can be extremely complex, especially in consolidated systems where multiple operating systems are used. This means that more effort needs to be expended on ensuring that the system configuration and its implementation is correct, in particular the hardware resource partitioning which needs to be performed manually.

This increase in complexity and effort is unwelcome, and has resulted in a trend of using *supervisor* software which runs on the cores beneath the OS and manages access to shared resources, reducing the complexity of the individual OS environments. The supervisor may also provide the ability to perform a controlled reboot of individual cores without affecting other cores.

There is also an emerging trend to use full virtualization, which takes the supervision concept a step further. In this case, a hypervisor runs across the cores, and is responsible for creating a virtualized environment for each core and will configure the memory protection required for each OS and will then load and boot the relevant operating system respectively. This provides strong separation between the operating environments on each core, and typically could be used to enable the consolidation of applications which used to run on separate processors onto a multicore architecture; typically this would involve a general purpose OS such as Windows or Linux, and a real-time OS such as VxWorks.

In critical systems, a robust hypervisor is the one multicore technology that holds the promise of the highest efficiency. During technology refresh cycles it is typically a very difficult step to move to a newer processor; a critical system based upon a proven and/or certified hypervisor abstracts away the hardware dependencies from the operating systems and applications, and may allow migration of application platforms onto new silicon with minimal re-testing and verification.

5 Convergence

In the previous sections we have reviewed the trends for safety, security and multicore in isolation. It should be evident that whilst some trends are specific to their individual domains, there are some common trends which provide the potential for convergence.

5.1 Safety and multicore convergence

Consolidation is taking place in safety-critical systems through the use of IMA architectures to enable multiple applications to run concurrently on the same processor. This is also occurring as multiple independent applications are being migrated from single-processor platforms to cores within a multicore architecture. The next logical step is to consider whether multicore processors could be used in safety-critical systems, and which of the multicore software architectures is appropriate for safety.

SMP appears to be an attractive option for safety-critical systems on initial consideration, because it would enable an existing federated safety-critical application to exploit the increased performance of a multicore processor. However, using SMP will result in some loss of determinism, firstly because the time taken to access shared resources will not be predictable as it will be dependent on activity on other cores which may also attempt to access the shared resource, and secondly because of the difference in execution timings between a task being rescheduled on the same core on another core (due to the cache effects). In addition, SMP does not provide an obvious way to support multiple applications at different levels of safety-criticality concurrently. Therefore, it is anticipated that a convergence trend between SMP and safety-critical systems will probably not emerge.

AMP appears to provide the most potential for exploitation in safety-critical systems. The use of a hypervisor and virtualization to prevent applications on different cores from contending for shared resources could also be deployed to provide isolation between a safety-critical application running on one core, and a non-critical application running on another core. This approach is attractive for industrial process control and medical applications, as it enables the consolidation of a safety-critical control application running on an RTOS and a display application running on a general purpose OS onto a dual-core processor. Similarly, AMP could also be used to support multiple federated safety-critical avionics applications running on separate cores; and it could also support IMA applications running on an ARINC 653 RTOS separately on each core.

Although there is significant interest in the use of AMP multicore configurations in safety-critical avionics systems, there are still some barriers to adoption. This is due to the potential for coupling between applications running on different cores due to accesses to shared resources (including caches, memory controllers, and other devices) (Kinnan 2009), which could result in an application being blocked by an application on another core. This presents a challenge both for multiple applications running at the same level of criticality, and also applications running at different levels of criticality. In addition, some investigations have reported that the complexity of the multicore processor architecture means it is also more difficult to determine the worst case execution time (WCET), which is necessary for determining if the system will behave in a predictable manner under all conditions; however, it may be possible to alleviate these problems through smart configuration of the systems (Cullmann et al. 2010).

At present, the civil aviation certification authorities are taking a conservative approach to multicore certification under DO-254, but it is possible that the results on multicore avionics research programmes could produce guidance on the use of suitable multicore processors and configurations in the near future, and this might provide input into the design of new multicore processors to improve their suitability for safety-critical systems, for example the use of separate caches per core to provide better predictability for WCET analysis.

5.2 Security and multicore convergence

Consolidation is starting to take place in secure systems through the adoption of the MILS architecture to support multiple applications at different security classifications, where multiple processor platforms with 'air-gap security' have been used previously. However, there are a number of challenges which need to be addressed in order to use multicore processors in secure systems. Many of these apply to safety-critical systems, as discussed earlier, but there the adoption of multicore also presents a challenge which is unique to security, that of *covert channels of communication*.

In section 3.1, we considered the security threat of covert channels of communication on single processor systems. In multicore architectures, there is increased potential for covert channel communication, for two reasons. Firstly, there are usually resources shared between cores including and caches, memory controllers and interrupt controllers, and peripherals. Secondly, because there are now multiple cores executing *concurrently* (rather than multiple applications executing in turn on a single core) which increases the bandwidth of the covert channel. For example, a dual core processor which has as shared L2 cache provides the potential for a high-bandwidth cover covert communication channel, which could be avoided by providing a separate L2 cache per core.

Individual multicore processors can differ greatly in their architecture, ranging from dual-core and quad-core homogeneous architectures, to massively parallel devices and even heterogeneous multicore architectures comprising a general-purpose processor and processing elements. Therefore, it is difficult to make generalizations about the suitability of multicore processors for secure systems. However, it is expected that research into using multicore processors in secure systems will result in a set of generally accepted principles for multicore in secure systems, and this will pave the way for adoption in the future.

5.3 Safety, security and multicore convergence

We have already considered the potential for convergence between safety and multicore, and security and multicore. The next step, involving the convergence of all three presents an even greater challenge, as there is an implicit tension between safety and security requirements which adds to the overall complexity. For example, in a multicore system which has both safety and security requirements, how should the failure of one core be handled? Should the system try to restart the core or provide degraded capability using only one core, or should it assume that the system is under attack and shut down the other core in a secure state?

Although the convergence trend for safety, security and multicore has not emerged yet, it is expected that as the issues relating to safety and multicore, and security and multicore are addressed, then convergence will become an inevitable reality.

If we consider the software architectures which have the greatest potential to support safety, security and multicore, it is evident that an ARINC 653 safety-critical RTOS is unlikely to meet the security requirements due to the size of the kernel and because it may allow device drivers to be implemented in kernel space (this is discussed by Parkinson and Baker 2010). This contrasts with the hypervisor-based MILS implementations which provide the foundation for a secure system, which can also meet safety requirements through its separation and isolation capabilities, and therefore provides the best prospects for supporting multicore in a safe and secure environment.

6 Conclusions

There is already some convergence occurring between safety, security and multicore. ARINC 653 and IMA technologies have increased in technology readiness levels over the last decade, moving from the laboratory to successful deployment on civil and military aircraft programmes.

MILS is currently in an early adoption phase, and proof in technology demonstrators and deployment will lead to more widespread acceptance and use. Multicore is becoming all-pervasive as semiconductor manufacturers embrace this technology. Industry wants a unified solution for safety, security and multicore, but demand for this is growing faster than the technology is progressing, and although the fundamental technologies exist today, a unified solution is not available yet although hypervisor-based MILS architecture provides the greatest potential for meeting the needs of safety, security and multicore.

The maturing process for these technologies cannot be rushed but needs to be undertaken with due diligence because they are used in safety-critical systems where peoples' lives are at stake, and security-critical systems where national interests are at stake. Regulatory frameworks and increased connectivity demands in the domains of safety and security mean that we are likely to see positive, incremental steps towards a unified architecture in the near future, enabling more complex systems to be created on virtualized multicore platforms with high degrees of separation, thereby architecturally creating more robust environments for hosting both safe and secure critical applications.

References

Amdahl GM (1967) Validity of the single-processor approach to achieving large-scale computing capabilities. Proc Am Federation of Information Processing Societies Conf p483-485. AFIPS Press

ARINC (2003) Avionics application software standard interface. ARINC Specification 653-1

ASSC (2010) Allied Standards Avionics Architecture Council. Avionics Systems Standardisation Committee website. http://assconline.co.uk/asaac.asp. Accessed 9 August 2010

Barnes J (2005) Safe and secure software – an invitation to Ada 2005. AdaCore. http://www.adacore.com/home/ada_answers/ada_2005/safe_secure/. Accessed 9 August 2010

Bate I, Conmy P, Kelly T, McDermid J (2001) Use of modern processors in safety-critical applications. The Computer Journal 44:531-543

Cullmann C, Ferdinand C, Gebhard G, Grund D, Maiza (Burguière) C, Reineke J, Triquet B, Wilhelm R (2010) Predictability considerations in the design of multi-core embedded systems. Embedded real-time systems and software conference

DoD (1985) Trusted computer systems evaluation criteria, Department of Defense Standard 5200.28 (also known as Rainbow Series Orange Book). US Department of Defense. http://csrc.ncsl.nist.gov/publications/secpubs/rainbow/std001.txt. Accessed 9 August 2010

Holton G (2007) BAE SYSTEMS military air solutions, UK MOD Military Avionics Technology Exhibition.

ISO (2005) Common criteria for information technology security evaluation. ISO-15408 v3.1. http://www.commoncriteriaportal.org/index.html. Accessed 9 August 2010

Kinnan L (2009) Use of multicore processors in avionics systems and its potential impact on implementation and certification. 28th digital avionics systems conference

MAE (2010) First flight of carrier-based version of F-35 Joint Strike Fighter scheduled for this week. Military and Aerospace Electronics magazine, 3 June

Mann P (2002) Cyber security 'missing' from travel defenses. Aviation Week and Space Technology 8 July 2002 p41

NIAP (2007) US Government protection profile for separation kernels in environments requiring high robustness v1.03. National Information Assurance Partnership. http://www.niap-ccevs.org/pp/pp_skpp_hr_v1.03/. Accessed 20 September 2010

NSA (2000) National security telecommunications and information systems security policy (NSTISSP) No. 11, National Security Agency Information Assurance Directorate. http://www.cnss.gov/Assets/pdf/nstissp_11_fs.pdf. Accessed 9 August 2010

Parkinson P, Baker A (2010) High assurance systems development using the MILS architecture., Wind River technical white paper. http://www.windriver.com/whitepapers/. Accessed 9 August 2010

Perry W (1994) Specifications and standards – a new way of doing business. US DOD Memorandum, 29 June

Reagan R (1981) Executive Order 12333. The White House. http://www.ncs.gov/library/policy_docs/eo_12333.pdf Accessed 9 August 2010

RTCA (1992) Software considerations in airborne systems and equipment certification. RTCA DO-178B

RTCA (2000) Design assurance guidance for airborne electronic hardware. RTCA DO-254/EUROCAE ED-80

RTCA (2005) Integrated Modular Avionics (IMA) development guidance and certification considerations. RTCA DO-297/EUROCAE ED-124

Rushby J (1984) A trusted computing base for embedded systems. Proceedings 7th DoD/NBS Computer Security Conference, Gaithersburg, Maryland p294-311. http://fm.csl.sri.com/~rushby/abstracts/ncsc84-tcb. Accessed 9 August 2010

Wikipedia (2010a) Eurofighter Typhoon. Wikipedia. http://en.wikipedia.org/wiki/Eurofighter_Typhoon. Accessed 9 August 2010

Wikipedia (2010b) Blue Pill (malware). Wikipedia online encyclopedia. http://en.wikipedia.org/wiki/Blue_Pill_%28malware%29. Accessed 9 August 2010

Wikipedia (2010c) Moore's Law. Wikipedia online encyclopedia. http://en.wikipedia.org/wiki/Moore%27s_law. Accessed 9 August 2010

Wind River (2004) Smiths Aerospace selects Wind River for use in Boeing 7E7 common core system. Wind River press release. http://www.windriver.com/news/press/pr.html?ID=71. Accessed 9 August 2010

A Pragmatic View of Formal Methods: the Hi-Lite Project

Robert Dewar

AdaCore and New York University

New York, USA

Abstract Formal methods can be applied in a variety of different modes. Even if the notion of proving an entire program correct is of limited applicability, we can still achieve more modest goals, such as proving specific properties of programs, and in fact there are existing examples where such approaches have been success-ful. The inability of formal methods to carry 100% of the burden means that the overall development process must rely on a combination of tools and techniques spanning the range from formal proof to testing. We thus need tools, languages, and development environments that allow easy integration of these various ap-proaches. The Hi-Lite project aims to meet this need.

1 Introduction

> 'In theory there is no difference between theory and practice. In practice there is.'
> variously attributed to Yogi Berra, Albert Einstein, and others

One can imagine one of those HSBC bank's 'different viewpoint' ads at airports featuring a page of dense specification, with three captions: *Complicated, Interest-ing, Expensive*: *Complicated* from the programmer with limited mathematics skills who is wary of formalism, *Interesting* from the academic computer scientist more interested in researching the theory of programming than actually writing pro-grams in the real world, and *Expensive* from the aircraft manufacturing executive who already feels they spend a lot on software.

Everyone can agree on the importance of techniques that enable us to write re-liable programs. Our very lives depend on the reliability of software in this age when there are millions of lines of critical code not only aboard every aeroplane we fly on, but also in the cars we drive, the medical devices we rely on, the cell phones we use to keep in touch, and the cameras we use to record important mo-ments in our lives. A failure in any one of these could have serious adverse conse-

C. Dale, T. Anderson (eds.), *Advances in Systems Safety*, DOI 10.1007/978-0-85729-133-2_14,
© Springer-Verlag London Limited 2011

quences, from losing a once in a lifetime chance to record a wedding, to losing one's life in a car crash. The stakes are very high.

The term *formal methods* is a bit of a catch-all phrase covering many techniques and approaches. But the essence is to regard programs as formal mathematical objects, about which we can reason in a rigorous manner, using the tools and techniques that mathematicians have developed from centuries of experience. Potentially we can use such techniques in many different circumstances, but programs seem a particularly promising target, since they are constructed using artificial formal languages that in fact bear considerable similarities to the language used by mathematicians. The idea of being able to formally prove that a program is correct and reliable is definitely interesting, and we keep coming back to this fundamental notion. At a simpler level, we can at least perhaps prove important properties of programs, or use formal techniques to reason about programs, to find problems, and to provide information about existing programs.

In this paper, we will have a look at what has been achieved with existing techniques, and present some thoughts about what we may be able to do in the future. The more extreme visions of what can be achieved are probably unrealistic, but on the other hand, we can achieve (and indeed have achieved) remarkable results with current technology. Finally we will look at a new collaborative project, Hi-Lite, which attempts to bring together a number of existing techniques to allow more widespread use of effective approaches in the future.

2 Reliability and correctness

In the academic world, we often encounter a viewpoint that merges the concepts of reliability and correctness. That's not surprising: it is easy enough to investigate and publish papers on theories of correctness, but reliability is much more elusive. Since we are taking a pragmatic viewpoint in this paper, it is worth spending some time pointing out that these two concepts are very different.

Correctness means that a program's behaviour adheres to some formal model. Typically it is phrased in terms of conformance of a program to a formal specification. *Reliability* means that a program works well enough in practice to be acceptable. A program can most certainly be correct with respect to some specification, but still unreliable because of an incorrect or incomplete specification. On the other hand, a program may be reliable even though it has errors if the errors are infrequent enough or unimportant enough to be acceptable. I once had a student who had a summer job working for a major publisher in the United States. He noticed that their main mailing program had a bug that caused the first 500 names on the list to be discarded every time it was run. He proposed fixing this obvious error. His manager responded: 'Don't touch that program, it's totally reliable, there are millions of names on the list, and it doesn't matter if we lose a few every now and then.' It would be hard to imagine a formal specification for this program including such freedom.

A common viewpoint in the academic world is that all large software programs have serious errors, and that this is to be expected. I attended a lecture by a well known lawyer in the area of product liability who proposed that we need special laws for software since it was not possible to write software without serious flaws. Some time ago, I testified on behalf of a large computer manufacturer who was being sued by a customer who complained that the operating system was fraudulent because it contained serious errors. Basically we argued: 'Judge, we know the OS was full of serious bugs, but that's industry standard practice.' The judge was unconvinced and found for the plaintiff, but the damages were minimal because the judge could not understand why the plaintiff had struggled with the obviously unusable system for ten years trying to work around problems. Today, decades later, we still find it perfectly normal that modern systems like Windows contain hundreds of serious flaws allowing our computers to become infected with spyware and other malware.

But this common viewpoint is itself flawed. In fact we have technology for developing reliable programs that from a pragmatic point of view works extremely well. The DO-178B certification standard (RTCA/EUROCAE 1992, Chilenski 2002, Souyris et al. 2009) used for commercial (and increasingly for military) avionics system is definitely not in the realm of formal methods. In fact it really has no formal basis at all. But it works well: we have never lost a life on a commercial airliner because of a software bug. That's why the hypothetical airline executive looks with suspicion on formal methods: they sound like an expensive way of fixing something that does not need fixing. On the other hand, we have had some hair-raising close calls, such as the Malaysia Airline B777 incident in August 2005. As stated in the findings of an investigative report (ATSB 2007), 'An anomaly existed in the component software hierarchy that allowed inputs from a known faulty accelerometer to be processed by the air data inertial reference unit (ADIRU) and used by the primary flight computer, autopilot and other aircraft systems.' Moreover, we are increasingly using advanced techniques, such as Object-Oriented development and so-called modeling languages, where we cannot be so certain about relying on empirical experience. The development of the follow-on standard DO-178C (McHale 2009) addresses these areas, and interestingly opens the doorways to more extensive use of formal methods. We will discuss these specific points later.

To convince people that it makes sense to use formal methods, we need to recognize that the competition comes from software developed carefully following existing certification standards, rather than from typical commercial software produced with far less care. It is certainly a concern that so much critical software is developed using less than best practices. Most notably it is remarkable that we have no standards comparable to the avionics standards in the automobile area, even though typical cars have more lines of software aboard than a plane, and far more people die in car crashes. Has anyone died in an automobile accident because of a software bug? We simply do not know the answer to that question. Car crashes are not investigated with the same thoroughness as aeroplane crashes. The recent Toyota woes have served to draw attention to this issue, but we still don't have anything like full information.

3 Safety and security

Broadly speaking, safety is about making sure that software does not kill people, and security is about making sure that bad guys cannot hack into software systems (possibly also killing people). When we developed the Ada 95 standard (ISO 1995), we decided that the language should address safety and security issues, and we made extensive attempts to interact with these communities. We were surprised to find that the two communities were very distinct and did not seem to talk to one another, despite the fact that their technical concerns seemed very similar.

Back in those days, security seemed a much less pressing problem. I was involved with the certification of the Boeing 777 software, and we were very concerned with reliability and safety, but I can't remember the issue of security ever coming up.

The modern world, with its increasing reliance on computer software for critical systems, and what seems at some points to be an unending supply of bad guys with significant software skills, has changed that picture considerably. It is hard to imagine any safety-critical program that is not also security-critical in this day and age, so security issues are always on the table. A while ago, there was a publicized concern about the Boeing 787 systems combining passenger internet traffic and critical avionics software on the same bus (FAA 2008). This was resolved, but the fact that this concern made the national press shows the shift in viewpoints.

Are avionics and traffic-control systems vulnerable to outside attack? Popular TV series like *24* and *Alias* certainly seem to think so. Perhaps that's just in the realm of fiction, but we should remember that the first case of terrorists crashing a plane into a building occurred in a novel by Clancy years before 9/11. We can't afford to be complacent.

From a technical point of view, safety and security concerns are certainly similar, but there is one very important difference. While we can get a reasonable confidence level from a safety point of view by empirically observing reliability (this plane has flown thousands of hours with not one observed safety defect), we are not nearly so ready to accept this kind of empirical evidence for security. The fact that someone could walk by the World Trade Center buildings every day for decades and see them still standing did not prove they were invulnerable to attack. When it comes to security, the use of formal methods becomes more attractive. It is comforting to be able to prove mathematically that a program meets its security requirements. We will discuss later on whether this is achievable in practice.

4 Proving entire programs correct

The goal of proving an entire program correct has always been an attractive one. Thirty years ago, there was huge enthusiasm in the academic sector for this vision, but then that interest seemed to die out, and certainly we did not see a transformation of industry standard practice. So what was the problem?

Proving a program correct typically means proving that the program meets the specification. This presumes that you have a full specification, and that it is sufficiently formal to be used as a basis of a mathematical proof. There are a number of fundamental problems that stand in the way of using proof of correctness as a technique to validate an entire program, and they centre on the issue of producing this full formal specification.

4.1 Difficulty and expense of producing a formal specification

A full formal specification of a program is a large complex object. Essentially it involves writing the entire program at a different level of abstraction using some formal specification language such as Z (Spivey 2001). This is not an easy task; i.e., it is a potentially expensive task. Part of the difficulty is that formal specification languages tend to be unreadable by anyone outside a small group of experts who are unlikely to also be experts in the problem domain. Grace Hopper recognized early on the value of a programming language being readable by a non-programmer, and when we see in a COBOL program something like:

```
IF BALANCE IS NEGATIVE THEN
    PERFORM SEND_BILL
ELSE
    PERFORM RECORD_CREDIT
END-IF
```

we can expect even someone at the management level to read such code and agree it looks reasonable. This goal is of course not always uniformly accomplished in the COBOL world, but on the other hand, it's hard to imagine that many managers and designers of air-traffic control systems can comfortably read pages and pages of Z code.

Now if producing a full formal specification was a panacea, it might still be worth the expense, but as we discuss below, that's not the case. So it is legitimate to question whether the gains we get from the considerable extra expenditure of effort justify the costs.

4.2 Errors in the specification

The specification is, as we have noted, basically a large program. Yes, it's in a language with a high level of abstraction, which helps avoid low level coding errors, but on the other hand it's a complex language understood only by a small number of experts, and it is usually impossible to test this large program. It is hardly surprising that large specifications themselves are prone to errors. Proving that our final program is equivalent to a specification with errors is not exactly what we had in mind. In practice, proving this equivalence does find and avoid programming errors, but experience shows that a significant number of problems in final products arise from errors in the specifications. It is not at all clear that making the specification more formal helps solve this problem, and indeed it may actually make things worse.

4.3 Incomplete specifications

Since specifications are written at a high level, they tend quite deliberately to omit low level implementation details, but in practice problems can easily arise at that level. During the first moon landing there was a serious last minute glitch in which the CPU became overloaded and was losing low-priority tasks. Luckily a priority scheduling system was used, so only noncritical tasks were lost, and the landing was successful. Later analysis showed that the problem stemmed from a change in procedures that had required switching on a particular system before the landing rather than afterwards, and this used up a significant number of CPU cycles. That sort of detail can lead to major problems, but is unlikely to be caught in the formal specification process.

4.4 Things that cannot be formally specified

Some important aspects of programs just do not lend themselves to formal specification. For example, if we are writing a compiler, a critical criterion of quality is the output of easily understandable informative error messages and effective error recovery. I see no way of specifying this at a high level of abstraction. We know what we mean (it is reminiscent of Steven Potter's famous observation on pornography 'I know it when I see it'). But how is that to be specified formally? We could specify the exact error messages we want, but then we are simply doing the job of writing a compiler at the specification level. After all, any program is in some sense a specification of its own behaviour, but the whole point of formal specification is to use a high level of abstraction without over-specifying.

Similarly, the requirement for a user interface that is simple and intuitive is often critical. An over-complex display on a pilot's screen or an air traffic controller's console may result in dangerous human errors. For another example, one of the Mars missions was lost because a measurement was input in the wrong units, which was not an error in the program *per se*, but could have been prevented by a clearer interface. Again, how can we formally specify what it means for a user interface to be intuitive? That's a very tough problem.

4.5 Partial versus total correctness

When we talk of proving a program correct with respect to its specification, we are almost always talking about proving partial correctness. In functional terms, that means that if the program or some particular piece of the logic terminates, then it terminates with the right result. Proving termination is often much more difficult. Now in some circumstances this is not so critical. For example, if we can prove a compiler partially correct, we know that if the compiler terminates then it has produced a correct program. If there is a case where the compiler never terminates, that's an annoying bug, but it does not lead to an incorrect program.

On the other hand, in real-time systems termination is often vital. When the pilot moves the control stick, we have to be sure that appropriate systems respond. In fact, not only is termination a critical issue here, but in hard real-time systems of this kind, critical components must terminate within a specified period of time. A lot of work has been done on proving real-time performance in this sense, but it definitely complicates the process substantially, and in practice we usually rely on a combination of testing and safety margins to gain confidence in timing behaviour.

4.6 Programming language specification

When we write a formal specification, we certainly use some language that itself has a complete formal definition. But the final program is likely to be written in a language that lacks a formal specification. There have been some attempts to use formal definition techniques for real languages (notably the ANSI PL/I standard and the Algol-68 definition), but such formal definitions are notoriously difficult to read, which means that few people read them, which means they are more likely to contain errors. None of the languages in common use (C, C++, Ada, Java, etc.) have formal definitions, and, worse still, they are full of ambiguities where code that looks reasonable is in fact erroneous. Some languages are better than others. For example, Ada is much better defined than C. Nevertheless the full Ada language is still too large and complex and too ill-defined to be fully comfortable for formal development.

There have been attempts, more or less successful, to define suitable subsets. One example is MISRA C (MISRA 2004) but the definition is far from formal and complete. A much more successful attempt is the SPARK language (Barnes 2003) about which we will have more to say later. The success of SPARK derives from both the design objectives (it was always conceived to be used in the context of formal verification), and the fact that its starting point was Ada (with features such as scalar ranges that allow the programmer to specify useful properties of data objects).

5 Proving properties of programs

The previous section of this paper was rather discouraging, but it was the bad news preceding much better news. While it seems unlikely that the approach of full correctness proofs for entire programs will ever play an important part in practical development approaches, for the reasons we have discussed, the notion of proving certain properties of programs is much more promising. Actually we can be much more positive, this is not just a promise for the future: there are many examples where this approach of proving certain properties has been used successfully.

5.1 Proving freedom from run-time errors

A pervasive source of errors in programs comes from low-level run-time errors. Some interesting work at Microsoft (Moy et al. 2009, Hackett et al. 2006) discusses the buffer overflow problem in C, and describes a semi-formal approach that has been used in conjunction with Windows code to find thousands of potential buffer overflows. These buffer overflows have often been the source of security weaknesses. For example one (in)famous worm program worked by sending a huge subject for an email. The programmer had defined a large array ('no one could possibly need a subject longer than *xxx*') and did not check for overflow of this array. The attacking program sent a long subject that was in fact executable code and arranged to overwrite a stack return address to point to and execute this code. After buffer overflows, the second most serious source of errors in C programs has to do with integer overflows, because an integer overflow on the size of a buffer readily translates into a buffer overflow. In C, integer overflows are particularly tricky to prevent, because of standard practice (which does not distinguish between numbers and their machine representation) and overly complex rules of implicit conversions.

Ada programs can have the same kind of errors. A buffer overflow corresponds to an attempt to index an array with an out-of-bounds value, and of course integer overflow is still possible. The difference is that in Ada, both situations result in well defined behaviour, namely the raising of run-time exceptions.

Obviously you don't want such run-time errors to occur. If they do occur, then the Ada approach (termination with an error message saying that an exception has been raised) is generally preferable to a random malfunction. However, it is pretty useless for a pilot of a plane to see a message on the command console announcing that a Constraint Error exception has been raised in critical avionics guidance code.

Obviously we want to be sure that a program is entirely free of such run-time errors. So what about the approach of constructing a mathematical proof of freedom from such errors? We don't need a specially written formal specification, so most of the potential problems described above (Section 4) disappear. We do need a well-defined target language, so that we have a proper formal definition of what we mean by a run-time error.

It turns out that this approach is not only promising, it is practical and has been used on some large real-life applications written in SPARK. SPARK is well suited to this technique, because it is well-defined, has the same semantics as Ada for run-time errors, and is designed to be used in a formal proof context. Several large programs, including a real-time air-traffic control system and a helicopter cockpit control program, have been proved to be free from run-time errors (Chapman 2000). In C terms, this means these programs cannot possibly suffer from buffer overflow or integer overflow problems. That's a pretty impressive claim to be able to make. If Microsoft were able to prove the same level of reliability for the Windows code, we would undoubtedly have far fewer security problems with this software. Unfortunately, you really have to start from the beginning with such an approach in mind. Trying to retrofit this to 50 million lines of existing code is an overwhelming task.

5.2 Proving security properties

Security-critical programs have an interesting property: they don't have to work! That's right; it's annoying but not a security-problem for such a program to malfunction provided that it does not violate security requirements. For instance a program guarding access to a secure facility might fail to admit the four-star general with full clearance. That will make him hopping mad but will not violate security. On the other hand if a janitor can get in because his cell phone somehow unlocks the security controls accidentally, then *that's* a problem. If an ATM machine fails to respond to a user's attempt to insert a debit card, then that's annoying, but if it displays the contents of someone else's account and allows access, then that's a serious security violation.

If we are writing a security-critical program, we can envision a partial specification that falls far short of the difficult attempt to specify the entire program. This partial specification includes only security requirements. The formal proof then can simply focus on making sure that the program does not violate these specific requirements, and we can use more conventional means, e.g. exhaustive testing as discussed below, to verify reliable behaviour (we don't want the general to get mad!)

The attractive aspect of this approach is that it is practical without incurring the expense and difficulty of producing a full formal specification and proving it correct. Furthermore, it is in the system's security properties where we most feel the advantage of a formal proof. Proving that a system is impregnable to specified kinds of security failures is far more convincing than any amount of testing. It is interesting to note that MILS (Alves-Foss et al. 2007) at the highest Evaluation Assurance Levels (EAL 6 and 7) requires the use of formal approaches.

Again, we are not talking about some future technology. Using appropriate tools such as SPARK, it is quite practical to achieve these proofs of correctness. At the system level, both Wind River Systems and Green Hills have announced operating system kernels meeting very high level MILS EAL levels with formal proofs of the related security properties. For an interesting use of SPARK in this connection, see details of the Tokeneer project (AdaCore 2009). This was a demonstration program sponsored by NSA to show that it was practical to create application software and prove that it meets the highest security levels. The Tokeneer system controls entry to restricted systems using biometrics. What is particularly interesting is that the cost of producing this software was comparable to, or even somewhat less than, the cost of using conventional techniques. That's really important. If formal methods = lots of money, it will be hard to make much headway. If formal methods = cost savings, then people are much more interested.

6 The role of testing

So far we have concentrated on the role of formal proofs, but we should not neglect the importance of testing as part of the software development process. First of all, as we have described, there are limits to what we can achieve by formal proof. Second, even for a system proved correct, we will increase our confidence if we have done at least some testing. I don't think I am willing to get on a plane where the only assurance of the reliability of the software is some big mathematical proof, and the software has never been actually run before. Of course in some cases (moon landings, nuclear missile defences, dealing with reactor meltdown, etc.), you can't test under real deployment circumstances, but you can still gain important information from testing under simulated conditions.

Much of the effectiveness of the DO-178B certification standard for avionics comes from its prescription of extensive, complete, specified approaches to producing comprehensive sets of tests. Just constructing these tests often turns up problems with requirements, or discrepancies between requirements and implementation, and of course running the tests finds more such discrepancies on the one hand or gives us a considerably higher level of confidence on the other hand.

Of course testing can never be comprehensive (the Malaysia Airline incident mentioned in Section 2 turns out to be a real example of a software bug escaping detection despite comprehensive testing).

In an ideal world where cost is no object, we would prefer to do comprehensive testing as well as proof where practical using formal methods. However, that sounds expensive, and you are unlikely to make much headway if that is your approach. The airline executive in charge of cost-control will not listen to you, and historically there has been some antagonism to formal methods based on this concern of increased costs.

On the other hand, if you can show that using formal proof techniques can reduce the burden of testing or other required activities, so that the costs are the same, or perhaps lower, then you have got the attention of that executive. At least that is the experience at Airbus, where unit proofs have replaced unit testing in some cases (Souyris et al. 2009).

DO-178C will likely specifically admit the possibility of replacing testing with formal proofs in some specified circumstances. To get an idea of what is possible, let's look at one particular problem, namely dynamic dispatching. In Object-Oriented programs you declare a hierarchy of types derived from parent types and inheriting their properties. A dispatching call might appear in the code simply as:

```
Object.Draw (x, y);
```

The problem is that **Draw** may at run-time execute any one of a whole collection of different methods or subprograms depending on the run-time nature of **Object**. That's a problem for testing, because we have to test all possibilities. If there are 20 different possibilities for **Draw**, we should test all of them, because we don't know what **Object** will be at run-time. But constructing such tests may be impractical. Not only is producing 20 separate tests for each such call an alarming prospect in itself, but constructing the tests may be impossible because of logical constraints on the possible values of **Object** at this particular point in the program.

An approach currently being examined in the context of DO-178C is to require the members of a type hierarchy to obey the Liskov Substitution Principle (Liskov and Wing 2001). This is a formalization, in terms of preconditions and postconditions, of the principle that the behaviour of a derived member should be similar in a formal sense to its parent's behaviour, so if the **Draw** call works for one, it is guaranteed to work for all.

This is a well known approach, but how do we know that the members of a hierarchy obey this principle? We could conceivably try to demonstrate this with testing, but that's not easy. It may be much easier to use formal proof techniques to prove this limited property.

This is just one example where testing and proof can work together rather than be seen as antagonistic approaches. Any comprehensive approach to the use of formal methods in development scenarios must properly accommodate the integration of testing. As we have mentioned in the case of security-critical systems, we can envision proof techniques being used to address specific security issues, and comprehensive testing to address the general reliability issues.

7 Using formal approaches to reasoning about existing programs

So far, we have concentrated on the notion of formal proof, but there is another interesting application of formal reasoning techniques, and that is to examine existing programs. Humans do this all the time using informal reasoning. What can be achieved by adding formal mathematical reasoning, carried out by automated software, to this process?

The current interest in static analysis programs such as PolySpace and Code-Peer shows that such an approach can indeed be valuable. This is typically an after-the-fact application of formal reasoning. It is not easy at this stage to add full formal proof, e.g. of freedom from run-time errors, but it is most definitely practical to look for some cases of run-time errors. A tool that finds a significant fraction of buffer-overflow errors in a C program is definitely useful, even if it can't guarantee to find them all. It won't eliminate the need for comprehensive testing, but finding errors earlier can often significantly reduce costs and improve reliability. One way of looking at these tools is that they provide an automatic version of traditional code review techniques (Ganssle 2010, Taft and Dewar 2009).

In addition to looking for errors, such analysis programs can usefully find information about existing programs that can be very helpful. CodePeer, for example, has the advantage of starting with Ada, which is easier to reason about because the programmer provides more information (e.g. the allowed ranges of all integer types). This tool can generate preconditions and postconditions, which can be very useful in understanding what a subprogram actually does, as opposed to what it says it does in incomplete or inaccurate comments. CodePeer can also generate test vectors suggesting ranges of values of input variables needed to achieve complete coverage.

If you are following DO-178B to the letter you never do any reverse engineering of this kind, since you can generate your tests solely from the requirements and not from the code itself. At the other extreme you might be working with a legacy system that you would like to certify, in which case everything needs to be reverse engineered. In real life, many programs fall between these two extremes, and tools like CodePeer can be very valuable in this process. For example, in the US, the FAA is being much stricter these days about requiring full DO-178B certification of military planes such as UAVs flying through civilian space. In theory we could redo the avionics from scratch to comply with DO-178B, but in practice we use some degree of reverse engineering on existing code. Indeed, it is not clear that restarting from scratch *would* be ideal, since it would lose the confidence that comes from years of experience with the existing code base.

Further discussions of static analysis can be found in (Fisher 2007, Taft and Dewar 2009, Bessey et al. 2010, Chess and West 2007). For an interesting specific example, see (Moy and Wallenburg 2010) which discusses the application of static analysis to Tokeneer. This investigation found a number of potential bugs. None of these affected the proved security properties, but this is an interesting example of synergy between different approaches to the use of formal reasoning.

8 Putting it all together: the Hi-Lite project

As discussed above, formal reasoning about programs can play an important part in the development of reliable programs, and indeed it seems clear that increased use of and reliance on formal methods is happening now, and will continue to be more important in the future. However, it also seems clear that testing will continue to play a significant role, since some properties can only be addressed in practice by testing.

This means that our methodology for program development must integrate the use of formal methods at different levels (formal proof of properties, reasoning about existing programs), with conventional systematic testing. In particular, it seems clear that integration testing cannot be eliminated, and unit testing as an adjunct to the use of formal methods will continue to play an important role.

If we accept that our development methodology must integrate these diverse approaches, then we need tools and languages that address this integration. At the current time, we have a mix of separately developed tools and techniques that do not integrate well. Let's in particular look at the programming language issue. At present we typically have to deal with multiple notations and environments that make it hard to take full advantage of possible interactions between tools.

As an example, consider the role of preconditions. The notion of preconditions, which specify a set of requirements that must be met on entry to a particular piece of code, typically a function or procedure, is an old one, which has appeared in many contexts. Preconditions can potentially serve a number of different purposes.

First, they can act as formalized comments. Compare the following:

```
procedure Verify_Pressures (Inner, Outer : Pressure);
-- Note: on entry Inner must always be greater than Outer
procedure Verify_Pressures (Inner, Outer : Pressure) with
   Pre => Inner > Outer;
```

We most certainly prefer the second form. Precise notations are always preferable to the vagaries of natural language if we can find a clear way to write things, as in this case. Even more importantly, comments are notoriously hard to keep up to date (testing does not test comments, and formal reasoning about comments written in English is definitely more in the science fiction realm). On the other hand, you have to keep preconditions up to date, or tests will fail.

Second, they simplify and extend the utility of testing. Preconditions can be compiled into actual run-time checks that will fail in a clear manner if the preconditions are not met. Such failures may help to locate potential or latent bugs which would not otherwise show up. The case of latent bugs is particularly interesting. You may have a case where, due to the particular code in place, no test could be written that fails if the precondition test is omitted, but if legitimate later changes are made to the procedure, then failure to meet preconditions could cause problems at some call site. Such problems are a major issue in maintenance programming, and being able to catch them before they occur can lead to significant cost savings and improved reliability.

Third, they provide a focus for formal proof systems. For calls, the task is to formally prove that the preconditions are met. For the procedure or function, the task is to prove that satisfaction of the preconditions is sufficient to guarantee required properties, e.g. freedom from run-time errors. This allows proofs to be modularized, which is helpful from a number of points of view. As an example of this focus consider the issues raised by DO-178C mentioned earlier in this paper. In addition to proving the basic adherence to the preconditions, we would also want to prove that derived types had preconditions that were proper weakening of preconditions (languages like Eiffel and Ada 2012 which provide for automatic weakening of preconditions can be helpful in this task).

Fourth, they provide a useful way for static analysis programs to summarize information they can determine about the current behaviour of the code. Normally we think of writing preconditions first, then writing code that adheres to these preconditions. But we can also generate preconditions automatically by looking at the actual code. These preconditions can then serve any of the first three purposes.

Now that we see the various purposes of preconditions, it is not surprising to find that they are addressed in the various tools we use, but there is no integrated systematic approach. In the AdaCore technology alone, we have four different syntaxes for preconditions:

- the *Precondition* pragma implemented some time ago in the context of Ada 2005
- the *Pre* aspect defined as part of the new Ada 2012 language
- the precondition annotations used in SPARK for formal verification purposes
- the syntax used by CodePeer to output preconditions deduced from the code.

Obviously, it would be desirable to have a single notation. An important goal of the Hi-Lite project is to define a common language of annotations covering preconditions and other similar aspects. By defining this common language Hi-Lite will allow industries to switch from an all-testing policy to a more efficient use of modern assurance methods. Much of this annotation language is expected to be included in the next version of the Ada language, Ada 2012, making it an international standard. The vision is to define a viable subset of Ada 2012, possibly with some extensions for further annotations. This will involve some interesting work on the relationship between static and dynamic approaches (Ernst 2003).

Hi-Lite will create a set of workflows for critical software verification based on existing tools already used in industry, some of which were mentioned earlier. These workflows will focus on separate verification through the use of annotations like the precondition shown above, which could be as beneficial to critical software development as separate compilation was beneficial to software development in general. The goal is to reduce the entry cost of formal verification sufficiently so that non-experts will be able to apply separate verification early in the development of systems in common languages like Ada and C. This is in contrast with current practice where formal verification is the responsibility of experts working with specialized formal languages of limited accessibility.

One critical asset in this effort is the decades of experience of industrial formal verification with SPARK, which Hi-Lite has leveraged to define an extended SPARK programming language and more powerful SPARK verification tools. The goal here is to extend the benefits of SPARK verification to software using common programming abstractions like containers and Object Oriented programming. Traceability of verification activities and results will facilitate software certification. It will also provide the basis for an easy-to-use verification system, which can help bring the advantages of agile software methods (Beck et al. 2001) to the certification arena.

It is expected that various products will be defined and commercialized based on these workflows by the owners of the base tools: AdaCore, Altran, CEA and INRIA. The large-scale experiments performed by industrial partners Altran, Astrium and Thales will certainly provide invaluable feedback concerning the benefits of this approach in an industrial context.

9 Conclusion

An earlier vision of total proof of correctness of programs as a panacea that would ensure totally reliable programs and eliminate the need for testing and the presence of errors in programs is certainly unrealistic now, and is likely to remain so indefinitely. However, it is increasingly clear that a more directed use of formal methods and proof techniques can be an extremely valuable approach. The history of work on programming is full of examples of someone coming along and saying, 'I have a wonderful new technique for building programs, the only catch is that you have to throw out all your existing tools and techniques.' A far more realistic approach is to recognize that programming is and will remain a complex and difficult task, and we need a variety of tools and techniques to address these problems in a world of increasing complexity and concerns. The Hi-Lite project is intended to provide a framework in which a variety of approaches spanning the range from formal proof to conventional testing can play easily and effectively together.

References

AdaCore (2009) The Tokeneer project. http://www.adacore.com/home/products/sparkpro/toke neer/?gclid=CK_x243uk6QCFYs65QodHVGXXQ. Accessed 11 October 2010
Alves-Foss J, Harrison W, Oman P, Taylor C (2007) The MILS architecture for high assurance embedded systems. Int J Embed Syst 2: 239-247
ATSB (2007) Australian Transport Safety Bureau, In-flight upset event, 240 km north-west of Perth, WA, Boeing Company 777-200, 9M-MRG, 1 August 2005, Report No 200503722
Barnes J (2003) High integrity software: the SPARK approach to safety and security. Addison Wesley
Beck K et al (2001) Manifesto for agile software development. http://agilemanifesto.org/. Accessed 11 October 2010

Bessey A, Block K, Chelf et al (2010) A few billion lines of code later: using static analysis to find bugs in the real world. Commun ACM 53(2):66-75. http://cacm.acm.org/maga zines/2010/2/69354-a-few-billion-lines-of-code-later/fulltext. Accessed 11 October 2010

Chapman R (2000) Industrial experience with SPARK. ACM SIGAda Ada Letters XX(4)64-68

Chess B, West J (2007) Static analysis as part of the code review process. In: Chess B, West J Secure programming with static analysis. Addison-Wesley

Chilenski J (2002), Software development under DO-178B, Open Group http://www.opengroup. org/rtforum/jan2002/slides/safety-critical/chilenski.pdf. Accessed 11 October 2010

Ernst M (2003) Static and dynamic analysis: synergy and duality. In: WODA 2003: ICSE Workshop on Dynamic Analysis. Portland, OR

FAA (2008) Department of Transportation, FAA. Special conditions: Boeing model 787-8 airplane; systems and data networks security – isolation or protection from unauthorized passenger domain systems access. Federal Register

Fisher G (2007) When, why and how to leverage source code analysis tools. http://www.kloc work.com/resources/white-paper/static-analysis-when-why-how. Accessed 11 October 2010

Ganssle J (2010) A guide to code inspections. http://www.ganssle.com/inspections.pdf. Accessed 11 October 2010

Hackett B, Das M, Wang D, Yang Z (2006) Modular checking for buffer overflows in the large. In: ICSE '06: Proc 28th Int Conf on Softw Eng, New York. ACM

ISO (1995) Ada reference manual ISO/IEC 8652:1995 with Technical Corrigendum 1. http:// www.adaic.org/standards/95lrm/html/RM-TTL.html. Accessed 11 October 2010

Liskov B, Wing J (2001) Behavioral subtyping using invariants and constraints. In: Formal methods for distributed processing. Cambridge University Press

McHale J (2009) Upgrade to DO-178B certification, DO-178C to address modern avionics software trends http://www.militaryaerospace.com/index/display/avi-article-display/369873/ar ticles/avionics-intelligence/features-and-analysis/2009/10/upgrade-to-do-178b-certification-do-178c-to-address-modern-avionics-software-trends.html. Accessed 11 October 2010

MISRA (2004) MISRA-C: Guidelines for the use of the C language in critical systems. http:// www.misra-c.com/. Accessed 11 October 2010

Moy M, Wallenburg A (2010), Tokeneer: beyond formal program verification. Embedded Real Time Software and Systems (ERTS^2 2010), Toulouse, France

Moy Y, Bjorner N, Sielaff D (2009) Modular bug-finding for integer overflows in the large. http://research.microsoft.com/apps/pubs/?id=80722. Accessed 11 October 2010

RTCA/EUROCAE (1992), RTCA SC-167/EUROCAE WG-12. RTCA/DO-178B. Software considerations in airborne systems and equipment certification

Souyris J, Wiels V et al (2009), Formal verification of avionics software products. FM 2009. LNCS 5850. Springer

Spivey J (2001) The Z notation: a reference manual. http://spivey.oriel.ox.ac.uk/~mike/zrm/. Accessed 11 October 2010

Taft T, Dewar R (2009) Making static analysis a part of code review. Embedded Computing Design. http://embedded-computing.com/making-static-analysis-part-code-review. Accessed 11 October 2010

Safety Standards

CE Marking – the Essential Requirements

Mervyn Playle

Quintec Associates Limited (part of the Thales Group)

Basingstoke, UK

Abstract The European Union (EU) harmonisation project introduced the CE marking of products to enable the free, unhindered movement of goods throughout the European market. The CE mark replaced the EC mark in the mid 1990s and is fundamental to the New Approach Directives. When a product falls within the scope of a New Approach Directive the manufacturer must comply with the 'goal setting' *essential requirements* of the directive, to follow one of the conformity assessment procedures provided for, and to draw up the technical documentation specified. Although not mandatory, a manufacturer can choose to satisfy the *essential requirements* through the application of European harmonised standards.

1 Introduction

This paper is intended to increase awareness of CE marking, and to be informative and useful to those with related responsibilities, including safety practitioners with an interest in the safety of products and systems, and those seeking an introduction to the subject. It provides an overview of CE marking only, for a fuller understanding the reader should refer to the vast range of information to be found on the Internet and elsewhere, for example the European Union's (EU) website (EC 2010a), the European Commission's 'Guide to the implementation of directives based on the New Approach and the Global Approach' (EC 2000), and the guideline documents on individual directives, for machinery (EC 2010b), electrical equipment (EC 2007) and electromagnetic compatibility (EC 2010c). See also the guidance documents produced by UK Government departments for business and by Notified Bodies [1].

The paper introduces product liability law in Section 2, CE marking in Section 3 and product compliance requirements in Section 4. References to the *essential requirements* of four New Approach Directives are given in Section 5. Section 6 briefly discusses the term 'product' and Section 7 looks at 'products in combina-

---

[1] A Notified Body in the European Union, is an organisation that has been accredited by a Member State to assess whether a product meets certain preordained standards.

C. Dale, T. Anderson (eds.), *Advances in Systems Safety*, DOI 10.1007/978-0-85729-133-2_15,
© Springer-Verlag London Limited 2011

tion'. Section 8 discusses European harmonised standards, and Section 9 the 'conformity assessment' procedures provided for by directives. A CE marking process is given in Section 10 and the EC declaration of conformity (D of C) is introduced in Section 11. Six key questions for producers to address at the outset of the CE marking process are posed in Section 12 and Section 13 overviews the CE marking of a complex product. Finally, key points relative to CE marking are summarised in Section 14.

2 Product liability

Product liability is the area of law in which manufacturers, distributors, suppliers, retailers, etc. are held responsible for the injuries their products cause. Traditionally, product liability has been limited to tangible personal property.

Product liability legislation is overarching, covering all products including those covered by CE marking legislation. It developed following moves to ensure manufacturers and suppliers take responsibility for the safety of the products they produce and distribute. A strict liability regime in Europe began with the Council of Europe Convention on Products Liability in regard to Personal Injury and Death (the Strasbourg Convention) 27 January 1977. This resulted in the Product Liability Directive 85/374/EEC (EC 1985) that was adopted by the European Economic Community on 25 July1985 and transposed into UK law in the Consumer Protection Act (HMSO 1987).

The Product Liability Directive set down specific rules, including:

Article 1
The producer shall be liable for damage caused by a defect in his product.

Article 3
1. 'Producer' means the manufacturer of a finished product, ... any raw material or ... a component part and any person ... putting his name, trademark or other distinguishing feature on the product presents himself as its producer.
2. ... any person who imports ... a product for sale, hire, leasing or any form of distribution in the course of his business shall be ... a producer ... and ... responsible as a producer.
3. Where the producer of the product cannot be identified, each supplier of the product shall be treated as its producer unless he informs the injured person ... of the identity of the producer or ... person who supplied ... the product. The same shall apply, in the case of an imported product, if this product does not indicate the identity of the importer, even if the name of the producer is indicated.

Article 5
Where ... two or more persons are liable for the same damage, they shall be liable jointly and severally ...

Article 6
1. A product is defective when it does not provide the safety which a person is entitled to expect, taking ... into account
   a. The presentation of the product;

b. The use to which it could reasonably be expected that the product would be put;

c. The time when the product was put into circulation.

Article 12

The liability of the producer ... may not, in relation to the injured person, be limited or excluded by a provision limiting his liability or exempting him from liability.

The term 'producer' in product liability law is interpreted widely and is not restricted to the person who made the product. As product liability law developed European CE marking law also developed to require any person responsible for producing or supplying a product in the course of a commercial activity, whether for payment or free of charge, to *demonstrate* that products 'put into service' in the European Economic Area (EEA)[2] are in compliance with certain *essential requirements* relating to the safety of that product.

Generally, new products are subject to the CE marking directives, however, another non-CE marking directive, e.g., the Marine Directive (the 'wheel mark'), an Automotive Directive (the 'e-mark'), or the General Product Safety Directive (EC 1997) (no marking) may apply. A manufacturer must determine which marking scheme applies and follow the applicable conformity assessment rules.

3 What is CE marking?

The CE marking symbol is shown in Figure 1 and is the abbreviation of the French phrase 'Conformité Européene' which means 'European Conformity'. Initially the term used was the 'EC Mark' but was officially replaced by the 'CE Mark' by Directive 93/68/EEC (EC 1993).

Fig. 1. The CE Marking Symbol

The CE marking system is part of the European single market harmonisation project and is invoked via pan-European New Approach Directives that lay down the minimum protection requirements to be met by apparatus, known as the *essential requirements*. References to the European single market means the European Economic Area (EEA).

Directives are issued by the European Commission and incorporated into the laws of the member states, by the member states themselves. In the UK, directives become regulations published as statutory instruments (SI). Technical solutions to

---

[2] In 1994 the European Union Member States and the countries of the European Free Trade Association (EFTA) (except Switzerland) joined to become the European Economic Area (EEA).

achieve the required level of protection are defined in European harmonised standards known as European Norms (EN): these will be discussed in Section 8.

CE marking was introduced in 1993 by Directive 93/68/EEC and came into force on 1 January 1995. Products could still be placed on the market under the old rules until 1 January 1997, after which it became mandatory to comply.

Note that the New Approach Directives apply to 'new' products and not to those 'in service', 'refurbished' or 'safety-enhanced' which are covered by the General Product Safety Directive (GPSD) (EC 2001). The GPSD is not a CE Marking Directive, and products within its scope must not be CE marked. However, where an 'old' product is modified to have significantly enhanced performance and capability compared to the original product then it should be treated as a 'new product' and be CE marked prior to 'placing on the market'[3] and 'putting into service'.

The CE mark should *not* be confused with the certification marks of international approval agencies, such as ASTA or BSI (UK), VDE (Germany), DEMKO (Denmark) and NEMKO (Netherlands). Certification marks on products show they meet the requirements of a standard, e.g. British Standard (BS) 1363 covering plugs, socket-outlets and connection units in the UK. Products carrying agency certification marks have undergone rigorous safety testing to approve a product type. Approval certification data should be included as evidence in a Technical File (TF) to show component suitability for the purpose used.

The CE mark on a product must be distinguishable from other marking and be a minimum of 5mm high. It is a manufacturer's *declaration* that his product complies with the *essential requirements* of the relevant European product safety directives to which the product should conform. The manufacturer's *claim* of conformity entitles the product to be legally placed on the European market and to enjoy free unhindered movement throughout the EEA.

Whilst CE marking enables free movement on the single market it also permits the withdrawal by the enforcement authorities of member states, of non-conforming products. Where this occurs, withdrawal of products must be formally notified to the European Commission via the RAPEX notification system, the EU rapid alert system for dangerous consumer products covering both foodstuffs and industrial products. It is also applicable to consumer products covered by the New Approach Directives.

---

[3] Placing on the market is the making of a product available for the first time on the Community market, with a view to distribution or use in the Community regardless of the legal instrument of transfer, e.g. sale, loan, hire, leasing, gift. Putting into service takes place at the moment of first use within the Community by the end user.

4 Product compliance requirements

A product must be in compliance with *all* of the safety directives that apply to it and a manufacturer declares that his product satisfies all the *essential requirements* of the directives via the EC declaration of conformity (D of C), discussed in Section 11.

For systems comprising equipment, sub-systems and incorporated apparatus several safety directives may apply, therefore, each relevant part of the system must comply with the *essential requirements* of the directive(s) applicable to that part. Note that the *essential requirements* of individual directives are quite diverse and broad ranging. Where one system forms part of another, for example a pressure containment system forming part of a machine, the pressure system must comply with the *essential requirements* of the Pressure Equipment Directive (EC 1997) and as an integrated system with the requirements of the Machinery Directive (EC 2006a).

An apparatus covered by a CE marking directive *must* comply at the moment of first 'making available', so long as the supply is for distribution and/or use within the EEA. *Making available* generally occurs when the apparatus moves from the manufacturing phase to the market.

Products not intended for the EEA market are not required to be CE marked, even if they originate in the EEA. If re-imported they must be fully compliant when 'made available' for the first time on the market of the EEA. This applies to all imported products, including second-hand, of whatever origin.

The CE marking signifies compliance of a product with all the directive(s) applicable to it, and each of these must be identified on the declaration of conformity drawn up by the manufacturer or his authorised representative.

Only the manufacturer or his authorised representative established in the Community are authorised to affix the CE marking. An authorised representative is the person(s) expressly appointed to act on behalf of a manufacturer in respect of the regulations. The authorised representative must be established in the EEA and hold the technical documentation at the disposal of the authorities, on request. Where a manufacturer does not CE mark his product and has no authorised representative, then the person making the product available takes responsibility; refer to European Parliament and Council Decision 768/2008/EC (EC 2008), Article R4.

Following issue of a safety directive there is a transition period, usually three years, before becoming mandatory. During this period a manufacturer can declare compliance with the directive and affix the CE marking, or market the product under the current system. After the transition period ends *all* products must comply with the new requirements.

Where a manufacturer resides outside the EEA and there is no authorised representative, the importer assumes regulatory responsibility. If the importer is not established in the EEA, any other person resident in the EEA who places an apparatus on the market assumes the obligations of the directive(s).

5 The essential requirements of directives

The *essential requirements* are published in the Annexes of the specific directives and the implementing legislation. Essential requirements are numerous, detailed and specific to product type. The references given below relate to the four principal directives relevant to the complex product discussed in Section 13:

- Low Voltage Directive 2006/95/EC (EC 2006b), Annex I: Principal elements of the safety objectives for electrical equipment designed for use within certain voltage limits
- Electromagnetic Compatibility Directive 2004/108/EC (EC 2004) Annex I: Essential requirements referred to in Article 5
- Machinery Directive 2006/42/EC (EC 2006a) Annex I: Essential health and safety relating to the design and construction of machinery
- Pressure Equipment Directive 97/23/EC (EC 1997) Annex I: Essential safety requirements

6 'Product'

The term 'product' in directives has various meanings, with objects referred to by New Approach Directives as:

- accessories
- apparatus
- appliances
- assemblies
- components
- devices
- equipment
- fittings
- instruments
- material
- products
- safety components
- systems
- units.

CE marking obligations apply regardless of the quantity of a product type produced, or its size. Single and multiple units, large machines, product combinations and assemblies not qualifying as 'fixed installations' fall within the scope of directives and must meet the *essential requirements*.

7 Combinations of product

7.1 Systems and assemblies

A manufacturer of a system of different products and parts, designed or put together as a combination, should consider the combination as *one finished product* and CE mark it. The manufacturer of the combination is responsible for selecting suitable products to make up the combination, for putting the combination together so that it complies with the *essential requirements*, and to fulfil all the requirements of directives applicable to the assembly.

Whilst combinations of product are generally considered a single product, some combinations assembled from individually CE marked units do not have to comply as such. A hi-fidelity domestic music system, for example, is deemed to comply as an assembly because products have been designed specifically for the domestic market and integration with compatible units. The manufacturer has no control over the final combination so he designs his system with interfaces at 'safe extra low voltage' (SELV) and with assembly requiring only simple skills. For particular hazards such as connection to the 230Vac mains supply, the manufacturer supplies components that are approved for the purpose and provide a minimum of two levels of protection. Also, full instructions in an appropriate language are provided.

7.2 Partially finished products

Certain products may be CE marked but not considered 'finished products' until incorporated into another apparatus that is itself required to meet a directive's *essential requirements*, for example, a CE marked open-frame power supply. The 'open-frame' unit will only fully comply with the *essential requirements* of the Low Voltage Directive (EC 2006b) once installed in a final product. The power supply manufacturer has no control over the product's final use so he provides instructions and warnings for installation and use. The final installer satisfies the *essential requirements* by incorporating the power supply into a suitable enclosure and by the provision of a system of insulation for protection against electric shock.

The Machinery Directive provides for a declaration of incorporation (D of I) that enables machines that are 'partially finished' products to be put on the market for incorporation into other apparatus. The D of I identifies the essential safety requirements with which the partially finished product complies, the machine becoming fully compliant when incorporated into a final apparatus that complies with an appropriate directive.

7.3 Fixed installations

'Fixed installations' are a special case, a definition of which includes the requirement 'intended to be used permanently'. This condition would be satisfied if the constituent parts of the installed apparatus were to be used in the defined location for the expected lifetime(s), however, if during that lifetime the constituent parts will be moved and taken into service at another location, the requirement would not be satisfied.

In the Electromagnetic Compatibility Directive (EC 2004) a combination of products 'installed in a specific place for a specific purpose' can be deemed a 'fixed installation' and therefore not require CE marking, however, the system must still meet the *essential requirements* of the EMC Directive, therefore the building's 'responsible person' must construct a Technical Assessment File to demonstrate compliance of the 'fixed installation' with the directive.

Other products to be installed in buildings must be CE marked, e.g. a lift system must be marked in accordance with the Lifts Directive (EC 1995). Another example would be lifting equipment that must be CE marked under the Machinery Directive (EC 2006a).

For 'fixed installations' the specific directive(s) should be consulted, it should not be assumed that equipment does not require CE marking.

8 Harmonised standards

A harmonised standard is a standard adopted by one of the European standardisation bodies listed in Annex 1 to Directive 98/34/EC (EC 1998), as follows:

- CEN – European Committee for Standardisation
- CENELEC – European Committee for Electrotechnical Standardisation
- ETSI – European Telecommunications Standards Institute

Harmonised standards, known as European Norms (EN), provide solutions that enable compliance with the essential requirements of New Approach, or other relevant, Directives. They provide a *presumption of conformity* but for this to apply the standard must have been published in the Official Journal of the European Union (OJEU). Standards are produced by the European Standards Organisation for a technical sector, e.g. electrical and machinery, and published by national standards bodies, e.g. British Standards Institute (BSI), DIN in Germany, NF in France.

From time-to time the European Commission publishes in the OJEU the titles and references of harmonised standards issued. Generally, the publication provides:

- the European standardisation organisation
- the reference and title of the standard

- the reference of the superseded standard
- the date after which the superseded standard can no longer be applied.

The *essential requirements* of directives are goal-setting objectives and do not provide technical solutions, and the role of harmonised standards is to provide guidance on factors to be included in the safeguards. Although not mandatory, their use could be influential in any legal argument over whether a safeguard is 'reasonably practicable' or not.

When selecting standards it is sometimes thought that one standard is easier to comply with than another. At first reading, this may appear true, however, the user should refer to the list of 'normative references' as these become part of the standard and can be quite numerous. Any claim of compliance with a standard includes the normative references.

Standards should be selected on the basis of the product type and the risks its poses. Where a standard does not cover all risks then additional standards must be used.

Systems will almost certainly require the use of multiple standards. For example, an information technology (IT) product complying with EN60950-1 (BSI 2006a) will also need to be assessed under the Machinery Directive if incorporated in a machine. This is because the operational environment of the host machine will be different, probably harsher, than that for which the IT equipment was designed. For EMC, the IT equipment may be satisfactory in an office environment but not the industrial environment of a host machine. Before incorporation in a host machine, systems designers should check which standards the sub-assemblies have complied with in order to avoid unpredictable outcomes requiring expensive rework.

For machinery, there is a mandatory requirement for a risk assessment, this should be conducted using the European machinery safety standard EN ISO14121 (ISO 2007).

Note that standards do not always align with each other. For example, the hazardous voltage levels in the following harmonised standards that both relate to the safety of electrical equipment:

- EN 60204-1 (BSI 2006b) (Machinery Directive)

  Any voltage above PELV (Protective extra low voltage), i.e. 25V ac or 60V ripple-free dc

- EN 60950-1 (BSI 2006a) (Low Voltage Directive)

  Any voltage above 42.4V peak or 60V dc

9 Conformity assessment procedures

To declare a product in conformity with applicable legislation, a manufacturer must follow one of the conformity assessment procedures allowed by the legislation, the most common method being 'self-declaration'. The manufacturer designs his product to satisfy the *essential requirements* of the legislation and manufactures it under internal system controls. He assembles the technical documentation specified and draws up a declaration of conformity (D of C) in which he declares under his sole responsibility that his product is in compliance with the legislation. He affixes the CE mark. There is no third party involvement.

The self-declaration process is that provided by Module A of the Conformity Assessment Procedures of Annex II of Decision 768/2008/EC of 9 July 2008 (EC 2008). Conformity assessment procedures (Modules) cover both design and production phases and shown in Table 1.

Table 1. Conformity assessment procedures

Module	Description
A	Internal production control
A1	Internal production control plus supervised product testing
A2	Internal production control plus supervised product checks at random intervals
B	EC type-examination
C	Conformity to type based on internal production control
C1	Conformity to type based on internal production control plus supervised product testing
C2	Conformity to type based on internal production control plus supervised product checks at random intervals
D	Conformity to type based on quality assurance of the production process
D1	Quality assurance of the production process
E	Conformity to type based on product quality assurance
E1	Quality assurance of final product inspection and testing
F	Conformity to type based on product verification
F1	Conformity based on product verification
G	Conformity based on unit verification
H	Conformity based on full quality assurance
H1	Conformity based on full quality assurance plus design examination

The particular module(s) that a manufacturer must follow is based on the level of risk associated with his product. For example under the Pressure Equipment Directive (PED) (EC 1997) pressure components and systems are assessed and categorised by the manufacturer as being in a particular risk class. The result determines which conformity assessment modules allowed for in the PED that the manufacturer can choose from.

For risk Categories II to IV it is mandatory to involve a notified body and their identification number must follow the CE marking on the CE label. Category I pressure equipment can be placed on the market under the PED or the Machinery Directive (EC 2006a). Pressure equipment below Category I is produced under 'sound engineering practice' (SEP), in which case it must be traceable to the manufacturer but *not* be CE marked.

It should be noted that conformity assessment procedures are not the primary purpose of Decision 768/2008/EC (EC 2008). The legislation provides a framework for the marketing of products, laying down common principles and provisions for legislators to apply across a wide range of safety legislation. Article 1 sets out the following general principles:

1. products placed on the market shall comply with all applicable legislation
2. when placing products on the Community market, economic operators shall, in relation to their respective roles in the supply chain, be responsible for the compliance of their products with all applicable legislation
3. economic operators shall be responsible for ensuring that all information they provide with regard to their products is accurate, complete and in compliance with Community rules applicable.

10 The CE marking process

A manufacturer is considered knowledgeable and competent in his particular field of expertise and is expected to bring a high degree of professionalism to the design, production and supply of his product. For compliance purposes, a manufacturer must demonstrate 'due-diligence' with respect to the requirements of the regulations. The following is an outline CE marking process:

1. identify the directive(s) applicable to the product
2. identify the entry route of products into the EEA; imported goods must meet European requirements and should not be assumed to comply even if marked with other international safety marks
3. establish the compliance schedule and action dates during design and production
4. identify the 'route to compliance', either through:

   a. self-certification and use of relevant harmonised European standards
   b. technical assessment or technical construction file, with or without notified body approval
   c. notified body involvement and approval of the system of design and/or production.

5. identify any national requirements of the destination country; these may still exist in Europe and affect the products design prior to market placement

6. design the product to comply with the essential safety requirements of applicable directive(s)[4]

7. where applicable, work with the notified body to complete the design analyses, the system and document assessments, and the product compliance testing. Ensure the applicable conformity assessment procedures are satisfied

8. prepare the supporting technical documentation required by the directive to demonstrate compliance

9. draw up the declaration of conformity for signature by the organisations 'nominated representative'[5]

10. affix the CE mark to the product and/or its packaging and accompanying documentation

11 The EC declaration of conformity

The EC declaration of conformity (D of C) is the manufacturer's statement that he has fulfilled the requirements of all the Community harmonisation legislation relating to his product. The declaration identifies the product or type (for traceability) and all the legislation and standards (in whole or in part) with which conformity is declared.

As an example, the requirements for a declaration of conformity from Annex III of the Low Voltage Directive are given below. In all cases, refer to the directive(s) specific to the product to determine the actual requirements.

Low Voltage Directive 2006/95/EC Annex III

B.   EC declaration of conformity

The EC declaration of conformity must contain the following elements:

- name and address of the manufacturer or his authorized representative established within the Community,
- a description of the electrical equipment,
- reference to the authorized standards,
- where appropriate, references to the specifications with which conformity is declared,
- identification of the signatory who has been empowered to enter into commitments on behalf of the manufacturer or his authorized representative established within the Community,
- the last two digits of the year in which the CE marking was affixed.

In cases where a third party has been involved, the notified body registration number must be put on the declaration of conformity. In the case of the Pressure Equipment Directive the CE marking label must contain system pressure limit data and the notified body registration number.

---

[4] National differences may be identified within harmonised standards.

[5] The nominated representative is an individual authorised to commit the organisation legally and is the person to whom the authorities will refer in the first instance.

Where an authorised representative acts for a manufacturer, the authorised representative signs the declaration of conformity on behalf of the manufacturer.

The D of C is an integral part of the technical documentation required by a directive and must be retained by the manufacturer or his authorised representative, for the authorities on request. For some directives, e.g. the Pressure Equipment Directive, it is mandatory to issue a copy of the D of C when supplying the pressure component or product. Often, a manufacturer includes a copy of their D of C in the supplied documentation.

12 CE Marking – getting started

Figure 2 *identifies* six key questions for a product manufacturer to consider at the start of the CE compliance process.

Fig. 2. Key compliance questions

The manufacturer should:

1. determine what type of product he produces, e.g. electrical equipment, machinery, medical device
2. determine the intended market sector and the applicable marking scheme
3. identify the applicable legislation and the *essential requirements*
4. decide if harmonised standards are to be used for the technical solutions, and if so, which; if not, the alternative(s) that will be used

5. determine which conformity assessment procedures are allowed by the applicable directive(s)
6. determine the required compliance documentation to draw up and the content of the declaration of conformity.

12.1 Product safety considerations

The manufacturer, in meeting the *essential requirements* must assess his product with respect to *potential use and foreseeable misuse* when the product is operated and maintained as stated in the supporting literature. Foreseeable misuse should be considered if this is likely due to the nature of the product. Product designers should consider the following:

1. personnel affected by the product
2. production manufacturing controls to ensure that product conforms to and maintains the design safety intention
3. storage and transport
4. deployment and recovery
5. installation and commissioning
6. service and maintenance
7. disposal
8. product manuals and safety information, and the language(s) used.

13 CE compliance of a complex product

Let us assume that a manufacturer produces a large complex system that comprises electrical equipment, moving machinery and pressure containment systems, and by virtue of the integrated electrical and electronic equipment electromagnetic compatibility must also be assessed.

The manufacturer conducts a full risk assessment of his product against, for example EN ISO 14121 (ISO 2007), and draws up a list of potential directives and standards that cover the product type and the hazards exposed. A review of the scope of the directives enables the manufacturer to decide whether his product is within scope or not. The decisions taken are recorded in the product's technical documentation as evidence of 'due-diligence' in meeting the *essential requirements*.

For a product whose predominant risks are electrical in nature the Low Voltage Directive (EC 2006b) (LVD) will apply. The manufacturer reviews the LVD and finds that it applies to systems whose *voltage rating* falls within the range of 50V ac to 1,000V ac and 75V dc to 1,500V dc, therefore his complex system is within scope. The manufacturer notes that the LVD covers *all* hazards associated with the electrical equipment and not just those of an electrical nature.

For machinery, an interconnection of parts, one of which moves under power, causes the complex product to fall within the scope of the Machinery Directive (EC 2006a) (MD). *All* hazards posed by the machinery are subject to the Essential Health and Safety Requirements (EHSR) relating to the design and construction of machinery and given in Annex I of the Machinery Directive. Note that apparatus that moves under purely manual effort is out of scope of the Machinery Directive, except for manually powered lifting equipment.

The manufacturer decides that his complex apparatus and its installation pose prominent moving machinery and electrical hazards and is, therefore, both a machine and electrical equipment, therefore is subject to the *essential requirements* of both the MD and the LVD.

The complex machine incorporates a pressurised system that moves a heavy mechanical load, therefore the manufacturer reviews the Pressure Equipment Directive (EC 1997) (PED) and notes that it applies to pressure equipment having a maximum allowable pressure (PS) > 0.5 bar. It is noted that the PED applies to fluids, gases and vapours under pressure, and combinations of them.

Being a pressure *system* rather than a *component*, a 'global' assessment is required against the predetermined criteria in the PED. Assessment is based on fluid group (Group 1 or 2), pressure (PS) and system volume (V), with PS.V results in *bar-litres*. The system contains hydraulic oil at a maximum working pressure of 133 bar, and nitrogen gas at 68 bar in a volume of 50 litres. The highest system risk determines system category and this is on the gas (Group 2 fluid) side, with a PS.V result of 3,400 bar-litres. PED Annex 2 Table 2 places the system in Category IV so a notified body is required in the conformity assessment process.

Because our complex assembly contains complex electrical and electronic equipment it is susceptible to electromagnetic phenomena and may suffer interference or interruption from the system itself, or from co-located systems, or may interfere with those systems. The electromagnetic compatibility of the assembly will therefore be addressed in accordance with European EMC standards for industrial environments. Note that whilst the EMC Directive is not a safety directive, it is a CE marking directive and therefore applicable to the assembly.

Table 2 provides a compliance decision matrix for our complex product, identifying the applicable directives and the route to compliance. The matrix can be used to communicate compliance decisions to the organisation, and should be incorporated in the Safety Management Plan as well as the technical documentation.

Compliance with the Low Voltage and Machinery Directives will be self-declared following Module A conformity assessment procedure. For the EMC Directive the manufacturer has decided to include a notified body in the compliance process to review, underwrite and reinforce the manufacturer's EMC technical assessment.

Compliance with the Pressure Equipment Directive will be declared after (mandatory) notified body involvement. Assessing the pressure containment system as being in Category IV of the PED the manufacturer chooses to follow Module H1 conformity assessment procedure. This decision is based on the fact that the organisation both operates a certified quality system covering design and production, and produces apparatus on a regular basis. The Pressure Equipment Directive provides alternative conformity modules for CAT IV equipment, e.g. Module G, however Module G requires unit verification by a notified body, rendering this procedure inflexible since it requires notified body personnel to be available according to the manufacturer's production schedule, which is unlikely.

Table 2. Compliance decision matrix

Applicable CE marking directives	Low Voltage 2006/95/EC	Machinery 2006/42/EC	Pressure Equipment 97/23/EC	Electromagnetic Compatibility 2004/108/EC
Pressure system category			IV	
Conformity route: self-declaration or notified body	SD	SD	NB	SD
Conformity assessment module applied	A	A	H1	A
Technical file, technical construction file or technical assessment file	TF	TCF	TF	TAF
Technical file/ technical assessment to notified body		✗	✓	✓
Declaration of incorporation		✗		
Declaration of conformity	✓ (A single declaration covering all directives)			
Declaration of conformity to include notified body number		✗	✓	✓

The decision matrix identifies no requirement for notified body involvement for the Machinery Directive because the product is not 'special equipment' according to the Machinery Directive (EC 2006a) Article 12 and Annex IV. Also, because our complex product is not 'partially completed' equipment for incorporation into other apparatus, a declaration of incorporation (D of I) drawn up in accordance with Annex IIB of the Machinery Directive is not required.

For each CE marking directive the manufacturer assembles the technical documentation demonstrating the product's compliance and keeps it for the period specified by the directive(s); in our case for ten years after the shipment of the last product of the type.

The content of the technical documentation required by directives varies considerably; however, the technical documentation models are broadly similar so, by way of introduction, the Low Voltage Directive is cited here:

The manufacturer shall establish the technical documentation. The documentation shall make it possible to assess the product's conformity to the relevant requirements, and shall include an adequate analysis and assessment of the risk(s). The technical documentation shall specify the applicable requirements and cover, as far as relevant for the assessment, the design, manufacture and operation of the product. The technical documentation shall, wherever applicable, contain at least the following elements:

- A general description of the product
- Conceptual design and manufacturing drawings and schemes of components, sub-assemblies, circuits, etc.
- Descriptions and explanations necessary for the understanding of those drawings and schemes and the operation of the product
- A list of harmonised standards and/or other relevant technical specifications, the references of which have been published in the Official Journal of the European Union, applied in full or in part, and the descriptions of the solutions adopted to meet the essential requirements of the legislative instruments where those harmonised standards have not been applied. In the event of partly applied harmonised standards, the technical documentation shall specify the parts which have been applied
- Results of design calculations made, examinations carried out, etc., and test reports.

Figure 3 illustrates the document flow leading to the declaration of conformity of our complex apparatus. The requirements stem from the four principal directives and only when all the routes to conformity are followed and the documentation is drawn up in accordance with each directive can the CE mark be affixed.

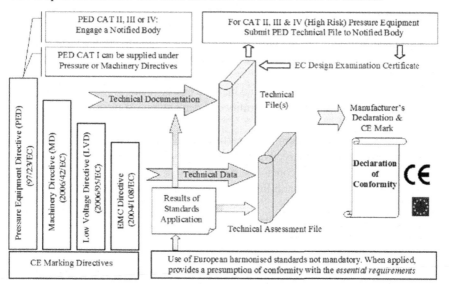

Fig. 3. Complex product-conformity assessment for four principal directives

Conformity with the PED requires submission of the technical file to a notified body who, when satisfied that it meets the *essential requirements*, issues an EC Type Examination Certificate that entitles the manufacturer to produce copies of the pressure system until the certificate expires. During the period of certification, the notified body conducts scheduled and unscheduled annual audits of the manufacturer's quality systems to ensure ongoing compliance.

For the EMC Directive (EC 2004), the size of the complex machine prevents it being tested fully against the EMC standards, so conformity is based on EMC testing conducted in accordance with generic EMC industrial environment standards and notified body assessment of the manufacturer's EMC technical assessment file.

Compliance evidence to satisfy all directives is derived from a very wide range of sources. Our complex machine technical file will, as a minimum, include the following data:

- a product description
- the safety rationale adopted to ensure compliance of the machine in the user environment
- applicable EU legislation and UK statutory instruments
- a list of the machinery directive essential health and safety requirements and the essential requirements of other directive(s) complied with
- European standards, international standards, etc. applied
- safety management plan(s)
- hazard analysis and risk assessment for machinery
- facilities and services requirements including electrical power supplies
- machine access, working platforms, ladders, hot and noisy areas, barriers, overhead hazards, trip hazards, maintenance lighting, etc.
- lifting equipment and lifting register, special tools, handling aids
- escape and emergency facilities (emergency stopping, egress, lighting, signage, fire doors, noise control areas, safety training)
- list of safety related parts
- component safety approvals and materials safety data
- supplier declarations of conformity and declarations of incorporation
- supplier data: test results, etc.
- notified body type examination certification
- pressure equipment directive technical file (includes hazard and risk assessment for the pressure containment system)
- electromagnetic compatibility directive technical assessment file
- design safety test results
- production safety test results
- software safety analysis and test results
- safety audit results (commissioning audit – physical)
- list of supplied manuals/user instructions covering operation, maintenance and disposal

- manufacturer's declaration of conformity signed by the organisation's nominated person

Production line safety tests typically include:

- pressure system hydrostatic test
- earth bonding test
- operation of the emergency stop system, emergency lighting, system interlocks, etc.
- power supply trips, warnings, alarms, etc.

14 CE marking summary

CE marking is mandatory. There is a legal duty for a producer to comply with the *essential requirements* specified in the applicable legislation if:

1. The equipment is intended for supply to the European Economic Area (EEA) and
2. The product falls within the scope of a CE marking directive.

14.1 Key points

- Technical harmonisation of products is limited to the *essential requirements*
- Only products fulfilling the *essential requirements* may enter the market
- Application of harmonized standards provides a presumption of conformity to the *essential requirements*
- The application of harmonized standards is voluntary: manufacturers may choose any solution that provides compliance with the *essential requirements*
- In demonstrating conformity with the *essential requirements*, manufacturers may choose whatever conformity assessment procedures are provided for in the directives.
- A manufacturer must assemble the specified technical documentation and he or his authorised representative must retain it for the minimum period set down in the directive(s).
- For certain types of products posing high levels of risk, a notified body must be involved in the conformity process.
- Except in certain instances, for systems and products CE + CE ≠ CE. Systems and assemblies must be assessed as one integrated product.

- Product literature is an *essential requirement* and *must* be supplied since it informs the user how to install, operate and maintain the product safely.
- Products must comply when first made available on the market of the European Economic Area, regardless of the instrument of transfer, e.g. sale, loan, lease, gift.
- All imported products, new and second-hand, must comply with CE marking legislation when first made available on the European marketplace.
- It is an offence to 'make available' a non-compliant product, or to affix the CE mark fraudulently.
- CE marking legislation places legal obligations on all persons in the supply chain. If the manufacturer cannot be identified, or if he is not resident in the EC and no authorised representative has been appointed, the importer is responsible.
- The CE mark is not a safety mark. It is a *claim* that a product complies with legal obligations allowing it free movement on the market of the EEA.
- Since all products subject to New Approach Directives carry CE marking, the marking is not intended to serve commercial purposes.
- The CE marking is not a mark of origin, as it does not indicate that the product was manufactured in the Community.

References

BSI (2006a) BS EN60950-1:2006 Information technology equipment – Safety – Part 1: General requirements

BSI (2006b) BS EN60204-1:2006 Safety of machinery – Electrical equipment of machines – Part 1: General requirements

EC (1985) Council directive on the approximation of the laws, regulations and administrative provisions of the member states concerning liability for defective products. 85/374/EEC

EC (1993) Council Directive 93/68/EEC 22 July 1993 amending Directives 87/404/EEC (simple pressure vessels), 88/378/EEC (safety of toys), 89/106/EEC (construction products), 89/336/EEC (electromagnetic compatibility), 89/392/EEC (machinery), 89/686/EEC (personal protective equipment), 90/384/EEC (non-automatic weighing instruments), 90/385/EEC (active implantable medicinal devices), 90/396/EEC (appliances burning gaseous fuels), 91/263/EEC (telecommunications terminal equipment), 92/42/EEC (new hot-water boilers fired with liquid or gaseous fuels) and 73/23/EEC (electrical equipment designed for use within certain voltage limits)

EC (1995) European Parliament and Council Directive 95/16/EC of 29 June 1995 on the approximation of the laws of the Member States relating to lifts

EC (1997) Directive 97/23/EC of the European Parliament and of the Council of 29 May 1997 on the approximation of the laws of the Member States concerning pressure equipment.

EC (1998) Directive 98/34/EC of the European Parliament and of the Council of 22 June 1998 laying down a procedure for the provision of information in the field of technical standards and regulations and of rules on Information Society services

EC (2000) Guide to the implementation of directives based on the New Approach and the Global Approach. European Commission. http://ec.europa.eu/enterprise/policies/single-market-goods/files/blue-guide/guidepublic_en.pdf. Accessed 2 September 2010

EC (2001) Directive 2001/95/EC of the European Parliament and of the Council of 3 December 2001 on general product safety

EC (2004) Directive 2004/108/EC of the European Parliament and of the Council of 15 December 2004 on the approximation of the laws of the Member States relating to electromagnetic compatibility and repealing Directive 89/336/EEC

EC (2006a) Directive 2006/42/EC of the European Parliament and of the Council of 17 May 2006 on machinery, and amending Directive 95/16/EC (recast)

EC (2006b) Directive 2006/95/EC of the European Parliament and of the Council of 12 December 2006 on the harmonisation of the laws of Member States relating to electrical equipment designed for use within certain voltage limits

EC (2007) Guidelines on the application of directive 2006/95/EC. http://www.ilnas.public.lu/fr/publications/surveillance-marche/guides/lvd-guide-en.pdf. Accessed 2 September 2010

EC (2008) Decision 768/2008/EC of the European Parliament and of the Council of 9 July 2008

EC (2010a) European Commission website. http://ec.europa.eu/enterprise/sectors/index_en.htm. Accessed 2 September 2010

EC (2010b) Guide to application of the machinery directive 2006/42/EC. http://ec.europa.eu/enterprise/sectors/mechanical/files/machinery/guide_application_directive_2006-42-ec-2nd_edit_6-2010_en[1].pdf. Accessed 2 September 2010

EC (2010c) Guide for the EMC directive 2004/108/EC. http://ec.europa.eu/enterprise/sectors/electrical/files/emc_guide__updated_20100208_v3_en.pdf. Accessed 2 September 2010

HMSO (1987) Consumer Protection Act Chapter 43

ISO (2007) BS EN ISO14121 Part 1 – Principles, and Part 2 – Practical guidance and examples of methods

Introduction and Revision of IEC 61508

Ron Bell

ESC Ltd

London, UK

Abstract Over the past twenty-five years there have been a number of initiatives worldwide to develop guidelines and standards to enable the safe exploitation of programmable electronic systems used for safety applications. In the context of industrial applications (to distinguish from aerospace and military applications) a major initiative has been focused on IEC 61508, and other standards based on IEC 61508, which have emerged as key international standards.

This paper considers some of the key features of IEC 61508 (IEC 2000), which has now been available for over ten years, and indicates the main changes that have been incorporated into the new Edition 2 (IEC 2010a), published in April 2010.

1 Background

The International Electrotechnical Commission (IEC) set up a Task Group in 1985 to assess the viability of developing a generic standard for programmable electronic systems to be used for safety applications, the outcome of which was the setting up of a working group to develop an holistic, systems based, approach. A working group had previously been set up to deal with safety-related software. These two working groups collaborated on the development of an international standard that was to become IEC 61508 (IEC 2000).

The original scope of the Task Group (programmable electronic systems used for safety applications) was extended to include all types of electro-technical based technologies (electrical, electronic and programmable electronic systems (E/E/PE systems)).

Parts 1 to 7 of IEC 61508 were published during the period 1998-2000. In 2005 IEC/TR 61508-0 (IEC 2005) was published. A review process to update and improve the standard was initiated in 2002 and was completed with the publication of IEC 61508 Edition 2 (IEC 2010a) in April 2010.

C. Dale, T. Anderson (eds.), *Advances in Systems Safety*, DOI 10.1007/978-0-85729-133-2_16,

2 Structure of IEC 61508

The overall title of IEC 61508 is 'Functional safety of electrical, electronic and programmable electronic (E/E/PE) safety-related systems'. The Parts are as listed in Table 1.

Table 1. The Parts of IEC 61508

Part	Title
0	Functional safety and IEC 61508[1]
1	General requirements
2	Requirements for electrical/electronic/programmable electronic safety-related systems
3	Software requirements
4	Definitions and abbreviations
5	Examples of methods for the determination of safety integrity levels
6	Guidelines on the application of parts 2 and 3
7	Overview of techniques and measures

Parts 1, 2, 3 contain all the normative requirements[2] and some informative requirements. Parts 0, 5, 6 and 7 do not contain any normative requirements.

Parts 1, 2, 3 and 4 of IEC 61508 are IEC basic safety publications. One of the responsibilities of IEC Technical Committees is, wherever practicable, to make use of IEC 61508, in its role as a basic publication, in the preparation of their own sector or product standards that have E/E/PE safety-related systems within their scope.

IEC 61508 is both a stand-alone standard and can also be used as the basis for sector and product standards. In its latter role, it has been used to develop standards for the process, nuclear and railway industries and for machinery and power drive systems. It has influenced, and will continue to influence, the development of E/E/PE safety-related systems and products across all sectors. This concept is illustrated in Figure 1.

The application of IEC 61508 as a standalone standard includes the use of the standard:

- as a set of general requirements for E/E/PE safety-related systems where no application sector or product standards exist or where they are not appropriate
- by suppliers of E/E/PE components and subsystems for use in all sectors (e.g. hardware and software of sensors, smart actuators, programmable controllers)

---

[1] Part 0 has the status of a Technical Report and is purely informative.

[2] In IEC standards a normative requirement is prefaced by 'shall' and if that requirement is relevant in the particular application then it is necessary to comply with the requirement. A requirement prefaced by 'should' is informative and can be considered as a recommendation but is not normative in respect of compliance to relevant requirements in the standard.

- by system integrators to meet user specifications for E/E/PE safety-related systems
- by users to specify requirements in terms of the safety functions to be performed together with the performance requirements of those safety functions
- to facilitate the maintenance of the 'as designed' safety integrity of E/E/PE safety-related systems
- to provide the technical framework for conformity assessment and certification services as a basis for carrying out assessments of safety lifecycle activities.

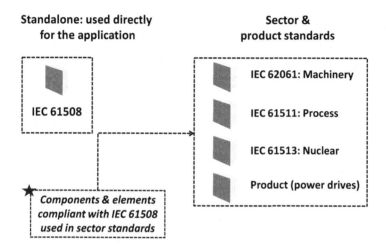

Standalone: used directly
for the application

Sector &
product standards

IEC 61508

IEC 62061: Machinery

IEC 61511: Process

IEC 61513: Nuclear

Product (power drives)

Components & elements
compliant with IEC 61508
used in sector standards

Fig. 1. Standalone and sector/product standards

Product or application sector international standards based on IEC 61508:

- are aimed at system designers, system integrators and users
- take account of sector-specific practice
- use terminology applicable in the sector to increase understanding for its intended users
- may specify particular constraints appropriate for the sector
- usually rely on the requirements of IEC 61508 for the design of subsystems.

3 Scope of IEC 61508

IEC 61508 is mainly concerned with E/E/PE safety-related systems whose failure could have an impact on the safety of persons and/or the environment. However, it was recognized that the consequences of failure could have serious economic implications and in such cases the standard could be used to specify any E/E/PE system used for the protection of equipment or product. This has important implications since it means that IEC 61508, which is identified with functional safety, can be used for the specification and implementation of systems where the functional performance parameter is not safety but, for example, environmental protection or asset protection.

Some of the key features of IEC 61508 are set out below.

- It enables the development of product and sector international standards, dealing with E/E/PE safety-related systems. This should lead to a high level of consistency (for example, of underlying principles, terminology etc.) both within and across application sectors; this will have both safety and economic benefits.
- It provides a method for the development of the safety requirements specification necessary to achieve the required functional safety for E/E/PE safety-related systems.
- It uses safety integrity levels (SILs) for specifying the target level of safety integrity for the safety functions to be implemented by the E/E/PE safety-related systems.
- It adopts a risk-based approach for the determination of the safety integrity level requirements.
- It sets numerical target failure measures for E/E/PE safety-related systems that are linked to the safety integrity levels.
- It sets a lower limit on the target failure measures, in a dangerous mode of failure, that can be claimed for a single E/E/PE safety-related system. For E/E/PE safety-related systems operating in:
  - a low demand mode of operation, the lower limit is set at an average probability of failure of 10^{-5} to perform its design function on demand
  - a high demand or continuous mode of operation, the lower limit is set at a average frequency of dangerous failure of 10^{-9} per hour.

4 Concept of functional safety

Safety is defined as the freedom from unacceptable risk of physical injury or of damage to the health of people, either directly or indirectly, as a result of damage to property or to the environment.

Functional safety is part of the overall safety that depends on a system or equipment operating correctly in response to its inputs. For example, activation of a level switch in a tank containing a flammable liquid, which causes a valve to close and prevent flammable liquid from entering the tank, is an instance of functional safety.

5 Strategy to achieve functional safety

The strategy for achieving functional safety is made up of the following key elements:

- management of functional safety
- technical requirements for relevant phases of the applicable safety lifecycles
- Functional Safety Assessment (FSA)
- competence of persons.

IEC 61508 uses three safety lifecycles in order that all relevant phases are addressed:

- the Overall Safety Lifecycle (see Figure 2)
- the E/E/PE System Safety Lifecycle (see Figure 3)
- the Software Safety Lifecycle (see Figure 4).

In order to deal in a systematic manner with all the activities necessary to achieve the required safety integrity for the E/E/PE safety-related systems, IEC 61508 adopts the Overall Safety Lifecycle indicated in Figure 3 (IEC 61508/Edition 2 shown) as the technical framework. The Overall Safety Lifecycle specified in IEC 61508 should be used as a basis for claiming conformance to the standard, but a different Overall Safety Lifecycle can be used to that given in Figure 3, providing the objectives and requirements of each clause of the standard are met.

The overall safety lifecycle encompasses the following risk reduction model:

- E/E/PE safety-related systems
- other risk reduction measures[3].

The portion of the overall safety lifecycle dealing with E/E/PE safety-related systems is expanded and shown in Figure 3. This is termed the E/E/PE System Safety Lifecycle and forms the technical framework for IEC 61508-2. The Software Safety Lifecycle is shown in Figure 4 and forms the technical framework for IEC 61508-3.

It is very important to recognize that the Overall E/E/PE System Safety and Software Safety Lifecycle figures are simplified views of reality and as such do not show all the iterations relating to specific phases or between phases. Iteration, however, is an essential and vital part of development through the Overall E/E/PE System Safety and Software Safety Lifecycles.

Activities relating to the management of functional safety, verification and functional safety assessment are not shown on the Overall E/E/PE System Safety and Software Safety Lifecycles. This has been done in order to reduce the com-

---

[3] Whilst IEC 61508 provides design requirements for the achievement of functional safety for E/E/PE safety-related systems, it does not provide design requirements for 'other risk reduction measures' but does take into account the risk reduction achieved by such measures.

plexity of the safety lifecycle activities. These activities will need to be applied at the relevant phases of the safety lifecycles.

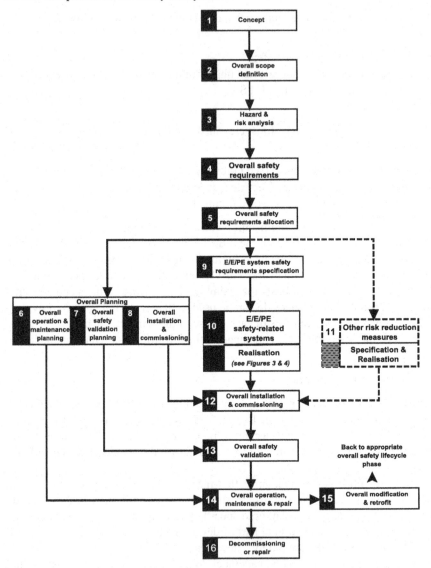

Fig. 2. Overall Safety Lifecycle from IEC 61508/Edition 2

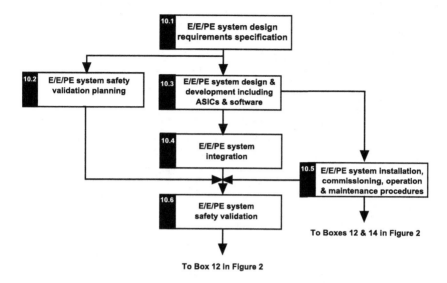

Fig. 3. E/E/PE system safety lifecycle (in realisation phase) from IEC 61508/Edition 2

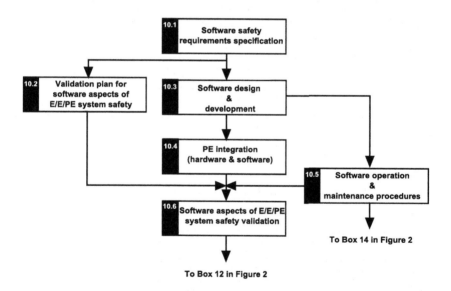

Fig. 4. Software safety lifecycle (in realisation phase) from IEC 61508/Edition 2

Evidence of the need to adopt an approach that covers all phases of the Overall Safety Lifecycle is illustrated in a study undertaken by the UK Health and Safety Executive (HSE 2003). The study analyzed a number of accidents and incidents involving safety-related control systems. Figure 5 shows the primary cause of failure for each lifecycle phase[4].

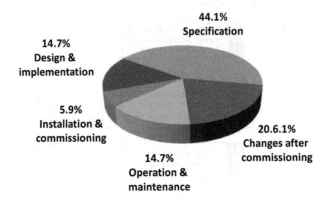

Fig. 5. Primary cause, by phase, of control system failures

The analysis suggests that most control system failures may have their root cause in an inadequate specification. In some cases this was because insufficient hazard analysis of the equipment under control had been carried out; in others it was because the impact on the specification of a critical failure mode of the control system had not been assessed.

Based on the HSE study, more than 60% of failures were 'built in' to the safety-related system before being taken into service. Whilst the primary causes by phase will vary depending upon the sector and complexity of the application, what is self-evident is that it is important that all phases of the lifecycle be addressed if functional safety is to be achieved.

6 Essence of functional safety

A cornerstone of functional safety is the safety function. The safety function is defined as follows:

> 'Function to be implemented by an E/E/PE safety-related system or other risk reduction measures, that is intended to achieve or maintain a safe state for the equipment under control in respect of a specific hazardous event.'

There is a need to specify the functional safety performance requirements for each safety function and this is the objective of the E/E/PE system safety requirements

---

[4] It is acknowledged that because of the small sample size the results of the analysis have low statistical significance, and therefore care needs to be taken in using these results to generalise for all control system failures. Even so, there are many useful lessons to be learned from summaries of incidents such as these.

specification which contains the requirements for all the safety functions being carried out by the E/E/PE safety-related system.

If the safety function is performed the hazardous event will not take place. The safety function is determined from the hazard analysis. It is the safety function that determines *what has to be done* to achieve or maintain a safe state for the equipment under control.

IEC 61508 adopts a risk-based approach to the development of the specification of the required safety performance of each safety function. The safety performance is referred to as the safety integrity and is determined from the risk assessment. This is illustrated in Figure 6.

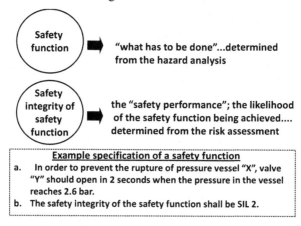

Fig. 6. Safety function and safety integrity of the safety function

7 Safety-related systems

A safety-related system is a system that is capable of carrying out the various specified safety functions and also capable of carrying them out with the required safety integrity. It is the safety integrity requirement of the safety function that sets the safety integrity requirements for the safety-related system. A safety-related system will carry out many safety functions and must be of sufficient safety integrity to carry out the safety function with the highest safety integrity requirement (unless special measures are taken).

8 Safety Integrity Levels

The failure categories in IEC 61508 relate to failures arising from both random hardware failures and systematic failures. The challenge to anyone designing a complex system such as a programmable electronic system is to determine how much rigour/assurance/confidence is necessary for the specified safety performance level. IEC 61508 tackles this on the following basis:

- that it is possible to quantify the random hardware failures
- that is not usually possible to quantify systematic failures.

IEC 61508 sets four Safety Integrity Levels (SILs). SIL 1 is the lowest and SIL 4 is the highest level of safety integrity. Each SIL has a specified target failure measure. The target SIL of the safety function(s) determines the measures that need to be taken in the design of the safety-related system.

Hardware Safety Integrity. This is achieved through meeting the quantified target failure measure for random failures together with meeting the Architectural Constraints for the specified SIL. The latter means that specified fault tolerance requirements (redundancy), graded to the SIL, have to be met but with a reduced fault tolerance requirement the greater the achieved Safe Failure Fraction[5].

Systematic Safety Integrity. 'Packages' of measures are used for different systematic failure mechanisms and these are in general qualitative measures with increasing rigour, assurance and confidence the higher the SIL.

Safety Integrity is made up of Hardware Safety Integrity (in relation to random failures) and Systematic Safety Integrity (in relation to systematic failures).

The above concepts are shown in Figure 7.

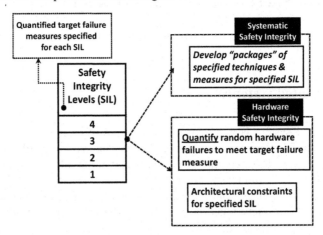

Fig. 7. Design strategy to achieve a specified SIL

---

[5] Safe Failure Fraction (SFF) is the ratio of the average failure rates of (safe failures plus dangerous detected failures) to (safe failures plus dangerous failures). The higher the ratio the greater the likelihood that a failure arising would be a safe failure or dangerous failure that has been detected.

The target failure measures for E/E/PE safety-related systems carrying safety functions of specified SILs are set out in Tables 2 and 3. It can be seen from these Tables that the SILs are linked to the target failure measures depending upon the mode of operation.

Table 2. Safety integrity levels: target failure measures for a safety function operating in a low demand mode of operation

Safety integrity level	Average probability of a dangerous failure on demand of the safety function (PFD_{avg})
4	10^{-5} to $< 10^{-4}$
3	10^{-4} to $< 10^{-3}$
2	10^{-3} to $< 10^{-2}$
1	10^{-2} to $< 10^{-1}$

Table 3. Safety integrity levels: target failure measures for a safety function operating in a high demand or continuous mode of operation

Safety integrity level	Probability of dangerous failure per hour (PFH)
4	10^{-9} to $< 10^{-8}$
3	10^{-8} to $< 10^{-7}$
2	10^{-7} to $< 10^{-6}$
1	10^{-6} to $< 10^{-5}$

The mode of operation is an important concept and is the way in which a safety-related system is intended to be used, with respect to the frequency of demands made upon it, which may be either:

- low demand mode, where the frequency of demands for operation made on a safety-related system is no greater than one per year [and no greater than twice the proof-test frequency][6]
- high demand or continuous mode, where the frequency of demands for operation made on a safety-related system is greater than one per year [or greater than twice the proof-check frequency][6]

Safety functions operating in a:

- low demand mode of operation would typically be implemented by a protection system architecture (see Figure 8)
- high demand mode of operation would typically be implemented by a protection system architecture or a safety-related control system architecture (see Figure 8)
- continuous mode of operation would typically be implemented by safety-related control system architecture (see Figure 8).

---

[6] Criteria in square brackets not included in IEC 61508/Edition 2.

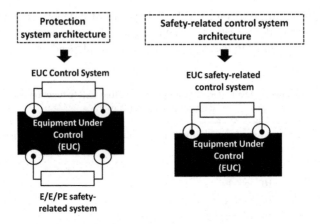

Fig. 8. Safety-related systems architectures

It should be noted that when determining the SIL, from a basis of knowing the target failure measure (which is established from the tolerable risk), the *demand rate* (i.e. the frequency the safety function is required to operate) is only relevant when the safety function is operating in a low demand mode of operation. It is not relevant when the safety function is operating in a high demand or continuous mode of operation.

9 Risk based approach

The required safety integrity of the E/E/PE safety-related system, with respect to a specific safety function, must be of such a level as to ensure that:

- the failure frequency of the safety-related systems is sufficiently low to prevent the hazardous event frequency exceeding that required to meet the tolerable risk, and/or
- the safety-related systems modify the consequences of the hazardous event to the extent required to meet the tolerable risk.

The failure frequency necessary to meet the tolerable risk, with respect to a specific safety function being carried out by the safety-related system, is determined taking into account any other risk reduction measures that are properly designed on functional safety criteria and properly managed throughout the life of the equipment.

The determination of this failure frequency, with respect to a specified safety function, allows the target failure measure to be determined and then the SIL to be established (from the target failure measure specified for each SIL in Table 2 or Table 3). The determination of the SIL for a specified safety function then allows the design process for the E/E/PE safety-related system to proceed (see Figure 7).

10 Revision of IEC 61508

As indicated in Section 1 of this paper, the review process to update and improve the standard was initiated in 2002 and was completed with the publication of IEC 61508 Edition 2 (IEC 2010a) in April 2010[7]. This section provides a summary of the revision process.

The procedure for revising an IEC standard is as follows:

1. Request from National Committees their views on the standard.
2. Based on the views of National Committees, prepare a Committee Draft (CD) and distribute to National Committees for their comments.
3. Assess National Committee comments from the CD consultation, prepare Committee Draft for Vote (CDV) and distribute to National Committees for vote.
4. If the voting results from the CDV consultation reach the required acceptance criteria, prepare Final Committee Draft International Standard (FDIS).
5. If the voting results from the FDIS voting exercise achieve the required acceptance criteria then the standard can be prepared for publication.

A key consideration during the revision process has been the need to ensure that any changes proposed added real value to the standard and to balance any perceived benefits made to the standard against the economic costs to users of the standard of implementing the changes.

Some of the key changes are considered below. Further information on IEC 61508, including Frequently Asked Questions, and a redline version that highlights the changes between Editions 1 and 2, can be found at the IEC Functional Safety Zone (IEC 2010e). IEC 61508 Standards+ version (IEC 2010f) was also issued in April 2010 and:

- shows the revisions referenced to Edition 1
- provides hyperlinked notes explaining the changes. This facility should prove particularly useful for those currently using IEC 61508/Edition 1.

10.1 Terminology

There have been several important changes to the definitions and it is important that where changes have been made they are examined to assess the implications since the change may affect the interpretation as understood in IEC 61508/Edition 1.

For example, the term *subsystem* was not a defined term in IEC 61508/Edition 1 but the usage of the term was not consistent; in IEC 61508/Edition 2 this is a defined term. A key feature of the definition is that a

---

[7] Parts 1-7 have been revised. Part 0 is currently planned for revision, beginning in 2010.

dangerous failure of the subsystem, with respect to a specified safety function, will result in the failure of the safety function. It should also be noted that for correct usage of the term it will be necessary to have knowledge of the dangerous failures associated with the specified safety function. That is, there is a need to know the application or specify the assumptions on which the dangerous failures are based in order to determine, for example, whether an element is also a subsystem.

Other examples of key definitions that have been changed or are new include *dangerous failure, safe failure, element* and *element safety function*.

10.2 Architectural constraints

There are two possible Routes to compliance:

- Route 1_H, based on hardware fault tolerance and safe failure fraction concepts;
- Route 2_H, based on component reliability data from field feedback, increased confidence levels and hardware fault tolerance for specified safety integrity levels.

There have been changes to the way in which Route 1_H is applied and together with changes to the definitions of safe and dangerous failures, some differences in the calculation of safe failure fraction may arise compared to the method specified in IEC 61508/Edition 1.

Route 2_H is a new concept for IEC 61508 and if Route 2_H is selected then clause 7.4.4.3.1 of the standard specifies the requirements as follows:

- a hardware fault tolerance of 2 for a specified safety function of SIL 4 unless the conditions in clause 7.4.4.3.2 apply
- a hardware fault tolerance of 1 for a specified safety function of SIL 3 unless the conditions in clause 7.4.4.3.2 apply
- a hardware fault tolerance of 1 for a specified safety function of SIL 2, operating in a high demand or continuous mode of operation, unless the conditions in clause 7.4.4.3.2 apply
- a hardware fault tolerance of 0 for a specified safety function of SIL 2 operating in a low demand mode of operation
- a hardware fault tolerance of 0 for a specified safety function of SIL 1.

Clause 7.4.4.3.2 specifies, *for type A elements only*, if it is determined that by following the HFT requirements specified in 7.4.4.3.1, for the situation where an HFT greater than 0 is required, additional failures would be introduced and lead to a decrease in the overall safety of the EUC, then a safer alternative architecture with reduced HFT may be implemented. In such a case this shall be justified and documented. The justification shall provide evidence that:

- following the requirements in 7.4.4.3.1 would introduce additional failures and would lead to a decrease in overall safety of the EUC, and

- if the HFT is reduced to 0 the failure modes, in the element carrying out the safety function, can be excluded because the associated dangerous failure rates are very low compared to the target failure measure for the safety function under consideration. That is, the sum of the dangerous failure frequencies of all serial elements, on which fault exclusion is being claimed, should not exceed 1% of the target failure measure. Furthermore the applicability of fault exclusions shall be justified considering the potential for systematic faults.

A note indicates that HFT is the preferred solution to achieve the required confidence that a robust architecture has been achieved.

If Route 2_H is selected then reliability data used for quantifying the effect of random hardware failures shall:

- be based on field feedback
- be collected in accordance with published standards
- be evaluated to estimate uncertainty levels
- address the data uncertainties when calculating the target failure measure
- improve the system until there is a confidence greater than 90% that the target failure measure has been achieved.

All type B elements used in Route 2_H shall have, as a minimum, a diagnostic coverage of not less than 60 %.

10.3 Modes of operation

The criteria relating to when a safety function is operating in a low demand mode of operation or a high demand/continuous mode of operation have been changed: the requirements relating to the proof test frequency have been removed.

10.4 Systematic safety integrity

There are three possible Routes to compliance:

- Route 1_S, requirements for the avoidance (prevention) and requirements for the control of systematic faults[8]
- Route 2_S, evidence that the equipment is 'proven in use' (PIU)[8]
- Route 3_S, for pre-existing software elements only.

For compliance with IEC 61508-2 it is necessary to meet the requirements of Route 1_S or Route 2_S, and for pre-existing software elements, Route 3_S.

---

[8] This covers both hardware and software.

10.5 Systematic Capability

Systematic Capability is defined as 'a measure (expressed on a scale of SC 1 to SC 4) of the confidence that the systematic safety integrity of an element meets the requirements of the specified SIL, in respect of the specified element safety function'.

Additionally, the concept of *synthesis of elements* with defined Systematic Capability has been developed. This would allow two elements meeting the requirements of Systematic Capability of SC 1 (for example) to be considered as a composite element of systematic capability of SC 2 but is conditional on there being 'sufficient independence' between the two elements.

10.6 Security

Malevolent and unauthorized actions have to be addressed during the hazard and risk analysis. If a security threat is seen as being reasonably foreseeable, then a security threats analysis *should be carried out* and if security threats have been identified then a vulnerability analysis *should be undertaken* in order to specify security requirements.

The rationale for this policy is that other IEC/ISO standards will be referenced that address this subject in depth.

10.7 E/E/PE requirements specification

The E/E/PE requirements specification in the current Edition of IEC 61508 comprised a single specification (i.e. a single step process). Two specifications are proposed (i.e. a two step process):

- Step 1: develop the E/E/PE system safety requirements specification (in IEC 61508-1)
- Step 2: develop the E/E/PE system design requirements specification (in IEC 61508-2).

10.8 Digital communications

The proposed requirements have been further elaborated and now comprise the concept of White and Black Channel architectures. Briefly:

- in White Channel architectures the entire communication channel (including protocol, services & network components) have to comply with IEC 61508 and either IEC 61784-3 (IEC 2010b) or IEC 62280 (IEC 2010c and 2010d)
- in Black Channel architectures, the interfaces have to comply with IEC 61784-3 or IEC 62280 (including services & protocols).

10.9 Management of functional safety

The clause has been restructured and now provides more comprehensive normative requirements, including:

- appointment of one or more persons by an organisation with responsibility for one or more phases necessary for the achievement of functional safety of an E/E/PE safety-related system
- identification of all persons undertaking defined activities relevant to the achievement of functional safety of an E/E/PE safety-related system
- all those persons undertaking defined activities relevant to the achievement of functional safety of an E/E/PE safety-related system shall be competent for the duties they have to perform[9].

10.10 ASICS and integrated circuits

Requirements for ASICs are now included:

- an appropriate group of techniques and measures shall be used that are essential to prevent the introduction of faults during the design and development of ASICs
- techniques and measures that support the achievement of relevant properties are given in an informative Annex
- special architectural requirements for integrated circuits (ICs) with on-chip redundancy are given in a normative Annex.

---

[9] This change in the competence requirements in IEC 61508/Edition 2 extends the normative requirements for competence across all safety lifecycle activities. In IEC 61508/Edition 1, the normative requirement for competence was restricted to the Functional Safety Assessment activity.

10.11 Safety manual for compliant items

The proposed revision sets out requirements for suppliers of products who claim compliance with the standard. The purpose of the safety manual for compliant items is to document all the information, relating to a compliant item, which is required to enable the integration of the compliant item into a safety-related system, or a subsystem or element, in compliance with the requirements of the standard.

Producers have to provide a safety manual for each compliant item they supply and for which they claim compliance with IEC 61508. The supplier is required to document a justification for all the information in the safety manual.

It should be noted that failure modes can only be classified as being safe or dangerous when the application of the compliant item is known and the following is stated to highlight this fact:

'No claims shall be made in the safety manual, in respect of the hardware fault tolerance or the safe failure fraction or any other functional safety characteristic that is dependent on knowledge of safe and dangerous failure modes, unless the underlying assumptions, as to what constitute safe and dangerous failure modes, are clearly specified.'

10.12 Software

The following are the key changes to IEC 61508-3 (software):

- the introduction of the idea of desirable *properties* (such as completeness, correctness and predictability) for the output of each lifecycle phase
- provision of extended requirement for the selection and justification of software development tools
- allowing software elements which were not originally developed with safety in mind to be re-used in safety related applications by the provision of suitable evidence including evidence of successful use in other applications
- revision to the set of techniques and measures in Annexes A and B, to remove obsolete or little-used techniques and introduce current methods.

In summary, the revision of IEC 61508 has tackled a number of important issues and provided more options in seeking compliance.

Acknowledgments The author thanks the International Electrotechnical Commission (IEC) for permission to reproduce information from its international publication IEC 61508 ed.2.0 parts 1 to 7 (2010). All such extracts are copyright of IEC, Geneva, Switzerland. All rights reserved. Further information on the IEC is available from www.iec.ch. IEC has no responsibility for the placement and context in which the extracts and contents are reproduced by the author, nor is IEC in any way responsible for the other content or accuracy therein.

References

HSE (2003) Out of control: why control systems go wrong and how to prevent failure, 2nd edn. HSE Books. http://www.hse.gov.uk/pubns/books/hsg238.htm. Accessed 17 August 2010

IEC (2000) IEC 61508 Functional safety of electrical/electronic/programmable electronic safety-related systems, Parts 1 to 7. International Electrotechnical Commission

IEC (2005) IEC 61508 Functional safety of electrical/electronic/programmable electronic safety-related systems, Part 0. International Electrotechnical Commission

IEC (2010a) IEC 61508 Functional safety of electrical/electronic/programmable electronic safety-related systems, Parts 1 to 7, Edition 2.0. International Electrotechnical Commission

IEC (2010b) IEC 61784-3 Industrial communication networks – profiles – Part 3: functional safety fieldbuses – general rules and profile definitions, Edition 2.0. International Electrotechnical Commission

IEC (2010c) IEC 62280-1 Railway applications – communication, signalling and processing systems – part 1: safety-related communication in closed transmission systems. International Electrotechnical Commission

IEC (2010d) IEC 62280-2 Railway applications – communication, signalling and processing systems – part 2: safety-related communication in open transmission systems. International Electrotechnical Commission

IEC (2010e) IEC functional safety zone. http://www.iec.ch/zone/fsafety. Accessed 26 September 2010

IEC (2010f) S+ IEC 61508 ed2.0. http://www.iec.ch/functionalsafety. Accessed 26 September 2010

Are we there yet? A Practitioner's View of DO-178C/ED-12C

Dewi Daniels

SILVER ATENA

Malmesbury, UK

Abstract   RTCA DO-178B/EUROCAE ED-12B is the industry-accepted guidance for determining that the software aspects of airborne systems and equipment comply with airworthiness requirements. DO-178B/ED-12B, published in 1992, is being updated to DO-178C/ED-12C. Nearly six years in the making, DO-178C/ED-12C is expected to be completed in December 2010. It will be accompanied by a new set of supplements providing additional and much-needed guidance on tool qualification, model based development and verification, object-oriented technologies, and formal methods. Written by a member of the DO-178C/ED-12C editorial team who is also a practising software developer and verifier, this paper provides a practitioner's view of the new standard and its supplements. It explains how they will affect your organisation, focusing on the practical implications of the many changes between DO-178B/ED-12B and DO-178C/ED-12C.

1 What is DO-178B?

RTCA DO-178B/EUROCAE ED-12B (RTCA 1992, referred to as DO-178B in the remainder of this paper) is one of the most influential documents in safety critical software development. Most of the software flying on commercial aircraft has to satisfy the objectives of DO-178B[1].

DO-178B was first published in 1992. It is published jointly by RTCA, Inc. as DO-178B and by the European Organization for Civil Aviation Equipment (EUROCAE) as ED-12B. It was written by a joint EUROCAE Working Group 12 (WG-12) and RTCA Special Committee 167 (SC-167), which had over 250 par-

---

[1] Formally, the FAA and EASA recognize DO-178B as an acceptable means of compliance to their respective regulations for software aspects of certification. Applicants can propose alternate means of compliance, but these have to be agreed with the certification authorities.

C. Dale, T. Anderson (eds.), *Advances in Systems Safety*, DOI 10.1007/978-0-85729-133-2_17,

ticipants. The document presents government and industry consensus on recommended practices for airborne software development and verification.

Some aspects of DO-178B worth emphasising are:

- It is an objective based document. It tells applicants what they need to achieve rather than prescribing specific software development life cycles, techniques and practices.
- It defines five software levels, ranging from Level A (software whose anomalous behaviour would cause or contribute to a catastrophic failure condition for the aircraft) to Level E (software that has no effect on safety).
- It emphasises requirements based testing, i.e. a test strategy where the tests are developed from the software requirements. It does not require structural testing, i.e. a test strategy where the tests are developed from the source code.
- It uses structural code coverage analysis to:

    - ensure that the code structure has been exercised by the requirements-based testing to the extent required for the software level
    - support demonstration of absence of unintended behaviour
    - establish the thoroughness of the requirements based testing.

- Traceability is required between system requirements allocated to software, software requirements and source code (also between source code and object code for Level A), and between software requirements and test cases. This enables verification that all the requirements have been implemented and that there is no undocumented code.

DO-178B has proved to be very successful. The fact that DO-178B has remained unchanged for 18 years shows that the authors of DO-178B were successful in their goal of describing the principles of safety critical software development and assurance without tying the text to specific software technologies, which have changed enormously during that time.

More importantly, not a single aeroplane accident in passenger service has been ascribed to software failure. The author knows of one hull loss accident that occurred during flight test that was ascribed to (developmental) software and which unfortunately resulted in the loss of an Airbus A330 test aircraft and the death of all seven people on board (DGA 1994).

There have been a very small number of incidents in passenger service that have been ascribed to software failure. The best-documented example is probably an in-flight upset on a Boeing 777 near Perth, Australia, in 2005. A contributing factor was found to be a software anomaly that allowed inputs from a known faulty accelerometer to be processed by the Air Data Inertial Reference Unit (ADIRU) (ATSB 2007).

Even so, this is an astonishing record given the number of commercial aircraft in service worldwide, and the number of critical aircraft functions now implemented in software. According to a Boeing report (Boeing 2010), there are 20,025 certified jet aeroplanes.

According to the same Boeing report, the hull loss accident rate is 1.59 accidents per million departures. This means that if you flew twice a day, it would be 2,178 years before you were involved in a hull loss accident, on average. The odds of being involved in a hull loss accident are considerably less than the odds of being struck by lightning (estimated at 1:280,000 by the US National Lightning Safety Institute).

Nevertheless, there are no grounds for complacency. Even though the risk to an individual of being involved in an aircraft accident is vanishingly small, there are so many aircraft in service worldwide that a large passenger aircraft crashes, somewhere in the world, almost every month. The Boeing report shows there were 17 hull loss accidents resulting in 415 fatalities in 2009. Given the increase in the number of aircraft in-service each year, and given the increasing complexity of software intensive aircraft systems and the reliance being placed upon them, it must only be a matter of time before airborne software is implicated in an aircraft accident.

2 Why DO-178C?

When DO-178B was published in 1992, software was typically designed using structured methodologies such as the Yourdon Structured Method (YSM). DO-178B was written assuming that the software would be developed using top down functional decomposition. In the 18 years since 1992, a number of new techniques and technologies have been adopted by the software industry. These new techniques and technologies include:

- Model Based Design (MBD)
- Object Oriented Technology (OOT)
- Formal Methods (FM).

Applicants found it difficult to interpret DO-178B when applying these new techniques and technologies, and certification authorities became concerned at the lack of consistency in their application. Some attempts were made to provide practical advice on the application of these new techniques and technologies, for example, the Federal Aviation Administration (FAA) Object Oriented Technology in Aviation (OOTiA) handbook (FAA 2004).

The certification authorities and the aviation industry felt it would be useful to update DO-178B to reflect these changes in software technology. RTCA and EUROCAE therefore established joint RTCA Special Committee 205 (SC-205) and EUROCAE Working Group 71 (WG-71) in 2005 and tasked it with creating DO-178C/ED-12C (referred to as DO-178C in the remainder of this paper), DO-248C/ED-94C, DO-278A/ED-109A and a number of new, technology specific supplements).

SC-205/WG-71 consists of about 150 active participants, organised into seven subgroups. The author has, at various times during the five year life of the committee, been an active member of SG2 (issues and rationale) and SG4 (model based development), as well as European chair of the Issue Paper 217 (IP217) tiger team and a member of the editorial team. The author's current sub group, SG2, is typical in that SG2 members participate in a telephone conference call and web meeting twice a week, while the entire committee meets twice each year.

SC-205/WG-71 aims to complete by December 2010. The committee plans to deliver:

1. DO-178C/ED-12C: the core text, which applies to airborne software
2. DO-278A/ED-109A: a variant for ground based software, specifically Communication, Navigation, Surveillance and Air Traffic Management (CNS/ATM) software
3. DO-248C/ED-94C: a set of Frequently Asked Questions (FAQs) and Discussion Papers (DPs) on DO-178C/ED-12C
4. a tool qualification supplement
5. a model-based development and verification supplement
6. an object-oriented and related technology supplement
7. a formal methods technology supplement.

3 DO-178C Core Text

3.1 Overview

The changes to the core text between DO-178B and DO-178C are evolutionary rather than revolutionary. The terms of reference for SC-205/WG-71 (RTCA 2009) required backward compatibility with DO-178B. If your organisation has existing software development and verification processes that are compliant with DO-178B, and you don't use model-based design, object-oriented technology or formal methods, then little or no change to those processes will be required to achieve compliance with DO-178C. The changes to the DO-178C core text are mainly to support the new technology supplements, and to provide additional explanation where the DO-178B text had been found to be unclear or ambiguous.

The following sections are not intended to enumerate all the changes to the DO-178C core text, but to draw attention to the most significant changes.

3.2 Section 1: Introduction

There are a number of changes to section 1. One of the main changes was to clarify the relationship between objectives and activities. There was much debate within the committee as to whether the activities ought to be mandatory[2]. Some members believed that the activities ought to be mandated, otherwise applicants would choose to omit activities that they considered unduly onerous, with no rationale for their omission. Others felt that applicants should be free to propose any set of activities that satisfied the objectives and that placing undue emphasis on a specific set of activities would encourage a checklist mentality, where applicants carried out a prescribed set of activities with no thought as to their context or purpose, missing the intent of DO-178B. The compromise that was reached was that the text now states that DO-178C describes the activities for meeting the objectives, but points out that applicants may adopt alternative activities, subject to the approval of the certification authority.

A closely related, and equally hotly debated topic, was the difference between the two terms 'guidance' and 'guidelines'. DO-178B had used the two terms interchangeably. Since the publication of DO-178B in 1992, the term 'guidance' had acquired a specific meaning, particularly in US federal aviation legislation. The terms of reference (RTCA 2009) define 'guidance' to be material that could be recognized by the authorities as a means of compliance to the regulations, whereas 'guidelines' provide supporting information and will not be considered as a means of compliance. Some committee members felt that using two terms that have very similar meanings in common English usage to make such an important distinction would create confusion, especially for readers whose first language is not English. The solution adopted was to remove the term 'guidelines' from DO-178C and to use the term 'guidance' only in normative text.

Section 1 has also been updated to draw attention to the existence of the new technical supplements, and to point out that it is the applicant's responsibility to check that the use of a specific supplement is acceptable to the certification authority.

3.3 Section 2: System aspects relating to software development

Section 2 has been substantially rewritten to make DO-178C consistent with ARP 4754A, the forthcoming update to ARP 4754 (SAE 1996), which describes the system life cycle processes for aircraft systems.

---

[2] Strictly speaking, nothing in DO-178B is mandatory. The purpose of RTCA, Inc. is to develop consensus-based recommendations. For this reason, DO-178B avoids using the words 'shall' and 'must', as stated in subsection 1.4.

In addition, DO-178B subsection 2.2 associated the DO-178B software levels (A to E) with the failure conditions defined in Advisory Circular (AC) 25-1309-A and Joint Aviation Authorities (JAA) Guidance Material (AMJ) 25-1309. These two documents related to the US and European regulations (as they existed in 1992), respectively, for the certification of transport category airplanes. DO-178B subsection 2.2 has been rewritten so that Code of Federal Regulations (CFR) 14 (the current US airworthiness standards for transport category airplanes) is used as just one example, since DO-178B could also be applied to other types of aircraft (such as light aircraft and helicopters), or even to systems outside the aerospace domain.

3.4 Section 3: Software life cycle and Section 4: Software planning process

DO-178C sections 3 and 4 are little changed from DO-178B sections 3 and 4. That is not to say that they are unchanged, only that the changes do not have a significant impact on the applicant's software development and verification processes.

3.5 Section 5: Software development processes

3.5.1 High-level and low-level requirements

DO-178B always allowed for the possibility of multiple levels of software requirements. For example, DO-178B section 5 refers to 'one or more successive, lower levels of requirements'. An early draft of DO-178B referred to high-level requirements, intermediate-level requirements and low-level requirements. The term, intermediate-level requirements, was felt to be confusing, so the published text of DO-178B names only two levels of software requirements: high-level requirements and low-level requirements.

An attempt was made to introduce a rigorous model of requirements and design into DO-178C that would define how multiple levels of requirements and design relate to each other (Jaffe et al. 2008). This proposal, IP217, was rejected because it was felt to be too big a change to be implemented correctly in the time remaining, although the authors were encouraged to continue refining their ideas for inclusion in a future revision of DO-178.

The retention of the extant DO-178B text means that there remains considerable ambiguity as to the intended relationship between high-level requirements and low-level requirements, these two terms being unique to DO-178B. High-level requirements are what most people outside the DO-178B community mean by software requirements. So what are low-level requirements? DO-178B defines low-level requirements to be 'software requirements derived from high-level requirements, derived requirements, and design constraints from which source code can be directly implemented without information'. So are low-level requirements simply high-level requirements developed to a greater level of detail, or are they the requirements for the software components within the software architecture? The former interpretation is implied by DO-248B FAQ #35, while the latter interpretation is implied by DO-178B paragraph 6.4.3, item c. DO-178C allows both interpretations.

Another related issue is that DO-178B allowed for the possibility of a single level of requirements, in which case the high-level requirements are also considered low-level requirements. The intent was to avoid forcing the creation of two levels of requirements even for trivially simple software applications. Applicants sometimes misuse this paragraph to justify producing a single level of requirements for complex software applications. This may result in a development process that does not comply with DO-178B. This was the topic of Certification Authorities Software Team (CAST) position paper CAST-15 (CAST 2003a). A note was added to section 5 that the applicant may be required to justify software development processes that produce a single level of requirements. A full discussion of this topic may be found in CAST-15.

3.5.2 Derived requirements

Another area of uncertainty has been concerning the meaning of derived requirements. The term was originally intended to describe those requirements derived from design decisions made during the software design process. DO-178B defines derived requirements to be 'additional requirements resulting from the software development processes, which may not be directly traceable to higher level requirements'. This definition suggests that the defining characteristic of derived requirements is that they are additional requirements resulting from the software development processes. They may (or may not) be directly traceable to higher-level requirements. However, DO-178B section 5 states, 'derived requirements are requirements that are not directly traceable to higher level requirements'. This text suggests that the defining characteristic of derived requirements is that they are not traceable to higher-level requirements. This inconsistency between section 5 and the glossary was compounded by the fact that in the French text of ED-12B (the European version of DO-178B), the definition of derived requirements is translated as additional requirements 'qui peuvent ne pas être directement traçables vers des exigences de plus haut niveau', that is, 'which cannot be directly traceable to higher level requirements'.

DO-178B requires that derived requirements be provided to the system safety assessment process. Some committee members were concerned that some requirements that should have been provided to the system safety assessment process were not, because they had been traced to higher-level requirements, however tenuously. They felt there is pressure (often self-imposed) on software engineers to trace as many requirements as possible to higher-level requirements, to minimize the number of requirements that have to be provided to the system safety assessment process. The solution adopted was to redefine derived requirements to include those that specify behaviour beyond that specified by the system requirements or the higher-level software requirements.

3.6 Section 6: Software verification process

3.6.1 Objectives versus activities

The entire document has been restructured to make for a cleaner separation between objectives and activities. This restructuring has affected section 6 more than any other section.

3.6.2 Verification independence

DO-178C subsection 6.2 now clarifies that the person who created a set of low-level requirements-based test cases should not be the same person who developed the associated source code from those low-level requirements. This recommendation resulted from CAST-26 (CAST 2006). A proposal that the person who created a set of low-level requirements-based test cases should not be the same person who developed the associated set of low-level requirements, which was also based on CAST-26, was rejected by plenary.

3.6.3 Requirements-based testing

Section 6 has been updated to clarify that test cases should be requirements-based, including robustness test cases (DO-178C paragraph 6.4.2) and the test cases used to gain credit for structural coverage (DO-178C subparagraph 6.4.4.2).

3.6.4 Requirements expressed by logic equations

DO-178B subparagraph 6.4.2.1, item d concerns the number of test cases required to verify a requirement expressed by logic equations. For example, consider the following requirement: 'A green light shall be illuminated when the nose landing gear is down and locked, and the right landing gear is down and locked, and the left landing gear is down and locked'. One approach would be to test all combinations of the variables. This would result in eight test cases for this example. The note following DO-178B subparagraph 6.4.2.1, item d points out that a different strategy could be developed. The example given is that, at Level A, test cases could be established to provide Modified Condition/Decision Coverage (MC/DC). This would result in a reduced set of four test cases for this example.

The reference to Level A in the note could be read to suggest that the number of test cases required to verify a requirement depends on the software level. This was not the intent of the original DO-178B authors. The note was meant to say that if the requirement test cases that have been developed are sufficient to achieve MC/DC coverage of the source code (which is only required at Level A), then enough testing has been done. It would not make any sense to claim that two test cases would be sufficient at Level B or that no test cases would be necessary at Level D.

The reference to MC/DC in the note might also create a link between normal range test cases and structural coverage analysis, which was not intended.

The note has been deleted from DO-178C and a new FAQ #78 added to DO-248C.

3.6.4 Modified condition/decision coverage (MC/DC)

DO-178B is infamous for requiring MC/DC at Level A. This is often claimed to be unduly onerous (e.g. Thomas 2007). This is ironic, since MC/DC was intended to reduce the testing burden, and was introduced as an alternative to testing all combinations of terms in a Boolean expression.

While the definition of MC/DC in the DO-178B glossary is disarmingly straightforward, the application of MC/DC to actual software projects has led to any number of uncertainties and misunderstandings. MC/DC has been the subject of two CAST position papers (CAST 2001, 2002) as well as an 85-page tutorial (Hayhurst et al. 2001). Examples of the questions that have arisen are:

- Is masking MC/DC[3] an acceptable alternative to unique-cause MC/DC?
- What is the difference between a decision and a branch?
- How does short circuit evaluation affect MC/DC?
- Is achieving MC/DC at the object code level equivalent to achieving MC/DC at the source code level?
- Should bitwise operators be considered Boolean operators?
- Is it sufficient to execute a given sequence of statements, or is it necessary to verify that the correct output has been produced? Some applicants have claimed that they can achieve a high degree of structural coverage just by powering up the system.

---

[3] Masking MC/DC is a variant of MC/DC that allows more than one condition in a decision to be changed between test cases. This is useful when conditions in a decision are coupled, i.e. the value of one condition depends upon the value of another condition within the same decision.

A proposal was made to create a more generalised notion of coverage that would provide a clearer means of compliance for the MC/DC coverage criteria. This was developed into the generalised model of requirements and design that was mentioned earlier (IP217). Following the rejection of IP217, a proposal was made to redefine structure coverage in terms of execution sequences, rather than Boolean expressions. It was felt that defining a decision to be a special kind of Boolean expression instead of a programming construct used to choose between two or more execution sequences was counter-intuitive. This proposal was also rejected, since it implied that Boolean expressions that did not influence the flow of control would no longer be considered for MC/DC, and it was felt that this would be lowering the bar. The compromise that was eventually reached was to make some small improvements to the existing definitions, the most significant one being to extend the glossary definition of MC/DC to allow masking MC/DC, and to provide further explanation in a discussion paper in DO-248C.

3.6.4 Analysis of data coupling and control coupling

Analysis of data coupling and control coupling is one of the least understood DO-178B objectives. DO-178B subparagraph 6.4.4.2, item c simply states, 'The analysis should confirm the data coupling and control coupling between the code components'. Data coupling is the dependence of a software component on data not exclusively under the control of that software component. Control coupling is the manner or degree by which one software component influences the execution of another software component. However, what does analysis of data coupling and control coupling mean?

CAST-19 (CAST 2004) explains that the authors of DO-178B were concerned that applicants could achieve the structural coverage objectives through unit testing alone. The intent of the analysis of data coupling and control coupling objective was to ensure that applicants did sufficient integration testing.

DO-178C clarifies that analysis of data coupling and control coupling is a structural coverage analysis that confirms that the requirements-based testing has exercised the data and control coupling between code components. It is not necessary (or desirable) to write specific tests to exercise data coupling and control coupling. The data coupling and control coupling should be exercised by the requirements-based hardware/software integration tests and the requirements-based software integration tests. The analysis of data coupling and control coupling identifies which requirements-based test(s) exercise(s) each data coupling and control coupling within the software.

3.6.5 Deactivated code

DO-178C clarifies how deactivated code is handled during structural coverage analysis resolution. There are two categories of deactivated code:

Category one. This is code that is not intended to be executed in any configuration used within any aircraft or engine. It should be demonstrated through a combination of analysis and test that the deactivated code cannot be executed inadvertently.

Category two. This is code that is executed only in certain configurations. Such code should be verified against its requirements.

3.6.6 Parameter data items

DO-178C introduces the notion of parameter data items. A parameter data item is a data set that influences the behaviour of the software without modifying the executable object code and which is managed as a separate configuration item. DO-178B did not provide any guidance as to how to manage such data items. Such guidance as is provided in DO-178C is welcomed, especially given the growing adoption of Integrated Module Avionics (IMA). DO-178C requires that:

- the executable object code should be verified to behave correctly with all realisable values of the parameter data items[4]
- the parameter data items are verified to contain valid values.

3.7 Section 7: Software configuration management process, Section 8: Software quality assurance process, Section 9: Certification liaison process, Section 10: Overview of aircraft and engine certification and Section 11: Software life cycle data

The changes to DO-178C sections 7–11 are relatively minor.

3.8 Section 12: Additional considerations

The main changes to section 12 are to reflect the introduction of the separate tool qualification supplement and formal methods technology supplement.

---

[4] Real and integer parameter data items can, of course, be exercised using equivalence classes and boundary values.

4 DO-278A

DO-278A is a variant of DO-178C aimed at CNS/ATM systems. These are ground-based, rather than airborne, systems. These systems typically make much more use of commercial off the shelf software (COTS), especially operating systems and databases, than do airborne systems. DO-278A defines six software levels (AL1 to AL6), as compared to five in DO-178C (Level A to Level E).

Mostly, the updates to DO-278A have tracked the corresponding updates to DO-178C. The main changes that are specific to DO-278A are:

- minor updates to the guidance in subsection 12.4 on the use of COTS
- expansion of the guidance in subsection 12.5 on adaptation parameter data.

5 DO-248C

DO-248C was still immature at the time of writing this paper, as most of the committee's effort had been focused on updating the DO-178C core text and the new technology supplements.

The errata from DO-248B have been removed, since the corrections have now been incorporated in the DO-178C core text.

The answer to FAQ #34: 'What is the concept of independence as used in DO-178C?' has been expanded considerably. It now includes a figure and a table illustrating the verification independence required by DO-178C at Level A.

The answer to FAQ #42: 'Can structural coverage be demonstrated by analyzing the object code instead of the source code?' has been expanded, largely based on CAST-17 (CAST 2003b). There has been a great deal of uncertainty as to whether measuring structural coverage at object code level is an acceptable alternative to measuring structural coverage at source code level. Opinions ranged from certain tool vendors claiming that measuring structural coverage at object code level is mandatory at Level A to certain FAA Aircraft Certification Offices (ACOs) ruling that measuring MC/DC at object code level is not acceptable at Level A. After discussion with some of the original authors of DO-178B, it was determined that both approaches have advantages and disadvantages, which need to be taken into consideration.

A number of new FAQs have been added. At the time of writing, these were:

- FAQ #77 on failure detection and safety monitoring requirements
- FAQ #78 on software requirements expressed by logic equations, which replaces the note following DO-178B subparagraph 6.4.2.1, item d
- FAQ #79 on technical standard orders (TSOs)
- FAQ #80 on inlining
- FAQs #81–84 on parameter data items.

A number of new Discussion Papers have also been added. At the time of writing, these were:

- DP #16 on cache management
- DP #17 on the use of floating point arithmetic
- DP #18 on the use of service experience.

A rationale for all the DO-178C objectives has been added in DO-248C section 5.

6 Tool qualification supplement

The tool qualification supplement is probably the single biggest change in DO-178C. The guidance on tool qualification has been increased from three pages in DO-178B subsection 12.2 to 117 pages in the new tool qualification supplement.

In DO-178B, tools were classified as one of two types:

Software development tools. These were tools that create software, and which could therefore introduce errors into the airborne software. Examples include developers, linkers and auto code generators.

Software verification tools. These were tools used to detect errors. They therefore cannot introduce errors, but can fail to detect them. Examples include test tools and static code analysers.

DO-178B required tools to be qualified only when they were used to automate a software development or verification activity without its output being verified. Software development tools were qualified by satisfying the same DO-178B objectives as for airborne software. Software verification tools were qualified by demonstrating that the tool complied with its requirements under normal operating conditions. A tool could be qualified only for use on a specific system, and needed further qualification to be reused on other systems[5].

In practice, qualifying software development tools to DO-178B Level A was very time-consuming and expensive. Most applicants avoided the need to qualify their software development tools by verifying the output (for example, reviewing and unit testing the source code generated by auto code generators). Very few commercially available software development tools have been qualified to DO-178B Level A. One example of such a tool is the SCADE KCG.

On the other hand, qualifying a software verification tool is relatively straightforward. A number of commercially available products have been qualified as DO-178B software verification tools.

DO-178C has replaced the existing two tool categories (software development tools and software verification tools) with five tool qualification levels (TQLs),

---

[5] This did not stop tool vendors from selling what they claimed to be 'qualified' tools.

ranging from TQL-1 (the most rigorous) to TQL-5 (the least rigorous). The TQL of the tool is determined by a combination of:

1. the impact on the airborne software of the tool inserting an error or failing to detect an error
2. the software level of the airborne software to which the tool is being applied.

For example, a tool whose output is part of the airborne software and thus could insert an error is determined to be TQL-1 if used to develop Level A software, TQL-4 if used to develop Level D software. Conversely, a tool that, within the scope of its intended use, could only fail to detect an error is determined to be TQL-5 regardless of whether it is used to verify Level A software or Level D software.

DO-178C subsection 12.2 describes how to determine the TQL for a particular tool. The objectives that are to be satisfied, the activities that are to be carried out and the qualification data that are to be provided for each TQL are defined in the tool qualification supplement.

A separate supplement was produced because:

- tools are different from airborne software and require specific guidance
- many tools are developed by teams other than those developing the airborne software.
- it is hoped that the supplement can be used for projects in other domains, not just airborne software.

The tool qualification supplement defines objectives, activities and qualification data analogous to the objectives, activities and lifecycle data defined in DO-178C. Just as the objectives are modulated by software level in DO-178C, so the objectives are modulated by TQL in the tool qualification supplement.

7 Model-based development and verification supplement

The model-based development and verification supplement has proved to be the most contentious of all the supplements. At the time of writing, it had still not been approved by plenary.

A model is an abstract representation of a system. In software development, models can be used to capture software requirements and/or software designs. Code can often be generated automatically from a design model. Examples of model-based development and verification tools include Simulink and SCADE.

Model-based development and verification promises many advantages for safety-critical software development:

- the use of the same modelling languages and tools by system engineers and software engineers improves communication between the two disciplines

- model-based development allows early simulation and analysis of requirements and designs expressed as models, rather than having to wait for the design to be implemented and for the executable object code to be executed
- model simulation can be used to supplement reviews and analyses to verify that a model is compliant with the requirements from which it was developed
- auto code generation reduces the time required to implement requirements and design changes.

However, model-based development and verification also presents a number of challenges:

- It risks blurring the distinction between requirements ('what') and design ('how'). When does a model represent requirements, and when does it represent design? Can it represent both at the same time?
- There is a risk that some applicants will try to collapse several levels of requirements and design into one, making it difficult to ensure compliance with the traceability and verification objectives. There have been cases where applicants have claimed that a single model contained all their system requirements, high-level requirements, software architecture and low-level requirements, and that the source code and test cases were auto generated from the model. This is not acceptable since all that can be demonstrated is that the executable object code is a faithful implementation of the model. What do you verify such a model against?
- Differences between the modelling environment and the target computer (for example, in its handling of floating point arithmetic) may mean that the executable object code behaves differently from the model. This limits the credit that may be taken for simulations carried out in the modelling environment.

A key principle encapsulated in the model-based development and verification supplement is that every model must be verified against the requirements from which it was developed.

The model-based development and verification supplement recognises two kinds of models that it considers relevant to software development and verification:

Specification Model. This is an abstract representation of the externally observable properties of the software. It defines what the software needs to do, but not how it does it. It does not define any software design details, such as internal data structures, internal data flow or internal control flow. A specification model may be used to express software high-level requirements. It may not be used to express software architecture or software low-level requirements.

Design Model. This defines internal data structures, internal data flow and internal control flow. A design model may be used to express software architecture and software low-level requirements. It may not be used to express software high-level requirements.

It is the applicant's choice whether to develop a specification model, a design model, or both. Any given model is either a specification model or a design model. It cannot be both.

The supplement introduces the notion of model coverage analysis, analogous to structural coverage analysis. The purpose of model coverage analysis is to detect unintended functions in the model.

The most contentious aspects of the supplement at the time of writing are:

1. The supplement proposes that model simulation could be used in combination with reviews and analyses to achieve some objectives that could previously only be achieved through reviews and analyses of the high-level requirements, low-level requirements and software architecture. Those opposed to this proposal point out that DO-178B required reviews as well as tests because reviews will detect errors that tests cannot detect. The supporters of this proposal point out that model simulation supplements reviews and analyses, it does not replace them, and claim that model simulation is more efficient (i.e. it detects the same set of errors more quickly) and exhaustive (i.e. it detects more errors) than reviews and analyses.

2. The supplement also proposes that model simulation could be used to claim credit for some testing of the executable object code on the target computer. The supporters of this proposal point out that DO-178B already allows for some tests to be performed in other than the integrated target computer environment (e.g. DO-178B paragraph 6.4.1) and that the supplement requires that the applicant be able to demonstrate that the model simulation provides at least the same level of defect detection as testing of the target code. The opponents of this proposal point out that it goes beyond DO-178B paragraph 6.4.1, and that model simulation can never substitute for any testing of the executable object code on the target computer.

8 Object-oriented and related technology supplement

As stated earlier, DO-178B was written at a time when structured design techniques such as the Yourdon Structured Method (YSM) were the predominant design techniques for embedded software development. The objectives and activities described in DO-178B fit very well with functional top-down design decomposition. The adoption of object-oriented design methodologies in the 1990s introduced a number of benefits for airborne software development (such as increased reuse of software for product families, for example), but also caused a number of difficulties.

In 2002 and 2003, the National Aeronautics and Space Administration (NASA) and the FAA sponsored two Object-Oriented Technology in Aviation (OOTiA) workshops, which resulted in the publication of the FAA OOTiA Handbook (FAA

2004) in 2004. The FAA OOTiA Handbook formed the starting point for the object-oriented and related technology supplement.

Traceability was relatively straightforward when structured analysis and design techniques were used. For example, using YSM, a textual requirement might be traced to a process in a dataflow diagram, from the process to a module in a structure chart, and from the module to a procedure in the source code. When using object-oriented techniques, it is very tempting to trace system requirements to use cases, and use cases to classes. However, the relationship between use cases and classes is typically many-to-many. Many classes co-operate to implement a single use case, and each class typically participates in the implementation of many use cases. The supplement recommends that traceability should be from requirements to the methods and attributes that implement those requirements, not to the classes, to preserve the granularity required to satisfy the intent of DO-178B. Classes are considered just an artefact of the software architecture for organising the requirements.

The supplement introduces an additional objective and related activities to verify type consistency. Type consistency is a complex subject. While the supplement allows the use of inheritance with method overriding and dynamic dispatch even at Level A, these techniques require additional verification activities that can be done either by testing or by formal analysis.

Object-oriented programming languages tend to rely on dynamic memory management. The supplement introduces an additional objective and related activities to verify dynamic memory management. The activities are aimed to ensure that none of the following vulnerabilities exist:

1. ambiguous references, where an allocator returns a reference to memory that is already in use
2. fragmentation starvation, where an allocation request fails because there is insufficient contiguous free memory
3. deallocation starvation, where an allocation request fails because memory that is no longer being used has not been reclaimed
4. heap memory exhaustion, where the program requires more heap memory than is available
5. premature deallocation, where memory is reclaimed while it is still in use
6. lost update and stale reference, where an object has been moved to avoid fragmentation of memory, but the program continues to reference the object at its old address
7. time bound allocation or deallocation, where the software is delayed unexpectedly by the garbage collector.

9 Formal methods technology supplement

Formal methods have a long history that may come as a surprise to some readers. Indeed, the application of formal methods to airborne software predates the use of MC/DC. The earliest instance of formal methods being applied to airborne software of which the author is aware was a series of program proofs carried out by Program Validation Limited (PVL) in the late 1980s (Clutterbuck and Carré 1988, O'Neill et al. 1988). The PVL team used the SPADE proof checker to carry out a proof of correctness of Lucas Control Language (LUCOL) code modules written in Z8002 assembly code, which were used in the fuel control unit of the Rolls-Royce RB211-524G. The work was later extended to carry out formal verification of the LUCOL modules for a whole family of jet engines, although the formal verification was not used for certification credit.

A much more recent example was the use by Airbus of the Caveat tool to conduct formal proof instead of unit testing of the Airbus A380 flight control and guidance unit (Souyris et al. 2009).

When DO-178B was written, there was much debate as to whether formal methods should be allowed to be used for certification credit. At the time, the majority opinion was that formal methods were not yet mature enough to be included in the core objectives and activities. However, formal methods were included as one of the alternative methods discussed in DO-178B subsection 12.3.

As part of the DO-178C effort, a formal methods technology supplement has been developed, which will at last allow credit for the use of formal methods.

The term, formal methods, encompasses a very wide range of tools and techniques, ranging from formal specifications written in languages such as Z (Spivey 1998), through model checking to program proof of source code written in programming languages such as SPARK (Chapman and Amey 2008).

Formal methods are mathematically based techniques for the development and verification of software aspects of digital systems. Because of their mathematical basis, formal methods have well-defined and unambiguous semantics, enabling precise communication between engineers and enabling formal analyses that provide objective evidence of program properties such as freedom from exceptions or correctness with respect to a formal (mathematical) specification.

DO-178B subsection 6.3 has always allowed analyses as well as reviews. The author's understanding is that the original authors of DO-178B mostly had reviews in mind, but were mindful that advances in technology during the lifetime of DO-178B would most likely to allow some of the objectives that had been satisfied by reviews (e.g. conformance to standards) to be satisfied by computer-based analyses.

The use of formal methods for requirements or design allows some of the verification objectives to be satisfied by the use of formal methods. The formal methods technology supplement provides specific guidance as to how formal methods can be used to conduct analyses of the high-level requirements, low-level requirements, software architecture and source code. Formal analysis of the executable object code may be used to establish specific properties of the executable object code. For example, formal methods can be used to demonstrate compliance of the executable object code with the low-level requirements. These formal analyses can replace some testing of the executable object code, although testing remains the primary means of verification of the executable object code.

10 Conclusions

So are we there yet? As far as DO-178C is concerned, we're nearly there. At the time of writing, DO-178C is expected to be completed by December 2010 and to be published in the first quarter of 2011.

DO-178C is an evolution of DO-178B. The changes to the core text are intended to clarify those instances in the text where misunderstandings and misinterpretations have occurred, rather than to impose additional objectives on applicants. The biggest change relative to DO-178B is the addition of the new supplements to provide additional guidance on the use of new technologies that have been adopted by the avionic software industry since DO-178B was published in 1992. It is anticipated that any new technologies that are adopted during the lifetime of DO-178C can also be addressed by creating new supplements, rather than having to revisit the DO-178C core text.

In another sense, we'll never reach our final destination, as there is always room for improvement, especially where safety is concerned. It is the author's opinion that DO-178B has proved successful in satisfying its main purpose, which is to ensure that airborne software performs its intended function with a level of confidence in safety that complies with airworthiness requirements. This is not to say that the document has been easy to use or that airborne software is defect free. Nevertheless, the in-flight incidents of which the author is aware were not caused by the airborne software failing to implement its requirements correctly; rather they were caused by the software faithfully implementing requirements that specified unsafe or otherwise undesirable behaviour or that failed to specify an appropriate response to abnormal inputs or conditions. For example, a contributing factor to the A320 accident at Warsaw in 1993 was the interlock logic resulting in delayed deployment of the spoilers, thrust reversers and wheel brakes (Ladkin 1996).

It is therefore the author's belief that future developments should focus more on ensuring that the requirements are the right requirements (in particular, that they specify safe behaviour). This is particularly challenging when creating systems of systems, such as IMA systems, since such systems can interact with each other in unexpected ways, especially under degraded operating conditions. The authors of DO-178B considered requirements validation to be a systems issue outside the scope of DO-178B, so addressing this important topic is likely to require further expansion of the systems-level guidance such as SAE ARP4754A.

Another issue facing the aerospace industry is the proliferation of software-intensive systems that affect safety. The current guidance addresses only airborne software (addressed by DO-178C) and CNS/ATM software (addressed by DO-278A). There is no guidance for ground-based software other than CNS/ATM. With increased integration between the ground-based CNS/ATM and airborne segments, the introduction of Unmanned Aerial Vehicles (UAVs) and systems such as Electronic Flight Bags (EFBs), flight planning systems and aircraft maintenance systems, there is a risk of software being deployed with insufficient consideration given as to its potential effect on safety. For example, the control software for a remotely piloted UAV carries out the same function whether it is implemented on the ground or on the aircraft, yet UAV ground control stations are often developed and deployed with no attempt made to satisfy the objectives of DO-178B. There is a need for clear guidance on the development and verification of any safety-related software, irrespective of whether it is ground-based or airborne. Such guidance is likely to come in the form of further evolutions of DO-178C and DO-278A.

References

ATSB (2007) In-flight upset event 240 km north-west of Perth, WA Boeing Company 777-200, 9M-MRG, 1 August 2005. ATSB Transport Safety Investigation Report

Boeing (2010) Statistical summary of commercial jet airplane accidents worldwide operations 1959-2009. Boeing Commercial Airplanes

CAST (2001) Rationale for accepting masking MC/DC in certification projects. CAST position paper CAST-6

CAST (2002) What is a 'decision' in application of modified condition/decision coverage (MC/DC) and decision coverage (DC)? CAST position paper CAST-10

CAST (2003a) Merging high-level and low-level requirements. CAST position paper CAST-15

CAST (2003b) Structural coverage of object code. CAST position paper CAST-17

CAST (2004) Clarification of structural coverage analyses of data coupling and control coupling. CAST position paper CAST-19

CAST (2006) Verification independence. CAST position paper CAST-26

Chapman R, Amey P (2008) SPARK 95 – the SPADE Ada 95 kernel (including RavenSPARK). Praxis High Integrity Systems Ltd

Clutterbuck DL, Carré BA (1988) The verification of low-level code. Softw Eng J UK 3:3:97-111. doi:10.1049/sej.1988.0012

DGA (1994) Commission d'enquête sur l'accident survenu le 30 Juin 1994 a Toulouse-Blagnac (31) a l'Airbus A330 N°42 d'Airbus Industrie Immatricule FWWKH. Rapport préliminaire. Direction Générale de l'Aviation. http://www.rvs.uni-bielefeld.de/publications/Incidents/DOCS/ComAndRep/A330-Toulouse/Rapport.html. Accessed 6 September 2010

FAA (2004) Handbook for object-oriented technology in aviation (OOTiA). Federal Aviation Administration

Hayhurst KJ, Veerhusen DS, Chilenski JJ, Rierson LK (2001) A practical tutorial on modified condition/decision coverage, National Aeronautics and Space Administration

Jaffe MS, Busser R, Daniels D, Delseny H, Romanski G (2008) Progress report on some proposed upgrades to the conceptual software engineering underpinnings of DO-178B/ED-12B. Proc of the 3rd IET Int Syst Saf Conf

Ladkin (1996) Report on the accident to Airbus A320-211 aircraft in Warsaw on 14 September 1993. http://www.rvs.uni-bielefeld.de/publications/Incidents/DOCS/ComAndRep/Warsaw/warsaw-report.html. Accessed 10 September 2010

O'Neill IM, Clutterbuck DL, Farrow PF, Summers PG, Dolman WC (1988) The formal verification of safety-critical assembly code. Proc SAFECOMP

RTCA (1992) DO-178B. Software considerations in airborne systems and equipment certification. RTCA, Inc.

RTCA (2009) Terms of reference for software joint special committee/working group software considerations in aeronautical systems. RTCA, Inc

SAE (1996) ARP 4754 Certification considerations for highly-integrated or complex aircraft systems. SAE International

Souyris J, Wiels V, Delmas D, Delseny H (2009) Formal verification of avionics software products, FM 2009: FORMAL METHODS Lecture Notes in Computer Science 5850/2009: 532-546. doi:10.1007/978-3-642-05089-3_34

Spivey JM (1998) The Z notation: a reference manual, 2nd edn. http://spivey.oriel.ox.ac.uk/~mike/zrm/zrm.pdf. Accessed 6 September 2010

Thomas M (2007) Unsafe standardization. IEEE Computer 40:11:109-111. doi:10.1109/MC.2007.407

AUTHOR INDEX

C. Dale, T. Anderson (eds.), *Advances in Systems Safety*, DOI 10.1007/978-0-85729-133-2,
© Springer-Verlag London Limited 2011